H. Schütz Wilson

**Studies in History, Legend and Literature**

H. Schütz Wilson

**Studies in History, Legend and Literature**

ISBN/EAN: 9783741124662

Manufactured in Europe, USA, Canada, Australia, Japa

Cover: Foto ©Andreas Hilbeck / pixelio.de

Manufactured and distributed by brebook publishing software (www.brebook.com)

H. Schütz Wilson

**Studies in History, Legend and Literature**

# STUDIES

IN

*HISTORY, LEGEND AND LITERATURE*

BY

H. SCHÜTZ WILSON

AUTHOR OF

'STUDIES AND ROMANCES,' 'ALPINE ASCENTS AND ADVENTURES,'
'THE TOWER AND THE SCAFFOLD,' ETC., ETC., ETC.

GRIFFITH & FARRAN

SUCCESSORS TO NEWBERY AND HARRIS

WEST CORNER ST PAUL'S CHURCHYARD, LONDON

E. P. DUTTON & CO., NEW YORK

1884

THIS VOLUME

IS

BY PERMISSION

𝔇𝔢𝔡𝔦𝔠𝔞𝔱𝔢𝔡

TO

J. A. FROUDE, Esq.,
M.A., Etc., Etc.

# NOTE.

THE Studies in this volume, on the subjects of
Lucrezia Borgia,
Struensee and Caroline Mathilde,
Elizabeth Stuart,
Eppelein von Gailingen, and
Goethe's Faust,
have appeared in the *Nineteenth Century*, *Cornhill Magazine*, and the *Westminster* and *Modern Reviews;* and are here reproduced (after due revision) by permission of the respective editors.

The Essay on Madame Roland has not appeared in any periodical.

# STUDIES IN HISTORY, LEGEND & LITERATURE.

## *LUCREZIA BORGIA.*

### I.—ROME.

> Vilest things
> Become themselves in her; that the holy priests
> Bless her, when she is riggish.
> *Antony and Cleopatra.*

LONDON is an instance of an old city rebuilt in modern times mainly by casing over the new above the old. The ancient sites remain, but the olden houses disappear; and in their places newer buildings, less picturesque possibly, though perhaps better suited to present needs, rise and rear their modern faces. The quaint and stately olden houses, which expressed the ideas and satisfied the needs of bygone states of society, vanish, and their place knows them no more.

So it is, in some instances, with history. Deeper knowledge of facts, readier access to old archives and records, a profounder insight into character, a nobler care for truth, have erected fairer structures on the very site of the olden habitations, and the new picture is painted over the former one. Perhaps the greatest instance of true historical rehabilitation is that of the character of Cromwell by Carlyle. The lampoons of the Restoration, the malignity of partisanship, the rarity of that profound insight which alone can worthily estimate a man so great as Cromwell, had combined to produce a caricature of the great Protector which was popularly accepted as a portrait till Carlyle came, and saw, and conquered. Upon a basis of exhaustive study, his profound and poetical insight penetrated to the very depths and mysteries of a nature so complex and so heroic: he saw that the deeds of Cromwell were the true outcome of his inner nature; and Carlyle recognised, through his own nobleness, the noble soul that he restored to history. There have been other instances of similar service, though I have no space to analyse them here. Still, Mr Froude's essay towards painting over the old popular portrait, current in our childhood, of Henry the Eighth, may be cited as another, and as a comparatively successful study in modern historical rehabilitation.

It may be said that the great poet is the best historian. The materials for a living portrait of

Greek Cleopatra were not clearly ample, were scanty rather than suggestive; but see how Shakspeare has fused all hints into a round and perfect whole; has, with the seeing eye of genius, looked into every phase of character and witchery of charm; and has presented through art to history a complete portraiture of the subtle and sumptuous serpent of Old Nile. Carlyle is a great historian because he also is a poet.

Rehabilitation is one thing, and mere 'whitewashing,' or covering over an existing portrait with the thick opaque plaster of sentimental negation, is another. Both processes are known to us in the present day. Great men re-create, and small men re-confuse. The success of the great ones tempts little men to their ruin; and criticism, which applauds true effort, should also expose mistaken sentiment.

An attempt has recently been made by a German writer, Herr Ferdinand Gregorovius, to repaint the character of Lucrezia Borgia. Analysis will enable us to judge whether his essay should be classified as rehabilitation or as whitewashing. Certain it is that his work possesses enough of merit, and enough of interest, to claim careful consideration. The popular estimate of Lucrezia Borgia is forcibly embodied in the drama of Victor Hugo and in the opera of Donizetti. The French poet is, as a dramatist, very indifferent to historic truth; a fact which may easily be verified by a reference to his portraiture of Cromwell. Gregorovius, indeed, says that Hugo has been solely intent, in his drama of *Lucrezia Borgia*, ' ein moralisches Ungeheuer für den Bühneneffect zu Stande zu bringen ; ' nor is the charge without foundation. In both opera and drama the popular conception of the character and deeds of the Duchess of Ferrara has been adapted to loosely imagined plots calculated only to produce effect upon the stage. In both productions Lucrezia appears, with eyes of baleful meaning gleaming through the mystery of a mask, with hands which grasp the dagger and the bowl, and with an indomitably wicked will which treads ruthlessly upon human lives in a dark progress from crime to crime. Environed by human hate, bearing a name which of itself excites a shudder and a loathing, the inflexible criminal hesitates at no wickedness which seems calculated to attain her purpose, and is only in so far not a mere monster that she murders in order to reach distinct ends and aims.

No monograph about Lucrezia Borgia is possible. Lucrezia cannot be drawn without reference to her dreadful father and to her terrible brother. As well might you attempt to depict Othello without reference to Iago. The three form a demoniac triumvirate of materialism, of superstition, of crime ; and the dark sinister figures stand out with terrible distinctness from the surroundings of the Vatican and the background of the Roman Catholic Church. Herr Gregorovius even attempts no palliation of Alexander or of Cæsar; although actuated possibly by

> The gallantry of man
> In lovelier woman's cause;

and, relying upon certain weaknesses of evidence, he labours hard to bring about a verdict of, at least, 'not proven,' in favour of Lucrezia. A frame will indifferently surround any picture. The picture may be true or false, good or bad. Its subject or its merits may be what they will; but the frame recks not of the thing it shall contain, and the Church of the Renaissance framed with entire indifference any crime or any criminal. The psychological interest of the Borgia triumvirate is deepened by their close connexion with the Roman Church. They form historical problems, and are indissolubly connected with the morbid pathology of romance. They illustrate the period to which they so intensely belonged. They are, indeed, the most pregnant embodiments of the early Renaissance in Italy; and no attempt, like that of Gregorovius, to set aside the contemporary verdict which time has long endorsed, especially if such attempt profess to be based upon *Urkunden und Correspondenzen*—that is, upon the discovery of original documents and letters—should be allowed to pass without critical examination.

It may, at starting, be said, without unfairness to Herr Gregorovius, that he is rather an advocate than a judge. He seeks, at times, to snatch a verdict for his client, by ignoring some, and even confusing other evidence. He speaks, in places, by innuendo instead of clear declaration; and he is—although perhaps unconsciously—a partisan. The historian who does not speak clearly, or who evades the full responsibility of his position, resembles the cuttle-fish which exudes ink with a view to secrete its personality; and Herr Gregorovius not unfrequently shrouds his meaning in a maze of words. He relies too much upon his newly-discovered documents, although they do not always bear out his conclusions; and he ignores too, persistently, contemporary historians—as, for instance, the well-known *Istoria d'Italia di Messer Francesco Guicciardini*. Guicciardini, born 1482 (within two years of the birth of Lucrezia), was, in the strictest sense, a contemporary historian, and was well acquainted with all contemporary sources of information. He was informed of all the mass of oral testimony of the day; and knew thoroughly that great floating body, form, and pressure of belief and knowledge which filled the very air of the land and time; which, in the absence of newspapers, and of all written and published journalistic history, is so invaluable to the student of problematical characters whose high places in the world throw a hush of silence round their path of unbridled passion and unchecked crime. Guicciardini throws light upon many a passage which Herr Gregorovius leaves very dark ; and I find it useful to refer constantly to the quaint, though long-winded, old historian while considering the work of the later German writer.

Before we decide upon the policy of exchanging old lamps for new, before we consider specially the distinct issue raised by Herr Gregorovius, it will be convenient to place before the reader a short *résumé*—stated, of course, with the utmost possible brevity—of the leading facts in the careers of the Borgian triumvirate. If we know what a man *is* we know what he will *do*. The mysteries of character, especially in connexion with human beings who lived so long ago, are most easily penetrated when we have before us, seen from a bird's-eye view, a picture (as clearly painted as may be) of their lives and times, of their position and action, and of the *Zeit-Kolorit* which surrounded their existence. The family of Borja, or Borgia, is of Spanish descent. The flattering science of heraldry failed, when Rodrigo had become Pope, to trace the then all-powerful house to any very noble origin ; but the founder of the family in Italy was Alfonso Borgia, who, born in Valencia in 1378, was in the service of King Alfonso of Arragon, and became Bishop of Valencia. This Alfonso was made a Cardinal in 1444, and in 1455 was raised to the Papal chair as Calixtus the Third. He was a vigorous opponent of the Council of Basel, and of the early German efforts towards the Reformation. His nephew, Rodrigo Borgia, then twenty-five years old, became a Cardinal in 1456.

The Borgias, as a race, were gifted with rare physical strength and beauty; were distinguished by intellectual force, by strong and ruthless wills, and by an absence of conscience. The Papacy is not, of course, an hereditary office; and it is noteworthy that, in very many instances, when a man became pope, he made the greatest exertions, during his lifetime, to found a dynasty in the Church, and to amass wealth and to accumulate power in his own family.

Calixtus the Third died in 1458; and was succeeded by Pius the Second, Paul the Second, Sixtus the Fourth, Innocent the Eighth. During the reign of Pius the Second, we get a very characteristic glimpse of Cardinal Rodrigo, then twenty-nine years old. He was in Siena, and the Pope wrote him a strong *Mahnbrief*, a letter of reproof and warning (1460) touching his life and conversation, and adverting particularly to one orgie, concerning which the Holy Father remarks 'that shame will not allow him to recount all that was there done.' Rodrigo was then already distinguished for that boundless sensuality which characterised his whole life. Gasparo of Verona, writing a few years later, describes Rodrigo as 'very handsome, of pleasant and cheerful bearing, gifted with sweet and elegant eloquence. Whenever he meets with charming women, he excites love in them in an almost magical way, and he attracts them to himself more strongly than the magnet does the iron.'

His *physique* must have been splendid. All the powers of the body were balanced in perfect harmony. His health was so fine that he was always cheerful and gay. It is recorded of him in his later days that 'Nothing causes him trouble. He grows younger every day.' Crime even could not trouble him through conscience. Judging from their lives, it is natural to imagine the members of the Borgia triumvirate dark, gloomy, and sinister. No conception can be more false. The men were splendidly handsome; the women singularly lovely. All were gay and charming. Cæsar's handsome face may, indeed, have been distorted for the time into something fiercely hellish or infra-human when actually engaged in some of his more violent deeds of blood; but the deed once happily completed, the face would recover its smooth serenity, and the eye its steady light. They were happy as handsome.

The sensuous vitalism of Cardinal Borgia gave a fresh proof of its magnetism, when, in 1466 or 1467, he met Vanozza Catanei in Rome. Vanozza is, it may be remarked, the 'caressing' version of the name of Giovanna. Of the family or descent of Vanozza nothing is certainly known; but it is known that she was born in 1442 in Rome, and that she fell a victim (probably a willing victim) to the seductive arts of the cardinal. A sensual nature framed in voluptuous beauty; strong will, and cunning sense—though unaccompanied by culture—enabled her to obtain great ascendency over her cardinal lover; and her hold upon him must have been strong, since, during the activity of the *liaison*, the number of his bastards by other women was inconsiderable. The children of Rodrigo and Vanozza were: Cæsar, born 1476; Juan, born 1474; Goffredo born 1481; and Lucrezia, born when her father was forty-nine and her mother thirty-eight, on the 18th of April 1480. After the birth of Lucrezia, Rodrigo married Vanozza to Giorgio della Croce, and Vanozza's future children were ascribed to her husband.

Upon the death of her first husband, the lady married, in 1486, Carlo Canale. Vanozza lived in great comfort, in a house on the Piazza Pizzo di Merlo, distant only a few steps from the palace of the cardinal, and situated near the Bridge of Sant Angelo and the Vatican. Rodrigo Borgia was one of the richest princes of the Church. His cardinal's income was added to by high offices in the Church, by many abbacies in Italy and Spain, by the three bishoprics of Portus, Carthago, and Valencia, and by his Vice-Chancellorship. He was one of the most successful of churchmen. In the year 1482, we find Rodrigo admitting the paternity of Girolama, Hieronyma, Pietro, Lodovico, and Giovanni di Borgia; also of another daughter, Isabella. The mother, or mothers, of these bastards have not been identified;

but Vanozza was not among them. Some of the above-named children were older than the Catanei family. Rodrigo provided splendidly for all his offspring. Guicciardini records, as a distinctive trait of Rodrigo, that whereas other popes and cardinals had always decently termed their illegitimate children *nipoti*, he openly, in legal documents, declarations, and correspondence, called his *figliuoli*, and *figliuole*.

The time, says Gregorovius, in which Lucrezia was born, must, in truth, be termed terrible. The Papacy had thrown off all pretence to priestly holiness, and was, politically, the most tyrannical and immoral of despotisms. Religion had become altogether materialised; and unbridled immorality was the law of manners. Wild war raged in the city of Rome between certain of the great houses; while, in 1480, the factions of Guelf and Ghibelline began their struggles. Savelli and Colonna were enemies of the Pope, but the Orsini were his furious partisans. A godless and inhuman time was that of the 'problem of civilisation,' the Renaissance, in Rome and in Italy, at the close of the fifteenth and the beginning of the sixteenth century. Savonarola's burning denunciations were well warranted by facts.

Lucrezia's first years were undoubtedly passed in the house of her mother; but while still in her girlhood she was transferred by her father to the care of Madonna Adriana, daughter of Don Pedro, a nephew of Calixtus the Third, and cousin of Rodrigo

Borgia. He married this lady to Lodovico, Lord of Bassanello, a member of the great house of Orsini, who died before 1489. Adriana, as a widow, inhabited one of the Orsini palaces in Rome. She had one son, Orsino Orsini, by her husband Lodovico.

Cardinal Rodrigo lived in closest intimacy with Madonna Adriana. She remained, until his death, the *confidante* of his crimes and his amours, his assistant in all his plans and intrigues; and knew better, perhaps, than any other person, the terrible secrets of the Vatican. Gregorovius presents us with an admirable picture of the state of female culture in the Italy of the Renaissance. That which we now call a 'blue-stocking' was then termed a 'virago;' and the appellation of a 'man-woman' was complimentary. Lady Jane Grey was found reading Plato; and the women of the time were, perforce, in the comparative absence of a great modern literature, driven back to the languages and literature of the two great cultured nations of antiquity. 'Style,' alike in speaking as in writing, in oratory as in composition, was the fashion of the day. The limited field of study made the renowned woman of the Renaissance in Italy—as Cassandra Fedeli, Ginevra Sforza, Ippolita Sforza—thorough in their knowledge; nor do they, as a consequence of learning, forego feminine charm and grace. Gregorovius even maintains that their education was superior to that of women in our day, even in much vaunted Germany. He says of his countrywomen, that their culture is now wholly superficial, baseless, and scientifically valueless; that they learn only two modern *Conversations - Sprachen* and something of pianoforte playing, accomplishments to which they devote an undue amount of time.

Devotion to the Church was the basis of the training of Italian women of the Renaissance. The aim was, not to awaken the heart, or elevate the soul, but to produce mechanical religious obedience and observance. Shelley says, in the admirable piece of definition prefaced to the tragedy of the *Cenci*, that religion, in the mind of an Italian Catholic, ' is adoration, faith, submission, penitence, blind admiration; not a rule for moral conduct. It has no necessary connexion with any one virtue. The most atrocious villain may be rigidly devout, and, without any shock to established faith, confess himself to be so. Religion is, according to the temper of the mind which it inhabits, a passion, a persuasion, an excuse, a refuge; never a check.' This passage will help us to understand the problem of the Borgias. Lucrezia was carefully brought up in religion of this sort; but her youth could scarcely have been exposed to worse moral influences.

Her father, the voluptuous cardinal, engaged, in 1489, in the most notorious of his many amours. Giulia Farnese, a young girl of a beauty so distinctive that she was called *La Bella*, married, on the

21st of May 1489, Orsino Orsini, the son of Madonna
Adriana. The marriage fêtes took place in the
palace of Cardinal Borgia. She was then fifteen,
and he was fifty-eight years old. Giulia, like Lucrezia, had golden hair, and must have been of a
surpassing loveliness. She inflamed the passions
of the magnetic cardinal, and within two years after
her marriage became the acknowledged mistress of
Rodrigo Borgia, receiving from the irreverent the
titles of the 'Concubine of the Pope' and the 'Bride
of Christ.' Her husband was suitably provided for
away from Rome, and Giulia and Lucrezia lived
with Adriana, who, in consequence of her compliant
assistance, became the most influential person in the
house of Borgia. She favoured Rodrigo's adulter-
ous connexion with the wife of her own son, and
was surely worthy of her hire. The fortunes of the
Farnese family were founded by the fair, if erring,
Giulia.

In 1491, her father first thought of arranging a
marriage for Lucrezia, then eleven years old ; and
the husband selected for her was Don Cherubin
Juan de Centelles, of Valencia, the brother of the
Count Oliva. The marriage contract was drawn up,
but Rodrigo, from causes not mentioned by historians,
suddenly broke off the projected marriage.

In 1492, Rodrigo Borgia attained the great object
of his ambition, and became Pope. Innocent the
Eighth died the 25th of July 1492, and the choice of

his successor lay between four candidates, Rafael Riario, Guiliano della Rovere, Ascanio Sforza, and Rodrigo Borgia.

The Papal chair was ultimately sold to the highest bidder; and that was Rodrigo Borgia, who reigned and is known in the annals of the Papacy as Alexander the Sixth.

Giacomo Trotti, the Ferrarese ambassador, wrote, 28th of August 1492, to Duke Ercole: 'Cum simonia et mille ribalderie et inhonestate si è venduto il Pontificato che è cosa ignominiosa et detestabile!' France and Spain weakly, Venice strongly, opposed the election; but all the states of Italy accepted the new Pope; and Rodrigo Borgia, once in the saddle, was not a man to be easily dislodged.

Perhaps no man ever looked the part better than did Pope Alexander the Sixth as he received homage after his election. His stately figure and majestic head, his noble bearing and eyes, triumphant indeed, but full of strong, clear will and purpose, his manner composed and yet awful, must have made him appear the theatrical ideal of a pope. His graceful way of giving his benediction to the admiring populace, as he rode upon his snow-white horse to the Church of Sta Maria del Popolo, enhanced the value of that singular blessing.

Vanozza and Giulia must have triumphed in the triumph of their lover. The Pope soon thought out another husband for his favourite daughter. She was contracted to Don Gasparo, the son of Don Giovanni Francesco di Procida, Count of Aversa. But this project was thrown aside in favour of a union with Giovanni Sforza, Count of Cotognola and sovereign lord of Pesaro. Sforza was a widower. His first wife was Maddalena, the sister of Elisabetta Gonzaga. Maddalena died the 8th of August 1490, in childbirth. Sforza, who was twenty-six years old, was tall and good-looking. His face is noble, but gives no impression of weight of will or commanding intellect. He was an independent sovereign ruler, and had political value as a member of the great house of Sforza, with which the house of Borgia was then intimately allied.

On the day of his coronation, the new Pope made his son Cæsar, sixteen years of age, Bishop of Valencia. The Vatican was crowded with the friends and relatives of the all-powerful Borgia. 'Not ten Papacies would suffice to satisfy all that mob,' wrote, in November 1492, Gianandrea Boccaccio to the Duke of Ferrara. Alessandro Farnese, brother of the 'Bride of Christ,' was made a cardinal, as was Juan Borgia, son of the Pope's sister. Alexander was certainly liberal towards his children, relatives, and supporters.

Alfonso, the heir of Ferrara, was, in 1492, in Rome, and made the acquaintance of Lucrezia. Neither could have thought at that time that he would become, nine years later, her third husband. Alfonso was then the husband of Anna Sforza, and Lucrezia was about to marry Giovanni Sforza. The proud house of Este was one of the noblest in Italy. Alfonso's mother was Eleonora of Arragon, daughter of King Ferdinand of Naples. She died 1493. His sister Beatrice had married Lodovico il Moro, of Milan ; and his other sister, Isabella, one of the loveliest and most learned women of the day—a true *virago*—had married, in 1490, Francesco Gonzaga of Mantua. Alfonso of Este was a witness of the preparations for the marriage of Lucrezia.

Lucrezia married Giovanni Sforza in Rome on the 12th of June 1493 ; and Madonna Giulia Farnese— ' de qua est tantus sermo,' says the Ferrarese ambassador—graced the nuptials with her presence.

The Duke of Gandia had married, in Spain, Donna Maria Enriquez, of noble Valencian family. The exact date of this marriage is not known, but it is supposed to have taken place at the end of 1492. The Duke left Rome to return to Spain on the 4th of August 1493. On the 16th, Goffredo, the youngest of the Catanei-Borgia children, was married, by procuration, to Donna Sancia, a natural daughter of the then Duke of Calabria. Cæsar Borgia was made cardinal on the 20th of September 1493. On the same day, Ippolito of Este and Alessandro Farnese received the red hat. The latter was termed, with reference to his sister's position, the apron-cardinal.' In 1492 Giulia Farnese had made his Holiness the happy father of a daughter, christened Laura. Her husband was living in Bassanello. The Pope appointed Giulia first lady of the Court of his daughter, Lucrezia. A remarkable letter of Lorenzo Pucci, dated the 24th of December 1493, gives us a picture of the house in Sta Maria in Portico, which was the palace of Lucrezia, where she lived with Madonna Adriana and Madonna Giulia. Pucci's object was to obtain the assistance of the latter towards procuring for him some Papal post, and his request was graciously granted. Madonna Giulia showed him her child, and Pucci remarks that the infant strongly resembled the Pope, 'adeo ut vere ex ejus semine orta dici possit.' Madonna Giulia then let fall her golden rain of hair, which reached down to her feet. Pucci was enchanted with her beauty. Madonna Lucrezia went out and changed her dress, returning in another splendid costume of violet-blue velvet. The three Papal ladies sat by the fire, and chatted gaily with their delighted visitor, who left them at vespers, and has left to us a letter which gives a glimpse of the interior, and the interior life, of Lucrezia's Roman palace.

Don Goffredo, now Prince of Squillace, in Naples, married there, on the 7th of May 1494, Donna Sancia; and her father, owing to the death of King Ferdinand, ascended the throne of Naples on the same day.

In consequence of a pestilence in Rome, Sforza carried his wife to Pesaro; and, at the request of the Pope, they took with them Giulia and Adriana. This occurred probably in May or June 1494. The union of Lucrezia with Sforza was childless; but I cannot find a word of clear evidence to prove whether it were loving or loveless. Freed from the gloom of Rome and the dark shadow of the Vatican, her residence in her husband's beautiful palace at Pesaro must have been for Lucrezia a time of calm and quiet. It was her first escape from family domination, and from the school of vice in which her youth had been passed.

In September 1494, Charles the Eighth marched into Italy, and this invasion had one romantic consequence. The Holy Father, writing to Lucrezia, recommended her to pray constantly to the Virgin, and expressed great displeasure at the long absence of Adriana and Giulia. They were therefore sent back to him, but on the way were seized by an advanced corps of the French army.

The Pope was beside himself with rage and anguish. The French captain, ignorant, perhaps, of the importance of his prisoners, demanded a ransom of 3000 ducats, and was laughed at by Lodovico il Moro, who said that his Holiness would willingly have paid 50,000 ducats, and that his ladies should have been detained as hostages to insure the political good conduct of the Pope. The 3000 ducats were paid at once; and when Giulia and Adriana returned to Rome, the old Pope rode out on horseback to meet what he termed 'his eyes and his heart,' attired as a cavalier, wearing sword and dagger, Spanish boots, a black velvet doublet brocaded with gold, and a velvet barret cap. The infatuated old lover behaved like a young gallant. Always supremely indifferent to 'public opinion,' he openly defied its censures by his public conduct at the *Einholung* of his female friends.

Even a Papal despotism is a despotism tempered by epigrams. Lodovico told Trotti, the ambassador, that while Adriana and Giulia were absent, the Pope had sent for three women, one from Valencia, the second from Castille, and the third, a particularly fine girl, of fifteen or sixteen years of age, from Venice. 'Man spricht hier in Mailand,' says Ambassador Trotti, through Gregorovius' translation, 'öffentlich über diesen Papst solche Schmähungen aus, wie man sie etwa in Ferrara über den Torta auslassen würde.'

In 1496, the Holy Father had all his Catanei children around him in Rome—the Duke of Gandia, the Cardinal Cæsar; and the Prince of Squillace, with his fair young wife, Donna Sancia; Lucrezia and her husband being also there. Sancia and Lucrezia held two separate, but splendid, *Nipoti* Courts in their respective palaces.

Donna Sancia caused the loudest scandal. Married to an immature boy—a sort of Italian Darnley—the least gifted of all the race of Borgia; she, beautiful and licentious, feeling herself the daughter of a king, lived in Rome a flagrantly voluptuous life. Young nobles, and Cardinal Ippolito of Este, were reported to be her lovers; and it was confidently stated, and generally believed, that her brothers-in-laws, Irian and Cæsar, were honoured by her favours. Lucrezia, though more circumspect, yet 'lived like the others.' She was, says Gregorovius, neither better nor worse than the rest. Fond of pleasure and of luxury, she sank completely into the ordinary life of a Borgia. The Courts of the times of Louis the Fourteenth and Fifteenth, of Augustus of Saxony, of Charles the Second, were dissolute enough; but none of these can at all be compared with the ruthless energy of crime, alternating with unbridled licence of passion, which distinguishes to special infamy the bastard's Courts which then flourished under the shadow of the seat of St Peter.

Lucrezia's first marriage was dissolved by violence and fraud, and with infamy. At Easter 1497, Sforza returned from serving as a *condottiere* in the army of Naples, and we find it recorded that, as son-in-law of Alexander the Sixth, he, together with Cæsar and Gandia, received from the hands of the Holy Father Easter palm branches in St Peter's. Shortly after, the Pope required of Sforza that he should consent to have his marriage annulled, and upon his refusal he was threatened with death.

One evening Giacomino, the chamberlain of Sforza, overheard a conversation between Cæsar and Lucrezia. Cæsar spoke freely to his sister, and told her that he had determined upon the murder of her husband. Hearing of this conversation, Sforza at once mounted his Turkish horse, and rode, in four and twenty hours, with 'loose rein and bloody spur' to Pesaro. Arrived there, the horse dropped dead.

This sudden flight saved the life of Lucrezia's husband, but was highly distasteful to the Pope and the Cardinal. If Sforza had remained in Rome, his marriage would have been effectually annulled by his murder; but in Pesaro he was safe, and the Pope was compelled to institute legal proceedings for a divorce on the alleged ground of nullity of marriage. Lucrezia seems to have lied freely, and to have submitted passively to the execution of the scheme of her father and her brother. In connexion with this divorce Messer Guicciardini affords evidence of value. He says:—

> Era medesimamente fama (se però è degna di credersi tanta enormità) che nell' amore di Madonna Lucrezia concorressero non solamente i due fratelli, ma eziandio il padre medesimo; il quale avendola, come fu fatto Pontefice, levata dal primo marito come diventato inferiore al suo grado, e maritatala a Giovanni Sforza, Signore di Pesaro; non comportando d'avere anche il marito per rivale dissolvè il matrimonio già consumato; avendo fatto inanzi ai giudici delagati da lui provare con false testimonianze, a dipoi confermare per sentenza, che Giovanni era per natura frigido e impotente.

The alleged cause for the dissolution of the marriage is transparently false. Sforza was married before he married Lucrezia; he married again after

his divorce from her; and he had issue by both these marriages. Lodovico il Moro, a rough, practical man, proposed that Sforza should give public proof of the falsity of the charge brought against him. Meanwhile, the Pope, who did not hesitate to play with the sacraments of the Church, succeeded in obtaining (December 20, 1497) the divorce which he desired. Of Lucrezia's real feelings in the matter there is no evidence whatever. Certain it is that she did not oppose—nay, that she assisted—the steps taken in Rome to annul her first marriage. A true woman of the Renaissance, she was full of beauty and of culture, of courage and intellect, of lust and cruelty; and it seems probable that her life never knew a real love or a true passion. Between her divorce and her next marriage she was, according to Sannazaro and Pontano, 'a measureless Hetaira;' and, during this period, an ambassador reports:—
'La Roma accertasi che la figliola del Papa ha partorito.' The report spread, and the satires written about Lucrezia at this period were, it is certain, well known in Ferrara.

Giovanni Sforza proclaimed aloud in all the courts of Italy the real causes of his flight, his intended murder, and his divorce.

Matarazzo relates that Sforza had discovered, after his return from Naples, the triple incest of his wife, and that this discovery led to the action of the Pope and the Cardinal.

About this time, Hieronymus Porcius, the Infallibilist, wrote maintaining the doctrine of the Papal infallibility, and asserting that he only is a Christian who worships and blindly obeys the Pope. To a hypercritical intellect it would almost seem that the theory of Papal infallibility, when applied to Alexander the Sixth, is subjected to some slight strain.

Alexander intended to promote the welfare of his eldest son, Gandia, in the world, and that of his second son, Cæsar, in the Church; he gave temporal benefits to Gandia, ecclesiastical benefits to Cæsar. But this arrangement was wholly unsatisfactory to Cæsar, whose ambition desired the crown of Naples, or the establishment of a kingdom of Middle Italy. Hence jealousy and ill-will between the brothers, rivals alike in love as in ambition. Hence the murder of Gandia by his Cain-like brother, Cæsar. The brothers supped together at the house of their mother; Cæsar reached home safely, but Gandia never returned, and his murdered corpse was found in the Tiber. Guicciardini says of this event, and of Cæsar Borgia, that 'non potendo tollerare che questo luogo gli fosse occupato dal fratello; impaziente oltre a questo ch'egli avesse più parte di lui nell' amore di Madonna Lucrezia, sorella comune, incitato dalla libidine, e dall' ambizione, lo fece una notte,' etc. The Pope ignored the deed, and screened the offender. None but secret inquiry was made into the murder of Gandia; but all Rome knew the truth.

The Ferrarese ambassador writes:—'Di novo ho inteso come della morte del Duca di Gandia fù causa il Cardinale suo fratello.' The Pope virtually made himself the accomplice of his son's Cain-like crime. Shortly after the murder of Gandia, Cæsar's relations with Donna Sancia became open and undisguised. Lucrezia withdrew, for a time, to the convent of S. Sisto, in the Via Appia. The motive assigned was her desire for a temporary religious retirement; but very other reasons were generally believed to have dictated the step; reasons which, says Donato Aretino, writing from Rome, on June 4, to the Cardinal Ippolito in Ferrara, 'cannot be trusted to a letter.'

Having cleared the way by the murder of his elder brother, Cæsar Borgia desired to quit the Church, and to enter upon a career of active temporal ambition; and it was proposed to make Goffredo cardinal in the place of Cæsar. The Pope projected a marriage between Cæsar—then a cardinal—and Carlotta, daughter of King Federigo of Naples; but this proposal was rejected with indignation by the Court of Naples. The schemes of the Borgias for obtaining a footing in, and ultimately the crown of, Naples, led to Lucrezia's second marriage. On the 21st of July 1498, she wedded, in the Vatican, Don Alfonso, Prince of Salerno, Duke of Biselli, brother of Donna Sancia, and natural son of Alfonso the Second of Naples. He was seventeen, and Lucrezia was eighteen years of age. The young Alfonso must well have known the infamous reputation of the woman whom he was compelled to marry. He was the handsomest youth, says Talini, that had ever been seen in Rome; but he was melancholy, silent, passive; and had in his face and manner something of that deep, still, inner dejection which, according to popular superstition, is seen in those doomed to a violent death. The Mantuan agent reported in August that Lucrezia had a real liking for her second husband.

On the 13th of August 1498, the most terrible of the Borgias, Cæsar, resigned his cardinal's hat, and soon after went to France, where he was created by Louis the Twelfth Duke of Valentinois, and where, in May 1499, he married Charlotte d'Albret, sister of the King of Navarre.

In 1499, Alfonso fled suddenly from Rome. His reasons were no doubt good, and he probably saved his life by flight. He left Lucrezia pregnant, and she is said to have wept his absence. Alfonso would seem to have been the one man who could elicit such tenderness as she may have possessed. Her father was rendered furious by the flight of Alfonso, and commanded his daughter to recall her husband. Did she know of his flight, or know the reasons which impelled him to fly? Here we know nothing. She wrote, but Alfonso did not return; and the Pope sent his daughter, as regent, to Spoleto. In Nepi,

Alfonso rejoined his wife, who was also regent of that place. On the 14th of October 1499, Lucrezia and her husband returned to Rome; and on the 1st of November she gave birth to a son, christened Rodrigo, after the Pope. The paternity of this child is generally ascribed to the Duke of Biselli. Cæsar Borgia was busy with his campaigns of conquest in the Romagna.

Guicciardini states that, in 1500, Alexander the Sixth had 'quest' anno creati con grandissima infamia dodici cardinali, non de' più benemeriti, ma di quegli che gli offersero prezzo maggiore.' Giulia Farnese was, according to Vasari, by command of His Holiness, painted by Pinturicchio as the Blessed Virgin in a picture of the Madonna and Child.

In 1500, Alexander was seriously hurt by the fall of a chimney in the Vatican. He was nursed and tended by Lucrezia, and by one of the ladies of her court who was a 'favourite' of the Pope—then seventy years of age. He ascribed his safety to the protection of the Virgin, to whom he presented a goblet filled with 300 ducats.

Cæsar hated the whole house of Aragon, and the marriage of Alfonso with Lucrezia had lost all political importance, as it could no longer bring Cæsar nearer to the throne of Naples. On the 15th of July 1500, Alfonso went, at eleven at night, to the Vatican to visit Lucrezia. As he ascended the St Peter's staircase, he was attacked by masked men.

They left him for dead, but, seriously wounded as he was by the daggers of the assassins, the young Duke crawled to the Papal residence. He was admitted, and Lucrezia fainted when she saw his condition. His life was despaired of, and he received absolution. Youth, however, triumphed, and Biselli returned to life. He was tended, in the chambers of the Vatican, by Lucrezia and Sancia, who themselves cooked all his food, while Alexander placed special guards round the Duke's chamber. The Venetian ambassador wrote to the Signoria to say that the attempt upon Alfonso's life was made by the person who had murdered Gandia. Cæsar must have had a deadly personal hatred of Alfonso. He visited the wounded man, and said, with his meaning smile, as he left the room, that 'that which is not done by noon can be completed in the evening.' On the 18th of August, Cæsar returned to the patient. It was nine at night, and he was accompanied by Capitano Michelotto. He drove Lucrezia and Sancia from the chamber of the young Duke, and then completed the murder. The body of Alfonso was carried into St Peter's.

Cæsar openly boasted of the murder. The Pope knew his son too well to trouble him with useless rebuke; and oblivion, as in the case of Gandia, soon gathered round the bloody deed. No man held aloof from the Borgias; no priest refused Cæsar entrance to a church; no cardinal ceased to greet him with reverence. Prelates hastened to him—for

Cæsar was, at the time, raising money by selling cardinal's hats to the highest bidders — to receive from his murderous hand the dignity which they had purchased. Surrounded by his *condottieri*, and, at the head of troops furnished by Alexander, Cæsar went gaily forth on his campaign in the Romagna.

Meanwhile we have no glimpse of Alfonso's widow. Such a murder must have had some shock for the nerves even of a Borgia; and she is thought to have loved her husband. No hint exists that can give us any clue to the feelings of Lucrezia. Was she indignant, but compelled to silence by dread of Cæsar? Did she acquiesce passively in the tragedy? One would like some answer to the questions on this point which naturally suggest themselves; but, alas! 'there lives no record of reply.' She knew well that her brother murdered Alfonso, but she certainly took no step to avenge her slaughtered husband, nor does any contemporary mention any grief or action on her part. One thing, however, is certain: she remained to the end of his life on intimate and even affectionate terms with Cæsar; their letters are familiar and friendly in tone; and Lucrezia, when Duchess of Ferrara, strained her influence to the utmost to serve the interests of the Duke of Valentinois. She was then in no fear of her brother, and her action could only proceed from warm sympathy with him and with his fortunes.

Hardly was the first Alfonso murdered, when there

was already talk of a second Alfonso. In November 1500, the Pope spoke of his project for a marriage between Lucrezia and the heir of Ferrara, Alfonso d'Este. Alfonso, twenty-four years of age, was a childless widower. The Venetian ambassador, on the 26th of November, reported the scheme to his Government, and said that the idea proceeded wholly from the Pope. It seems probable that the new marriage had been contemplated in the Vatican before the then existing marriage had been bloodily severed. The Duke of Gravina, an Orsini, was a candidate for the honour of Lucrezia's hand; but his claims were rejected in favour of Alfonso d'Este.

The reigning Duke, Ercole d'Este, was, at first, as indignant at this proposal as Federigo of Naples had been at the projected alliance of Cæsar with his house. The Duke's daughter, Isabella of Mantua, and Elisabetta of Urbino, were 'beside themselves' with rage and dismay. Alfonso himself refused to listen to the idea of such a marriage.

The Pope put pressure on Ferrara through France, and threatened the Duke with the direst enmity of himself, of Cæsar, and of Louis the Twelfth. Fear is an influential counsellor, and interest speaks with a still, strong voice. Duke Ercole at last gave way, and sought only to obtain from the Pope exorbitant concessions in return for his consent. Alexander exclaimed angrily that Ercole was a *mercatante*, but he had ultimately to accede to the very high terms demanded by the Duke. The Emperor Maximilian opposed the marriage with all his influence. Indeed, such a marriage was, as Guicciardini says, 'molto indegno della famiglia d' Este, perchè Lucrezia era spuria, e coperta di molte infamie.' Gregorovius says of Lucrezia, that at the time of the proposed Este marriage 'ihr Ruf war geradezu abschreckend.' It was felt on all hands that the honour of the proud house of Este was being basely trafficked away. Alfonso remained simply passive. He would take no step in the affair, and he never once wrote to Lucrezia during the negotiations for their marriage. Lucrezia's position must have been a degrading one for a proud woman. Her hand was being sold, by a forced sale, to a most unwilling purchaser. There could be no question of love, but there was every attribute of dishonour in the whole transaction. She, however, pressed on the marriage with feverish eagerness. She was, the envoys said, 'a better Ferrarese than the Ferrarese themselves;' and she removed all difficulties between the Pope and the Duke.

Her reputation was well known in Ferrara. When the Duke's envoys saw her in Rome, they reported that 'her appearance in no way answered to her sinister reputation.' They praised her great beauty; they were delighted with her grace and winning charm of manner, with her sweet gaiety, and with her clear intellect. In short, the envoys, like all other men who came within the charmed circle, were enchanted by the magic of Lucrezia's personality. It was early, though, for the widow of the recently murdered young husband to be showing such cheerfulness as the envoys complacently describe and dwell upon.

It should be here mentioned that the Pope, about this time, made the victorious Cæsar Duke of the Romagna. Ferrara was politically important to the new Duke, and he was dangerous to the possessions of Este. In the course of the campaign, Cæsar had seized Pesaro, and Giovanni Sforza was an exile in Ferrara itself.

Lucrezia seems to have looked upon her marriage with Alfonso d'Este with *naïve* vanity and ambition. It was the first time, in her experience of wedlock, that a throne had been offered to her, and that throne one of the oldest in Italy.

At this juncture a curious little episode occurred in Rome. One of the most perplexing infants in history—an unusually wise child if he knew his own father—then probably about three years old, had to be provided for by the Holy Father. This child is Giovanni di Borgia. In a bull, dated September 1, 1501, Alexander declares that the boy was the illegitimate offspring of Cæsar; but that he, the Pope, in virtue of his apostolic power, is pleased to legitimatise the child. In a second *breve*, dated directly after the former one, His Holiness explains that, although, 'for good reasons,' he had before ascribed the child to his son Cæsar, he now acknowledges it as his own. He speaks of the infant as 'nobili infanti Johanni Borgia nostro secundem carnem nipote.' Lucrezia was generally believed to be the mother of this boy. When Giovanni came in after years to Ferrara, the Duchess called him her 'brother.' If she were his mother, the paternity of the lad becomes a delicate problem.

At last, all difficulties were overcome, and on the 6th of January 1502, Lucrezia left Rome—for ever. A splendid escort from Ferrara accompanied her to her new home and new life. Alfonso received his bride with cold, silent politeness; but, during all the long festival which surrounded her marriage, Lucrezia is described as having been 'continuamente allegra e ridente.' Her beauty and her wonderful witchery of manner elicited the ecstatic admiration of Ferrara; and she became, at once, the idol of the Court and of the populace.

A new life had indeed opened to her. She had left her father, and her Holy Father, her brothers, her mother Vanozza, Madonna Giulia, Donna Sancia. Her experiences of life in Rome had been terrible and dark. Surrounded by lawless passions, crimes, and tragedies, knowing well the sinister secrets of the Vatican of the Renaissance, placed from her earliest youth in a school of almost unexampled wickedness; with the memories of two marriages, with one ex-husband living, and another festering in a bloody shroud—Lucrezia Borgia had acquired a fearful reputation, and had lived a dreadful life. The near personal support of Alexander and of Cæsar had ceased. They could no longer control or compel. Ferrara, compared to Rome, was noble and was pure. We shall never know whether, during her Roman life, she had been compelled into complicity with crime; or whether she, too, had been a genuine Borgia, and had shared contentedly the Borgia life of sin and shame. Was her eagerness for the Ferrara marriage a desire for a better life? or was it merely the result of an ambition which aspired to a throne? Again we know not, and can never know. Of regret, of remorse for the dark past, there is no sign or hint. She shared the magnificent *physique* of her race; had their temperamental cheerfulness, their equable temper, their powers of enjoyment, their strength of nerve, their want of conscience, their vanity, and their ambition. In her, also, the moral sense was non-existent, and superstition ruled where religion should have reigned. The final estimate of her character, the examination into evidence for or against her, must be reserved till later; but, taking the most favourable view of Lucrezia when she exchanged Rome for Ferrara, we must, at least, regard her as a woman of her race and of her time. She was a type of the Renaissance, and the daughter of the Borgia. This brief narrative of her life and ways here frees itself, gladly, from the gloom of Rome, and breathes a purer air in Ferrara. Henceforth Lucrezia Borgia, with the worst passages of her evil life left behind her, will move before us as the heroine of poet and of dramatist, as the delight of a Court, as the patroness of art, as the beloved of a people —as the renowned Duchess of Ferrara.

## II.—FERRARA.

*The days will grow to weeks, the weeks to months,*
*The months will add themselves and make the years,*
*The years will roll into the centuries,*
*And mine will ever be a name of scorn.—Guinevere.*

HERR GREGOROVIUS evinces a sympathetic acquaintance with the picturesque side of the Italian Renaissance, with its splendour and its art, with its masques and dancings, with its costume, ceremonials, and cavalcades. His description of the *fêtes* which delighted Ferrara at the nuptials of Lucrezia and Alfonso is minute, full, and graphic. Isabella Gonzaga did the honours, as lady representative of the house of Este, with scarcely dissembled unwillingness, and with a heart full of rage against her infamous new sister-in-law. The only voice which ever disputed Lucrezia's claim to beauty is that of Isabella, herself one of the fairest women of the day, who did not find the renowned bride so *very* beautiful

—considered, in fact, that Lucrezia's reputation for charms was somewhat exaggerated. The general welcome accorded to the Pope's daughter was, however, undoubtedly warm and hearty. Lucrezia's natural grace and charm were heightened by the radiant triumph which expressed itself in her whole bearing. The Pope was gratified by her reception in Ferrara. Madonna Adriana, at his wish, accompanied Lucrezia to her new home. Either by design, or under the pressure of necessity, the house of Este had prepared a selection of bastard daughters to receive Lucrezia in her palace. Arrived at the great staircase, she was greeted by another Lucrezia, a natural daughter of Duke Ercole, married to Annibale Bentivoglio ; by three illegitimate children of Sigismund of Este—Lucrezia, Countess of Cararra, the fair Diana, Countess Uguzoni, and Bianca Sanseverino. All agreed that the young duke's young wife was *venusta, gentile, graziosa, amabile*. Whatever prejudice may have existed against her, this remarkable woman succeeded without effort in enchanting all—with the exception of the noble Isabella Gonzaga—with whom she came in contact. Her happiness lent her an added force to the magic of great charm.

Alexander the Sixth was 'shut up in measureless content' at the success of the marriage which he had, with so much difficulty, brought about. He did not expect that Alfonso should love Lucrezia ;

but he desired that she should be treated with the honour due to a wife, and that she should be made the mother of a prince. He told the Ferrarese ambassador in Rome that, so long as Alfonso visited Lucrezia at night, he might run all day after other amours; and indeed, said the good old man, considering that my son-in-law is still so young, he does quite right to amuse himself in that way. Alfonso had no reason to dread any oppressively strict morality on the part of his respected father-in-law.

Cæsar, who had just strangled the young Astorre Manfredi in Sant Angelo, continued his campaign of successful rapine. He wrote the news of his triumphs to Lucrezia, and when, on the 5th of September, she was confined of a still-born child, he came to Ferrara to visit his sister. There is every evidence of intimate and cordial relations between the Duke of Valentinois and the Duchess of Ferrara. The Gonzagas listened to a proposal of marriage between their heir, Federigo, and Cæsar's daughter Luise. Cæsar, at this time, had all but attained the great object of his ambition—the crown of Middle Italy; when Louis the Twelfth interfered and forbade his further progress in that direction.

On the 18th of August 1503, Alexander the Sixth died of poison, and his son Cæsar was all but included in the same fate. We will let Guiccardini tell the tale in his own quaint way. He says :—

E cosa manifesta, essere stata consuetudine frequente del padre e sua [this refers to Cæsar] non solo di usuare il veleno, per vendicarsi contro agl' inimici, o per assicurarsi dei sospetti, ma eziandio per scellerata cupidità di spogliare delle proprie, facultà le persone ricche, cardinali e altri cortigiani, non avendo rispetto che da essi non avessero mai ricevuta offesa alcuna, come fu il cardinale molto ricco di S. Angelo, ma ne anche che gli fossero amicissimi e congiuntissimi.

In explanation of this allusion to Cardinal S. Angelo, it should be mentioned that the chamberlain of the murdered cardinal — the said chamberlain being executed for other and manifold misdeeds—confessed, before his death, that he had poisoned the cardinal under the express orders of Alexander and of Cæsar. Guicciardini's distinct statement of the Borgia practice of poisoning enemies or victims is borne out by the fact that Alexander and Cæsar were both poisoned by some (for them) mischance in an attempt to poison Adriano, Cardinale di Corneto. By an accident, the poisoned chalice, intended for another, was commended to their own lips. Cæsar, who was much younger than his father, saved his life by the timely use of antidotes, things with which he was probably well acquainted ; but Alexander perished miserably by the very poison which he had intended for the cardinal.

He died unregretted. Indeed, humanity seemed to breathe more freely when this monster was removed from the earth. Owing to the horrible effects of the Borgia poison, the corpse of the Pope had lost all shape and form, all distinction between length and breadth. A rope was fastened round the feet, and one porter dragged the body to its place of sepulture. Alexander's death-bed was not soothed by love. Neither Vanozza nor Giulia Farnese seems to have been near him. Lucrezia was in Ferrara, and Cæsar was suffering from the effects of the same deadly poison. Guicciardini says of Alexander the Sixth :—

> La sua immoderata ambizione, e pestifera perfidia, e con tutti gli essempj di orribile crudeltà, di mostruosa libidine e d'inaudita avarizia, vendendo senza distinzione le cose sacre e le profane, aveva attossicato tutto il mondo. E non dimeno era stato esaltato con rarissima e quasi perpetua prosperità dalla prima gioventù insino all' ultimo della vita sua, desiderando sempre cose grandissime, e ottenendo più di quello desiderava.

The life, the actions, and the character of this Pope will for ever remain a moral problem. It must be remembered that he *was* Pope. He was not merely an almost incredibly wicked man, but he claimed to be the vicar of God. Apart even from the darkest crime which stains his infamous memory, his life was a long breach of the commandments which say, thou shalt not steal ; thou shalt do no murder ; thou shalt not commit adultery ; thou shalt not bear false witness against thy neighbour. Alexander the Sixth is, perhaps, the greatest and the foulest criminal in history ; and he is, furthermore, an occupant of the chair of St Peter, the infallible pontiff of a Church which claims to represent Christianity. His life, and his success in life, destroy completely all the mystical pretensions which the superstitions and the fancies of men have woven round the Papacy. The spectacle of Rodrigo Borgia as Vicegerent of Christ excites almost a demoniac tendency to unnatural, mirthless amusement. The contrast of man and office awakens a sort of hideous humour.

Alexander did not hate or contemn the world; he was no Titanic sceptic or atheist, whose profound disbelief in divinity, and raging scorn of humanity, led him to despise heaven and to defy hell. No, he believed—in his way; but he could turn from incest, from adultery, from murder, to worship the Virgin, to perform mass, to fulfil any of the highest and most mystical functions of sacerdotal sacredness. He was nearly always successful; he was habitually happy. His health was fine, and his *physique* superb. He was superbly ambitious for himself; and his love for his children made him ambitious for them. His sensuality was measureless, and his greed unbounded; but he shared his spoils with his offspring, and helped them to acquire for themselves. He had absolutely no conscience, no moral sense; and no dread whatever of the reward of crime. He too might say, with Cenci,—

> And I have no remorse, and little fear,
> Which are, I think, the checks of other men.

In him were blended materialism and superstition. He touches humanity chiefly in his love for his children, but is otherwise as infra-human as he is undivine.

It would almost seem as if some demon had, in mockery of men, created a being who should thrive through unsurpassed wickedness, and who—as the profoundest effort of most devilish satire—should be placed on high in the then chief office of Christendom, and be worshipped by millions as the infallible representative on earth of the all-wise, all-merciful, omniscient, and eternal God. He is reported to have said, when dying, 'I come; so is right; wait but a very little;' and human credulity delighted in a belief that he had made a compact with the Evil One to sell his soul for the Papacy and the satisfaction of his lawless desires. He was, said the report, to enjoy the holy seat for twelve years; and, in fact, he was Pope for that period. Seven devils were, it was stated, seen of men in his death-chamber; and the Faust character of the popular belief was heightened by the story of a black hound running restlessly about in St Peter's.

It is probable that Lucrezia did not see the letters of her father-in-law about the late Pope, her father. Ercole spoke his views plainly. Bembo describes Lucrezia as being in deep dejection when the news came; but sorrow may have been blended with apprehension about the influence of the Pope's death upon her own position. Alfonso was, however, loyal to his wife. If he did not love her, he found in her, assuredly, an astute ally and a valuable helpmate. When the race of Borgia was proscribed, and Cæsar himself was in ignoble flight, Lucrezia remained safely sheltered and duly honoured in Ferrara. She was not included in the fall of her race and name. The children, Rodrigo and Giovanni Borgia, were in Rome; and the Orsini raged for the blood of every Borgia. Lucrezia exerted her influence to the very utmost to save and serve Cæsar Borgia, whose conquests, including those in the Romagna, were fast melting away. She probably could not, certainly did not, have the children in Ferrara, but she exerted herself for their safety and welfare, and a list is still extant, in the archives, of the clothing with which she, at that time, supplied them.

On the 22d of September 1503, Cardinal Piccolomini succeeded to the Papal chair as Pius the Third. The good old man had twelve bastard children, and his tender efforts to provide suitably for them in the Vatican were frustrated by his untimely death, which occurred on the 18th of October.

Cardinal Rovere was next elected, on the 1st of November 1503, as Pope Julius the Second. He continued the political worldly policy of Alexander the Sixth. Although his interests led him to oppose the House of Borgia, he yet warmly admired their talents and successes.

In 1505, Alfonso, then on a visit to our Henry the Seventh of England, was hastily summoned back to Ferrara, and arrived in time to close the eyes of his father, Duke Ercole. He then became the reigning Duke, and Lucrezia the actual Duchess of Ferrara.

In 1506, Donna Sancia died childless; and on the 28th of August 1512, Lucrezia's son, Rodrigo, died, at the age of thirteen, in Bari. She never saw the boy after she left Rome.

After many misfortunes and vicissitudes, Cæsar, the most terrible of the Borgias, died on the 12th of March 1507; and the accomplished villain had the undeserved good fortune to die a soldier's death. As a mercenary, in the pay of Navarre, he was engaged in besieging the Conte di Lerin, in the castle of Viana, when he received his death-wound. Lucrezia's grief at the death of the murderer of her brother Gandia, and of her second husband, Alfonso of Biselli, seems to have been great and deep. She cared for his two bastards, Girolamo and Lucrezia, in Ferrara itself. In 1510, her first husband, Giovanni Sforza, died; he was remarried, and left a legitimate son. Cæsar's daughter, Luise, married first Louis de la Tremouille, and afterwards Philippe de Bourbon. Her mother, the widow of the Duke of Valentinois, retired from the world, and lived, until her death, in strict seclusion. Ercole Strozzi sang the glorious life and heroic deeds of Cæsar Borgia in pompous strains which he dedicated to Lucrezia. He depicts Lucrezia and Charlotte mourning the death of the brother and husband, as Cassandra and Polyxena wept for Achilles. He recites all Cæsar's violent victories and usurpations; but, while he exalts his hero as superior to all the heroes of antiquity, he omits any mention of his black crimes, all allusion to those many murders, a list of which would perhaps have swelled the poem beyond all reasonable length. The treachery of Sinigaglia alone would have occupied too much space.

Alfonso d'Este was a quiet, practical man; something hard, and cold, and stern, but true and loyal, and devoted to Ferrara's welfare. He was no 'expensive Herr,' but a prince who cared little for court splendour or personal expenditure, and occupied himself chiefly with politics, with fortifications, and with the casting of cannon. I observe something of the Hohenzollern nature in this quiet, strenuous, active Alfonso. The situation of Ferrara was an anxious and a dangerous one. It was threatened by powerful enemies—by the Pope and by Venice; and, but for Alfonso's vigilance and energy, his duchy would surely have been taken from him. He left to his lovely wife court ceremonials and festivals; he left it to her to patronise painting and poetry; while he perfected that artillery which, remarkable for its time, afterwards won, in 1512, that battle of Ravenna, in which the loss of Gaston de Foix changed French victory into mourning. 'Le bon chevalier, le seigneur de Bayard,' visited Ferrara after the great battle, and saw Lucrezia. Fresh from France, he knew, probably, but little of her dark past, and, like a chivalrous poet-hearted knight, Bayard was enchanted with Ferrara's lovely and winning Duchess. He wrote,—'J'ose bien dire que, de son temps, ni beaucoup avant, il ne s'est point trouvé de plus triomphante princesse, car elle était belle, bonne, douce et courtoise à toutes gens.' Lucrezia's manner must have been sweet and fine; the grace of the princess tempered by the charm of the charming woman. She, too, was one of those princesses who madden poets: she had her Rizzio and Châtelard—her Bembo and Strozzi. Both poets were deeply, passionately enamoured of her, and she, in some sort, returned their affection; though the question of the exact extent of her relations towards them is a point which must be relegated to the hypotheses of history.

Many of the letters which were interchanged between Lucrezia and Bembo are still extant, and writ in very choice Italian. Those of Lucrezia appear to express a warmer feeling than friendship; and the lock of her golden hair, still to be seen in the Ambrosiana of Milan, was given by the Duchess to her adorer, Bembo. Alfonso was not, however, a husband whose jealousy could safely be aroused. Bembo, no doubt under pressure from the Duke, suddenly quitted Ferrara; and Ercole Strozzi, who remained, met a tragic fate. On the morning of the 6th of June 1508, the young poet was found dead at the corner of the Palazzo d'Este, pierced with three-and-twenty wounds. Strozzi was the pride of Ferrara, and the popular excitement was great. No inquiry was instituted, 'and no man,' says Paul Jovius, 'dared to name the murderer.' Two theories were current: one was that the jealous Alfonso had caused the deed to be done; the other that the Duchess had instigated the destruction of a lover who had just transferred his affections to Barbara Torelli. The truth was known to but very few, and they were silent; but the ardent young poet, who had scorched his wings at his high and dangerous love, perished miserably by the assassin's dagger, and exchanged life, and love, and song for an early and a bloody grave.*

In November 1506, we again hear of *La Bella*, of that Giulia who had founded the fortunes of the house of Farnese by her adultery with the late Pope. When all the Borgia faction fled for life from Rome, she went with Madonna Adriana to Bassanello, and there remained in safety. Her husband was dead. Giulia and Lucrezia continued in constant and intimate correspondence. To the astonishment of Rome, this adventurous adulteress succeeded in marrying her daughter Laura, the bastard child of

* As a specimen of Ercole Strozzi's poetical homage to Lucrezia, the following verse may be cited :—

'Læto nata solo, dextrâ, rosa, pollice carpta ;
Unde tibi solito pulchrior, unde color ?
Num te iterum tinxit Venus ? an potius tibi tantum
Borgia purpureo præbuit ore decus ?'

Alexander the Sixth, to Niccolo Rovere, the 'carnal nipote' of the Pope Julius the Second. This was great advancement for the sister of even the Duchess of Ferrara. The marriage took place in the Vatican. It meant reconciliation between the houses of Rovere and of Borgia; but it excited general surprise, and produced many epigrams. It was, perhaps, the greatest triumph achieved in the romantic life of Giulia Farnese, and restored her to the highest ranks of Roman aristocracy. She knew well the advantages of Papal favour. In May 1506, Julius the Second had given his own illegitimate daughter Felice in marriage to Giangior Lano Orsini of Bracciano, and the house of Orsini was gained over to the house of Rovere. Giulia, still a beautiful and seductive woman, returned to a life of splendour and of luxury.

In 1513, the truculent Julius the Second died, and was succeeded by the 'false Medici,' Leo X. Pietro Bembo, the poet lover of Lucrezia, became secretary to the new Pope.

On the 26th of November 1518, Vanozza Catanei, the mother of Lucrezia, died in Rome. The old sinner had become, in her later days, rigidly devout. Gregorovius says of her, 'sie wurde eine werkheilige Bettschwester.' The archives of Ferrara contain nine of her letters, addressed to Lucrezia and to Cardinal Ippolito. She was also in correspondence with her son, the Prince of Squillace, and, in the year 1515,

she received into her house her grandson, of ten
years old, the son of Giuffré, or Goffredo. Her letters
show a woman of strong sense, of force of character,
very cunning, with a keen eye to her own interests,
and of rough culture. She must have had something
of the distinctive power of will which she transmitted
to her children. It is noteworthy that Rodrigo
Borgia's bastards, other than his Catanei children,
all sank into the dark background of their time,
and were absorbed by the ordinary life of the day;
whereas Cæsar, Gandia, Lucrezia, are figures with
force enough to stand out against the age, and have
made their mark in history, in story, and in song.
Vanozza signs herself, when writing to Lucrezia, 'la
felice et infelice quanto matre, Vanotia Borgia de
Cathaneis.' Her letters are not written with her
own hand, but have been dictated to some amanu-
ensis. During the evil days for the house of Borgia,
she fled at first to her son Cæsar, but she returned
to Rome so soon as it was safe to do so; and she
managed to retain her not inconsiderable property.
She left all that she died possessed of to the Church,
and was buried in the church of S. Maria del Popolo.
Her funeral was attended with almost the same pomp
as that of a cardinal, and Leo the Tenth sent his
chamberlain to do honour to her obsequies. A
splendid tomb, bearing a lying inscription, was
erected over her remains; but hate or shame, in
after years, destroyed her monument, and left not

a trace of inscription or of sarcophagus. The masses for which she had paid in advance, to purchase heaven, were read for two hundred years, but were at last stopped by the Church; less, perhaps, from the belief that enough had been done for the repose of the soul of Vanozza, than from a dread of modern criticism. She was a woman whose life contained many memories, and who knew much of the interior of the Vatican. She was also Lucrezia's earliest link to life.

Under Leo the Tenth, Don Michelotto, Cæsar's old captain, was examined, under torture, in S. Angelo, touching his complicity with Cæsar in the murders of Gandia, of Alfonso of Aragon, of Varano, of Camerine, of Astorre and Ottasiano Manfredi, of Bernardino of Sermoneta, of the Bishop of Cagli, and of many another victim. He confessed under the second application of the rack, and 'dixe che Papa Alessandro fu quello che fece ammazzare Don Alfonso, marito che fu della Duchessa.' This confession was reported forthwith to Ferrara.

Ariosto is the poet who forms the chief glory of Ferrara; and he has immortalised the house of Este in the *Orlando Furioso*. In his temple of distinguished women he has placed Lucrezia. Ariosto was in the service of the profligate and cruel Cardinal Ippolito. Titian and Raphael both painted for Alfonso, and Lucrezia had in her cabinet a marble Cupid by Michael Angelo; of which statue the gallant Ercole Strozzi sang that the god had been turned to stone by the glances of Lucrezia's eyes. Many portraits of Lucrezia were painted in her lifetime, but not one is now known to exist. Some of them are, no doubt, pointed out in Italian galleries by confident *cognoscenti* as the portraits of other women. The portrait which Titian, it is believed, painted of her is unrecognised. Like the lost portrait of Sir Philip Sidney by Tinteretto, it is now, doubtless, ascribed to some other original. A head upon a medal, a sumptuous reputation, and verbal descriptions by poets or ambassadors, are now the only evidences which we possess of the matchless beauty of the splendidly lovely Lucrezia Borgia.

During the troublous times of Ferrara, her husband, when away with the army, left Lucrezia regent ; and her rule was wise and prudent. She was, indeed, as her father had justly said of her, a woman of rare mental power and talent. Her conduct, during her later life in Ferrara, was blameless and even exemplary. As the lust of the eye and the pride of life departed slowly with youth, with beauty, and with vanity, Lucrezia, like her mother, turned more and more to religious observances. She seemed to forget her past, and her past seemed to be forgotten of men. Bigotry waxed as vice waned. She bore five children, presumably, to Alfonso ; and her son succeeded to the dukedom as Ercole the Second of Este. He married that Renée, the daughter of

Louis the Twelfth, who afterwards embraced the Reformation.

On the 14th of June 1519, Lucrezia was confined of a still-born daughter. It soon became evident that the illness consequent upon this confinement would prove fatal, and the Duchess prepared to pay the debt of nature. As a woman she had good grounds for a just estimate of Popes, but as a Catholic she desired the Papal benediction; and she wrote, describing herself as a sinner, to Leo the Tenth, for his blessing before death. On the night of the 24th of June, she died. Her husband was present, and showed grief for the loss of his valuable ally and life companion of so many years. Alfonso survived Lucrezia fifteen years. He died on the 31st of October 1534. Our George the Second assured his dying queen, Caroline of Anspach, that he should never marry again, but would manage to make out with mistresses. Alfonso acted on the same principle. He never again married; but a certain beautiful Laura Eustochia Dianti, of Ferrara, became his acknowledged mistress, and bore him two sons, Alfonso and Alfonsino.

The evil fame which Lucrezia's later life had partly silenced, broke out again after her death. When Guidobaldo the Second was about to choose a wife, his father warned him against the frequent misalliances of princes, and cited that of Alfonso of Ferrara, who married Lucrezia Borgia, a woman 'of a sort that every man knows.' The son agreed in this judgment; and said that he had, he knew, a father who would never compel him to marry a woman like Lucrezia, 'di quella mala sorte che fù quella, e con tante disoneste parti.'

We have now run through a necessarily very condensed narrative of the Borgia triumvirate, and I must devote a few final words to the examination of the arguments of those who, like Herr Gregorovius, contend that Lucrezia Borgia is a much maligned woman ; and that the general historical conception, both of contemporaries and of later writers, is essentially ungenerous and unjust. There is a full consentience of contemporary historical witnesses relative to even the darkest guilt which loads with infamy the memory of Lucrezia Borgia. The attackers are Guicciardini, Machiavelli (who is explicit touching the relations between his hero Cæsar and Lucrezia), Sannazaro, Pontano, Matarazzo, Priuli, Petrus Martyr, Marcus Attilius Alexius ; while from among the ranks of the olden assailants rises the towering crest of the great modern, Gibbon.

The defenders are Herr Gregorovius, Mr W. Gilbert, Roscoe, and the Marchese Campori, who is the author of *Una Vittima della Storia*. There are some minor admirers or whitewashers, as Monsignor Antonelli, Giovanni Zucchetti, Domenico Cerri, Bernardo Gatti ; but this latter list comprises no writer of special mark or importance.

In order to narrow the field of inquiry, it may at

once be remarked that the assailants all refer their grave charges to the Roman period of Lucrezia's life. The defenders are fond of dwelling upon the Ferrara time, and argue that a woman who could live so well in Ferrara could not have been guilty of such evil as is charged against her in Rome.

The leading tenets of the defenders are :—

1. That such heinous crime as is charged against Lucrezia Borgia is, in itself, a thing incredible.
2. That a woman so lovely and so charming as she admittedly was, could not have been guilty.
3. That the life in Ferrara contradicts the life which she is said to have led in Rome.

It is worth while to examine this defence in detail.

Contemporary poets were, in the Ferrara time, her panegyrists and flatterers; but no contemporary historian omits to mention, with all the calmness of conviction, the leading criminal charges against Lucrezia.

The defenders cannot proceed by way of rebutting or shaking evidence. They can only refuse to give credence to it, and allege sentimentally that it should not be believed. As the true colours on a frescoed wall may be obscured and hidden by a layer of whitewash, they seek to cover over evidence which they cannot refute.

Gregorovius maintains that the moral sense is outraged by believing the historical evidence against Lucrezia; but surely the moral sense exceeds its province when it assuages its disgust by ignoring evidence, or by tampering with facts. It is right that certain facts should revolt the moral sense ; but it is not moral to find an escape for the mind by denying or disguising facts. The question is one of fact ; not whether the facts are pretty. The history of the Renaissance in Italy is in itself a large fact which contains a great deal that must revolt the moral sense.

The merely sentimental desire to exculpate Lucrezia, in the teeth of evidence, arises rather from the feeling of a weakling than from the judgment of a critic. The beauty of Lucrezia lives after her, and men who have never seen her are influenced by it, as those who did see her were subjugated by the witchery of her exceeding loveliness, and by the magic of her manner. Mary Queen of Scots, in like manner, though long dead, yet speaketh. Women of transcendent charm work upon posterity, and find champions after death as they found lovers or victims during life. The enchantment of femininity is a thing apart from worth or goodness. The great witch-women of history stir up adherents who passionately refuse to believe evil where they are moved by beauty. The beauty of woman, whether divine or demoniac, is indeed one of the great powers of the world, and few things in history have had more influence upon the course of human affairs. Its power outlasts its possessor.

Beauty, like other fine entities, depraves some men as it ennobles others.

It may confidently be contended that there is no crime which the heart of man can conceive, of which a Borgia was not capable. There are no limits, absolutely none, to their capacity for crime. Without conscience or fear, ruth or remorse, they used unhesitatingly the dagger or the poison-cup, and certainly hesitated neither at adultery nor at incest. The very oscillations of opinion, in modern times, about Lucrezia's dark guilt, arise chiefly from the difficulty of realising the Renaissance, or comprehending the Borgia nature. We find it hard to believe that such beings were; and yet they were, and were the ripened fruit of their land, their time their Church. Contemporary historians found no insuperable difficulty in crediting the current knowledge of all men. They simply recorded facts— facts not to them very startling or very shocking— which were known at every court in Italy, and talked of, though with bated breath most softly drawn in fear, by every noble, by every churchman, by every citizen. It is a common thing to find persons who judge the deeds of a past age by the ideas and customs of their own. The transfusion of the mind into bygone manners requires a peculiar gift or training. The chief and most revolting crime of the Borgias was not unknown, was not even quite singular, in the Italy of their day. It is not necessary to grope long amongst Italian literature of the day for instances in the plural of incest; it will be sufficient to cite one example. Machiavelli (*Discorsi* i. 27), when he blame, Gianpolo Baglioni, of Perugia, for not having acquired eternal glory by murdering the Pope, Julius the Second, who had rashly ventured, with but a small escort, into the city which Gianpolo held with a large force, says that such cowardice is the more surprising because Gianpolo was a fine villain, who had murdered all the relations who stood in his way, and who was then living with his sister as his mistress—'usava con la sorella.' The case of the *Cenci* is awfully notorious.

The incidents which occur in boudoir or in bedchamber are less visible than actions performed upon a Papal throne, or in a camp in the Romagna. History, when it enters a lady's bower, must tread softly and speak low, glad if it can pick up a hint from a *soubrette*, or catch a whisper from a chamberlain. Such persons mainly preserve a silence dictated by fear, or inspired by interest; and yet a great, foul secret is never wholly kept. Tongues are loose, and the walls of palaces have ears. Lucrezia's dark secret would be hard to penetrate, were not her accomplices in it Rodrigo, Cæsar, and Gandia.

Facts and arguments form a ladder by which the seer attains to heights from which he gazes with passionate vision or clearer insight. We have to ask ourselves—what would Shakspeare have said of Lucrezia? If his English imagination had become familiar with the records of the Renaissance, how would he, he who drew Lady Macbeth, Queen Gertrude, Goneril, and Regan, have painted Lucrezia? It were bold to assume to answer for him, and yet I think, there can be little doubt. The creator of Cleopatra would have evolved a character of a fair fiend, demoniac in charm, detestable in wickedness. He would have fused into a living whole the picture of a being based upon the pregnant hints of black-letter history. Failing the help of Shakspeare, can we accept Gregorovius as our guide?

All the interesting documents discovered by the German Historian contain no refutation or rebutment of the contemporary historians. That broad current of human knowledge and belief upon which the record of the chronicler is partly based, remains entirely unchecked by Gregorovius' researches. For evidence we must go back to the original sources, and out of the old materials we have to construct our conception of a character at once so fair and so dark.

Roscoe says, writing in that weak and balanced style which is a result of the tendency of historians of his day to imitate Hume,—'We may be allowed to conclude that it is scarcely possible, consistently with the known laws of moral character, that the flagitious and abominable Lucrezia Borgia, and the respectable and honoured Duchess of Ferrara, could be united in the same person.' He shows here, as I contend, a want of constructive imagination, or imaginative insight. The commonly known 'laws of moral character' do not apply to the Borgias, who were the moral phenomena that they were in consequence of standing outside known laws, and being capable of any atrocity while maintaining serenity and retaining mental ability. Lucrezia's policy in Ferrara was clear, and her adherence to what was politic is a note or sign of her undoubted capacity. Her position in Ferrara, especially after the death of her father, was one of entire dependence upon the goodwill and benevolence of the house of Este, and of her husband. Alfonso, who had never loved his wife, and who had, most unwillingly, been constrained to wed her, was yet loyal and true to his useful partner; but Alfonso was a stern lord, and one who would, beyond a doubt, have made short work with a wanton wife. When Lucrezia first arrived in Ferrara, she was taken by Alfonso—and he probably had a meaning in what he did—to the Aurora, at the foot of the Lion's Tower, where, by order of Niccolo the Third, his son Ugo and his wife Parisina Malatesta were beheaded, in the presence of the father and husband, for incestuous adultery. Lucrezia, without support from father or brother, free from their influence, and in a regal position open to the 'fierce light that beats upon a throne,' may have desired to atone for her past by a better life. It is by no means, as I hold, difficult to reconcile the criminal Lucrezia of grand and gloomy Rome with the popular Duchess of the gayer and lighter Ferrara. Lucrezia was too wary and too wise to risk, in Ferrara, the loss of throne, of husband, and of life. Gibbon says, in his *Antiquities of the House of Brunswick*,—' The house of Este was sullied by a sanguinary and incestuous race—by the nuptials of Alfonso the First with Lucretia, a bastard of Alexander the Sixth, the Tiberius of Christian Rome. This modern Lucretia might have assumed with more propriety the name of Messalina; since the woman who can be guilty, who can even be accused, of a criminal intercourse with a father and two brothers, must be abandoned to all the licentiousness of venal love.' I think that Gibbon may well be left to answer Roscoe.

Of Guicciardini himself Sir W. Jones says,—' We have finished the twentieth and last book of Guicciardini's history; the most authentic, I believe (may I add, I fear?) that ever was composed. I believe it, because the historian was an actor in his terrible drama, and personally knew the principal performers in it; and I fear it, because it exhibits the woeful picture of society in the fifteenth and sixteenth centuries.' In fact, the testimony of the old chronicler has never been historically impugned. Beauty dazzles judgment, and sentimentalists may decide not to receive evidence which tells against their sentiment; but they cannot shake the evidence of Guiccardini. If we believe that Louis the Fourteenth had illicit relations with Madame de Maintenon, or that Charles the Second had love passages with Mistress Eleanor Gwynne, we may also believe the record of the Borgias. Herr Gregorovius asks, in one place, if it be possible to believe that Ariosto and the other poets of Ferrara would have sung Lucrezia's praises as they did sing them, if she had been guilty of the crimes imputed to her. I answer—most possible. The man who believes that their flatteries disprove historical evidence, shows a want of insight, and fails to comprehend the real tone of the *Renaissance*. In that time the nerves, as the morals of men, differed widely from the nerves or morals of men of a later day. There was then a subtle sympathy between the committers of great atrocities and contemporary society. In the Italian Renaissance persons so highly placed as were the Borgias could do pretty much what they would without exciting general moral reprehension; and a fair Duchess of Ferrara would meet with nothing but praise in her own capital. Besides, I can, I think, effectually dispose of the moral value of Ariosto's praise by a short but pregnant narrative. Ariosto was a poet, but was emphatically a Court poet, and that in an Italian Court of the Renaissance. The narrative is this: Lucrezia brought with her to Ferrara, Angela Borgia, then a lovely young girl. Cardinal Ippolito and his natural brother, Giulio d'Este, both fell in love with Angela. She preferred Giulio, and praised his 'beautiful eyes.' The jealous cardinal determined upon revenge, and hired assassins to waylay Giulio on his return from hunting, and to put out those eyes which had won the praise of Angela. This was done ; but the surgeons of Ferrara succeeded ultimately in saving the sight of one of Giulio's eyes. The cruel deed was committed on the 3d of November 1505. The cardinal was punished by slight and short exile from Ferrara ; but Giulio was dissatisfied with Alfonso's light dealing with so base an attempt, and the natural brother devised *his* very Italian scheme of vengeance. The plan was to take off Cardinal Ippolito by poison, and as this could not be done without drawing down capital punishment upon the originator, it was characteristically determined that Alfonso should be stabbed to death at a masked ball. The spies of the cardinal detected the conspiracy, and told all details to their master. Giulio fled to Mantua, but the Duke delivered him up to Alfonso. . Don Ferrante, also a natural son of Este, was to have been placed on the throne of Ferrara as successor to Alfonso ; and he also was seized and imprisoned. The two princes were to be beheaded in the court of the ducal castle of Ferrara ; but, when the day of execution came, when block and axe stood ready, Alfonso spared the lives of his brothers, and condemned them to perpetual imprisonment. Ariosto wrote an eclogue in praise of the deed of his patron, the cardinal, and vilified Giulio. This fact alone, to my mind, robs Ariosto's laudations of Lucrezia of all moral worth or value.

Again, Herr Gregorovius asks whether Lucrezia's letter to Leo the Tenth, in which she begged for his Papal benediction, could have been written by such a sinner as she is believed to have been. I answer, most emphatically—Yes! The letter is, indeed, highly characteristic of such a woman in such a time, and exemplifies curiously her views of her relations towards the Unseen. She, no doubt, believed in her superstitious way in the power of a pope to free her from all future consequences resulting from the commission of *any* sin. Herr Gregorovius further appeals to women, and asks if they can believe that Lucrezia could be guilty of the crimes imputed to her? By 'women' he must mean those of his own day: if he had put the same question to the women of Italy in Lucrezia's day, he would have received an answer but little favourable to his theory. In truth, that oscillation of opinion which tends to exculpate Lucrezia is a product of the sentimentalism of recent times. Some amiable persons do not like to believe things which cannot prettily be believed. The Renaissance know its own children better; though it is undoubtedly difficult for us to realise to our own minds the state of morals characteristic of that epoch. The chroniclers of the day, such men as Guicciardini, were honest and simple-minded recorders of facts of all but universal knowledge. It is not difficult to comprehend that they were the hearers of *viva voce* evidence of such cogency that, if we were to hear it now, it would dispel all tendency to sentimental 'whitewashing.' If we knew all that Guicciardini knew, Gregorovius' occupation would be gone. Alexander and Cæsar, despite their many heinous crimes, were the recipients of the most fulsome flattery; and, if they were, how much more would Lucrezia be the object of Renaissance eulogy! Nor is it an argument to say that the chief contemporary accusers, as Guicciardini and Sannazaro, wrote in Florence and in Naples. The answer is, that then to write in Rome history adverse to the Borgia meant certain death. Cæsar, for a less thing, daggered his father's favourite secretary, Pedro Calderon Peretto; and he slew Cervillon and Franceso Troche, the latter also a private secretary of the Pope. Still, though he is no historian, there lived and wrote in Rome, in the days of the Borgias, a diarist whose work belongs to the most remarkable of literary productions. This man was Burkard, a native of Elsass, and master of the ceremonies to five Popes, one of whom was Alexander the Sixth. To his employers he probably appeared a simple and harmless pedant; and they could have no idea that the solemn and punctilious official was daily recording for history many of the chief

events and crimes of the Vatican. Had Cæsar or
Alexander suspected Burkard's daily occupation, his
life would not have been worth an hour's purchase.
Roman Catholic writers are very bitter against Burkard; but they forget those reports of ambassadors—
the 'own correspondents' and reporters of the day
—to their respective courts, which confirm the record
of the master of the ceremonies. Many of these ambassadors' reports have disappeared, but the archives
of the Italian Courts still contain a great number;
and no historian of the Renaissance can now dispense with the assistance furnished by the contemporary reports of these—to us even—invaluable
ambassadors.

Burkard's diary is written with ultra-Tacitus-like
brevity and condensation; and is cold, brief, and
unimpassioned. If the events which he records ever
cause any emotion in that official soul, he, at least,
is careful not to show it. He seems to feel neither
love nor hate, neither admiration nor indignation.
Sometimes he is eloquently silent: sometimes he is
even unusually curt and dry. To my fancy, he
always writes in a kind of haggard dread, glancing
uneasily over his shoulder, and trembling at a noise
in the wall, or at the hint of a coming step. He
must well have known the danger of his occupation;
and the character of his work shows us that he did
realise the nature of the peril. He records those
orgies in the Vatican, at one of which fifty of the

leading *Hetairæ* of Rome assisted. Characteristic of the then state of Rome is the evidence, reported by Burkard, of one Giorgio Schiavoni, who happened to witness the throwing into the Tiber of the corpse of the murdered Gandia. Schiavoni, who was privately interrogated in the Vatican, stated that he saw two men on foot come down to the brink of the river, and look carefully about to see whether they were observed. Schiavoni was hidden in a boat. Seeing no one about, the two men beckoned, and another man appeared with a horse, across which lay a dead body, the head and arms of which were hanging down on one side of the animal, while the legs and feet hung down upon the other. The men then, with all their strength, flung the corpse into the water. Being asked by some man, apparently a cavalier, who was hidden in the darkness, whether the body were disposed of, they answered, audibly to Schiavoni, 'Signor, sì.' The dark master saw the deceased's mantle floating duskily upon the river, and when, speaking from out the gloom, he called attention to it, the other men threw stones upon it until it sank. Schiavoni was asked why he had not mentioned all this to the authorities; and he replied, that he had seen in his time a hundred dead bodies thrown into the river at the same place, without any inquiry ever being made respecting them, so that he had not considered the event a matter of any importance. The body was, however, that of the Pope's son and Cardinal's brother, the Duke of Gandia. The clothes on the corpse were not disturbed, and thirty ducats were in a purse. The body bore nine wounds, one in the throat, the others in the head, body, and limbs. The face of the *Signor* present may have looked at the time less calmly handsome than was its wont. It was, says Guicciardini, 'comune proverbio, che il Papa non faceva mai quello che diceva, e il Valentino non diceva mai quello che faceva.' Cæsar may have been taciturn on this occasion, but unless Alexander had known that the one son had murdered the other, inquiry would not have slept; and no ordinary murderer would have escaped the doom attaching to the assassin of a Pope's son.

I have now endeavoured to place before my readers a narrative, necessarily very brief, but yet, I hope, sufficiently comprehensive, of the leading events in the careers of the members of the Borgia triumvirate; and I have essayed to cite fairly the evidence for and against Lucrezia, and to state clearly the opposing views and opinions of assailants and of defendants. I am bound to admit that Herr Gregorovius does not, in my judgment, succeed in rebutting the contemporary and conclusive evidence against the 'fair devil.' He has partially succeeded in obscuring facts beneath a coat of whitewash, cleverly applied; but it is the office of criticism to remove the covering, and to restore the original picture in all its truth of drawing and force of colouring. This I have hoped to do. When, in the fifth act of *Othello*, Iago wounds Cassio in the leg, and then kills his unfortunate confederate, Roderigo, the very heinousness of the almost incredible wickedness provokes from spectators the relief of a grim, saturnine humour; and the transaction, especially when Iago is finely acted (I have seen Macready play it), produces dry, joyless laughter. Such a laughing audience knows nothing of the Italian Renaissance, and has never read Machiavelli. The very enormity of the atrocities which were committed, for so long a time, and with so much impunity, by the Borgias, stirs in us almost the same irritated feeling of morbid humour; and excites in many persons, weakly amiable rather than critically clear, a tendency to sentimental incredulity The infra-human is thought to be unnatural. And yet it was a state of society in which the Borgias were possible — nay, were actual — which led the maddened Savonarola to his bitter death, which stirred Luther into most active life, which revolted humanity and ripened the Reformation. We have no Shakspeare, we have no help even from Carlyle, to assist us in solving that problem of Lucrezia's guilt or innocence which is a problem only in consequence of the higher morality of later and of better times. We are left to our own imaginative insight or constructive imagination, and these, I think, condemn her, and judge Lucrezia as she was judged by those who, living with her in her own day, knew alike the day and knew her. The dark cloud which has rested so long upon her reputation, seems, at first sight, about to lift, when we begin to listen hopefully to Gregorovius; but, after further study and more mature consideration, the black cloud settles darkly down in even deeper duskiness. We give her up to dramatist and librettist. We feel that they can use her name and fame as a representative of charm and crime. At once so foul and fair, we know that Ferrara does not condone Rome; and that history contains no woman's name at once so famous and so infamous. We remain conscious that record, and that story, will brand for ever as a name of scorn that of the dark and fair, the lovely and yet desperately wicked LUCREZIA BORGIA.

# COUNT STRUENSEE AND QUEEN CAROLINE MATHILDE.

THE system of royal marriages which prevailed pretty generally throughout Europe up to the close of the last century, however admirable politically that system might be, did not in all cases restrain the impulses of human frailty, or entirely secure royal domestic felicity. Monarchs were not proof against temptation; nor did the morals and manners which then generally obtained remain without influence upon the occupants of thrones. Royal husbands were often grossly unfaithful: royal wives were occasionally—for femininely meaneth furiously—tempestuously untrue to marriage vows. History and romance record and depict two special cases which afford terrible illustrations of the tragedies to which such royal marriages sometimes led.

The first of these cases is historical. It is that of George Louis, Electoral Prince of Hanover (afterwards our George I. of England) and his princess, Sophia Dorothea. Mated with a dull, and coarsely unfaithful husband, poor Sophia Dorothea conceived an infatuated passion for that handsome, dissolute scamp, Philip of Königsmarck. With an insane devotion, exhibited through most reckless imprudence, the demented princess abandoned herself to her mad, perverse attachment to her worthless lover; and made, defiantly, the scandal of her sin a public notoriety. On the night of Sunday, 1st July 1694, Königsmarck (the Prince being then absent) left the apartments of the princess after having arranged with her the details of their joint flight from Hanover. As Philip quitted the palace of Herrenhausen, he was set upon by four armed men, and, after making some ineffectual resistance, was slaughtered. While the unhappy gallant was dying, that jealous old harridan, the Countess Platen—who also had loved *par amours* the bewitching Philip—stamped upon his mouth in order to tread out his dying curses. His body was burnt next day; and it was fondly hoped that secrecy would, in that way, be secured. Sophia Dorothea, then twenty-eight years of age, was immured for thirty-two long years in the castle of Ahlden; and when she died there, the tragedy was complete. In travelling over the dreary sand-wastes of the Lüneburger Heide, I have often thought of the long martyrdom of the guilty, but sorely tempted and heavily punished woman—a woman once so witty, bright, imperious —I have tried to fancy the lonely imprisonment of a princess whose heart was full of such memories and sorrows, while her equally guilty husband was reigning phlegmatically as a king, and was solaced by the society of many mistresses.

The other case—and for this we must turn to romance—is the Princess's tragedy recounted by Thackeray in 'Barry Lyndon.' If the case be not an actual fact, it is yet a truth; and is based upon the necessary result of those inhuman royal marriage customs of old Europe. The Princess Olivia, following in the steps of Sophia Dorothea, falls madly in love with a certain young De Magny, who, like Philip, is worthless and is dissolute. She wrongs her husband, Prince Victor, who, when her frantic guilt is made clear, procures De Magny to be poisoned in prison: and, in prison also, causes the mysterious *Monsieur de Strasbourg* to behead, at a quite private execution, the demented, guilty Princess. 'It had best be done now that she has fainted,' said the masked Prince Victor to the headsman, in that dark, vaulted room in the Owl Tower. This royal tragedy occurred in 1769.

The scope and object of the present essay is to depict that other royal marriage tragedy—prefigured by the two parallel cases just recited—of the hapless Queen of Denmark, Caroline Mathilde, and of the adventurer Struensee.

Three persons, two of them royal, one of lowly birth, born respectively in England, in Germany, in Denmark, gravitated together under the decree of an inexorable Fate, and became involved in a most tragic drama of sin, of love, of intrigue, of misery—of death.

Christian VII., King of Denmark, was born in Copenhagen, January 29, 1749. He was the son of King Friedrich V., and of Louise, daughter of George II. of England. His mother died 1751, and his father then married Juliane Marie, Princess of Braunschweig-Wolfenbüttel; who became the mother of Prince Friedrich, and was the stepmother of Christian VII. Friedrich V. died January 14, 1766.

Caroline Mathilde was born in London, July 22, 1751. She was the daughter of Frederick Louis, Prince of Wales, who was the son of George II., and her mother was Auguste of Sachsen-Coburg.

Johann Friedrich Struensee was born August 5, 1737, in Halle. His father, Adam Struensee, an obscure clergyman and a preacher in the St Ulrichs-kirche, was the son of a cloth-worker in Neu Ruppin. His mother was Maria Dorothea, the daughter of a Dr Carl.

The mother of Christian and the father of Caroline Mathilde were children of George II., and the Prince and Princess were therefore first cousins.

In 1757 Struensee removed to Altona, where he practised with some success as a physician. His characteristics were an esurient vanity, a restless ambition, and a love of pleasure. At one time he contemplated emigration to the East Indies. An ardent disciple of Rousseau and of Voltaire, he became a Freethinker and Materialist, and was of opinion that 'wenn der Mensch stürbe, Nichts weiter zu hoffen oder zu fürchten sey'—*i.e.*, that after death nothing was to be hoped or feared for man. He had a talent for self-assertion, and for pushing himself into notice. He was fond of 'heroic cures,' which, when successful, brought him into notice, and acquired for him reputation. His manners were insinuating and his personality was imposing. His eyes were blue and penetrating; his hair was light-brown; he inclined to stoutness, but was well built and of a striking figure. He was full of energy and tact, and succeeded in making friends and in extending influence. On April 5, 1768, he reached the turning-point in his career, and obtained the post of Leibarzt, or 'body physician,' to Christian VII., though this appointment was only to be given to him during the extent of a journey of some months, which the young king proposed to make.

Christian himself was badly brought up and badly educated. His father seems to have taken no care for the young Prince, and his stepmother preferred her own son, Prince Friedrich. Christian was placed under governors, by one of whom, the Kammerherr Detlev von Reventlow, he was treated with extraordinary severity. When, in 1766, he succeeded to the government, he was but ill-fitted for the cares and the duties of his rank. As a young lad, he was full of boyish pranks and of wanton mischief. The over-strictness of his early training disposed him to excesses of all kinds so soon as he became free from all restraint.

Caroline Mathilde was well brought up by a tender mother, and was an accomplished princess. She might be called beautiful, and was sprightly, bright witted, and charming. When a proposal of marriage—a proposal dictated by political expediency—came from Denmark to England, Caroline Mathilde, then only fifteen years old, fell into a melancholy at the prospect of exchanging the happy home of her youth for a cold and far-off northern throne to be shared with a stranger. However, the marriage was determined upon without much regard for the young girl's natural feelings; and on October 1, 1766, Caroline Mathilde was married by proxy, at St James's, to Christian VII. Her elder brother, our George III., represented the absent bridegroom.

The day before her departure from the England which she loved, and which loved her, the young bride was plunged in sorrowful thought. Her mother gave the girl, as a talisman, a ring with the motto, 'Bring me happiness!' and the unhappy princess, for whom we can yet deeply feel, left her country and her home, her mother, and her brothers and sisters, for a new life and a foreign throne, for an unseen husband — and for a most tragic future fate.

She had a stormy voyage, and was fifteen days at sea. At Roskilde she first met the King, who seemed charmed, as well he might be, with the grace and beauty of his gentle, modest, but brilliant consort.

For a short time, everything seemed to promise happiness to the young married couple; but very soon a rift within the lute began to mar the music of their wedded life. The young Queen soon showed coldness—why we can easily guess—to her husband; and he widened the breach between them by the crassest and the coarsest infidelities. The Queen was at this time just over fifteen, and the King a little more than seventeen years of age. Christian, when plunging into his course of debauchery, took a line which was, for a king, almost original. He did not devote himself to intrigues with the fine ladies, with the frail fair ones of the Court, but he, under the guidance of Count Holck, found his delight among the Hetairæ. His first mistress was a wanton known by the piquante name of *Stiefelettkathrine*;\* his second was one renowned under the title of *Myladi*. The King's brother-in-law, the Landgraf Karl von Hessen-Kassel, who married Christian's youngest sister, Louise, was well acquainted with

---

\* When Christian was away on his tour, Stiefelettkathrine (who was daughter of under-officer Benthaken) was exported to Hamburg, and was then incarcerated in the *Zuchthaus*, or House of Correction. When Struensee attained to power, he procured her release, and the renowned *Hetaira* married an advocate, one Maes.

all that happened at the Court of his brother-in-law, and has left a valuable record of his knowledge in his 'Memoires de mon temps,' tells us 'Il (Christian) fit la connaissance de la plus renommée à Copenhague. On la nommait Myladi. Il courait avec elle la nuit sur les rues, brisait des lanternes, cassait des vitres, enfin, menait une vie terrible.'

This most scandalous conduct of a young married king, wedded to a wife, pure, beautiful, and amiable, led, of course, to domestic unhappiness, and soon became matter of public notoriety.

On the 28th of January 1768, a prince (afterwards Frederick VI. of Denmark) was born to the King and Queen. The Queen was not yet seventeen.

His Majesty then determined to make a tour in other States of Europe, and decided that the Queen should *not* accompany him. Caroline Mathilde was left in solitary state in Copenhagen, and had her infant for her only solace. The young Queen must have been very lonely in that Court of Denmark. She was deeply attached to her child; but she cannot have liked the absence on such a tour of such a husband.

The Landgraf Karl thus paints Christian at the period of this journey:—'Il (le roi) manquait entièrement d'application, mais avait beaucoup d'esprit, qui etait très-vif même, avait la repartie extrêmément prompte, très-gaie, fort bonne mémoire, en un mot un jeune homme charmant qu'on ne put qu' aimer.

Il avait une passion demesurée de connaître des femmes,' etc. The tour lasted for seven months. It was a triumph of sensual pleasure and of social success. On such visits to foreign Courts, the young King showed to great advantage. He was pleased, and was anxious to please. He was naturally most delighted with London and with Paris. In London he lodged in St James's Palace, and was treated with great distinction. Frequent festivities were given in his honour. His stepmother, the widowed Princess of Wales, annoyed him terribly by her persistent inquiries after the health and happiness of Caroline Mathilde. *Cette chère maman m'embête terriblement*, confessed the King, who was not just then devoted to conjugal duty. He discovered a peculiar liking for the beautiful Lady Talbot. Christian endeavoured to return the hospitalities of London by a grand masked ball, to which three thousand persons of rank and distinction were invited. He also visited Garrick in the retired actor's country house on the Thames.

He saw the Paris of Louis XV., and was charmed with the gay, wicked Court and city. 'Mais vous Chrétien, vous êtes adoré,' Paris told him, and the handsome, pleasure-loving young King heard gladly the flattering compliment. He met d'Alembert, Diderot, Helvetius, Marmontel, and was kissed by the *dames de la halle*. Madame de Flavecourt excited Christian's particular admiration. His stay in Paris was one round of brilliant and depraved pleasure.

But below all royal honours and public festivities, there was another and more secret source of pleasure for the amorous king. Graf Holck was Christian's *Grand-Maître des plaisirs*, and assisted his monarch to continual orgies of the wildest and most sensual debauchery. The young husband was devoted to sexual delights, and wallowed in unrestrained voluptuousness, to the great injury of his health. Struensee was his travelling physician, and may have had enough to do to repair the waste of pleasure ; but there is no record of any protest on the part of the doctor against the soul and body-destroying courses of the wanton King. It was not usual for a highwayman to adopt a white horse for professional purposes ; and the wily Struensee did not repel his patron by any pretence of purity or assertion of morality. He had no desire to disgust Christian by playing the part of mentor. He did not pose as an adviser against evil. He sought to gain the King's favour by pandering to the King's worst excesses ; and exerted himself to be the sympathetic physician of a boundless voluptuary. Holck was an entire favourite of the dissolute Christian ; and to Holck the astute doctor attached himself.

Struensee returned with Christian to Copenhagen, and on the stage of that city the three persons who were to have so terrible an influence, each on the others, met together. Struensee was presented to the Queen.

When Christian returned to Denmark he was a changed man, and the change was for the worse. His Majesty had

'Overmuch consumed his royal person.'

His health was undermined, his nerves were shattered, his temper was uncertain. Contrasted with the joys of Paris and of London, he did not find Denmark or the Queen desirable. He had become the servant of sin, and, with a weakened will and failing powers, he yet lived chiefly for 'pleasure.' It was, however, noticed that the King's manners had become finer and more quiet since his return from travel.

Caroline Mathilde, as was natural, detested Holck. She knew the services which the favourite rendered to his master; and she had a shrewd idea of what a travelling physician to her husband meant. Hence she at first distrusted Struensee. Holck was overwhelmed with kingly favours; and the doctor began to climb. Holck little suspected that the obscure and complaisant medical man would soon supersede him, as first favourite at Court.

Struensee was appointed *Leibarzt* to the King in Denmark. His salary was to be 1000 dollars, and he received a gift of 500 to pay his debts. On May 12, 1769, Struensee was appointed *Étatsrath*, or Councillor of State, and had the right of attending the Court. When the King and Queen, in the summer of 1769, were residing at Friedrichsberg, Struensee lived in the castle. On January 17, 1770, he was called upon to dwell in the royal palace of Christiansburg in Copenhagen. His position was still so uncertain that he tried, but in vain, to reconcile the Queen to Holck. Struensee had taken warily the first steps on the steep and slippery path of Court favour; but he possessed all the cunning and the skill which were necessary to render his foothold secure. There was a wisdom in him which guided his ambition to act in safety.

On May 2, 1770, he successfully inoculated the Crown Prince, and the child was saved from small-pox. This service won for Struensee the full favour of the Queen, and he was appointed reader to the King, and Cabinet-Secretary to the Queen, with a yearly salary of 1500 thalers. On May 4, a year only after having been appointed *Étatsrath*, he was made *Conferenz-Rath*.

This rapid rise of a foreigner, who was not even noble, excited great surprise. The listless King, weary and exhausted from satiety of sensuality, was guided in all his actions by the Queen and by Struensee; and Holck began to feel a just apprehension of the progress of the new favourite.

Their Majesties made a short tour in their own dominions. On this occasion, the Queen, who was still bent upon getting rid of Graf Holck, went with the lethargic King. On June 13, the royal travellers arrived at Gottorp Castle, which was the residence of the Landgraf Karl, and of the King's sister, Louise. Struensee was now helping the Queen to depose Holck, and, as a counterpoise to the falling favourite, the Kammerjunker Enevold Brandt, Holck's greatest enemy, was recalled from banishment, and was appointed chamberlain to the King. Brandt waited upon the surprised Holck. 'I think, Monsieur le Comte,' said Brandt, 'that you are not afraid of ghosts?' To which Holck replied, bitterly, 'Oh, non, Monsieur le Chambellan, je ne crains pas les spectres, mais les revenants.' The Landgraf Karl records of this royal visit to his castle, speaking of the Queen :—

'Elle était toujours embarrassée avec moi dès que Struensee était présent. On dinait avec gêne à la table du Roi. La reine jouait alors au quinze : j'étais placé à sa droite, Struensee à sa gauche, puis Brandt, nouvellement arrivé, et Warnstedt, page de la chambre finit la partie. Je n'aime pas à me retracer les façons et les propos que Struensee se permettait publiquement d'adresser à la Reine, appuyant son coude sur la table à celui de la Reine. J'avoue que mon cœur était brisé de voir cette Princesse, douée de tant d'esprit et d'agrément, tomber à ce point et en de si mauvaises mains. Le Roi et la Reine allaient à Traventhal avec toute la cour qui les avait suivis à Gottorp. Nous ne fûmes point du voyage, ma femme et moi. On ne nous le proposa point, et avec raison, car Traventhal etait choisi pour les orgies les moins decentes.'

The Landgraf was sharpsighted enough to detect the relations which already subsisted between the Queen and Struensee.

Holck's influence with the King was on the wane,

partly because it was no longer easy to amuse His Majesty after the old fashion ; and a cabal, composed of Struensee, Brandt, and Graf Rantzau-Ascheberg— with the Queen behind the three—succeeded in procuring the dismissal of Graf Holck ; who was allowed a pension of 2000 thalers. The Queen had triumphed over one of her enemies ; but she had allied herself with an even more dangerous foe.

Brandt was commencing that splendid Court career, as assistant to Struensee, which in a short time was to conduct him to the same scaffold on which his master was to perish. The third ally in the new combination, Graf Rantzau-Ascheberg, was the man destined, a little later on, to bring his former colleagues to ruin and to death.

Schack zu Rantzau-Ascheberg was descended from one of the most ancient noble families of Holstein. Born in 1717, he was Major-General at thirty-five, and was then suddenly dismissed. He took refuge in Russia. Winning the confidence of the Empress Catharine, and of Count Orloff, he took an active part in the conspiracy against Peter III. Returning to Denmark, he found favour from Christian VII., but was again suddenly dismissed in consequence of a Court intrigue. He was separated from his wife, who, in consequence, fell into melancholy madness. The Count was a man of his day, and led a life of dissolute gallantry. He had been involved in many duels, and in one of a specially tragic character. Having seduced a young lady, he had to meet her father; and the father fell. Rantzau was inconsolable. He provided liberally for all the family, and did all in his power to remedy the irrevocable ill. He married his lady victim with the left hand. Rantzau was a man of distinctive ability. Struensee rejoiced with reason at obtaining so able an ally; but he learned too late that Rantzau was far too able for his purposes.

Brandt was born in 1738, in Copenhagen. In 1755 he became *Hofjunker*. He had studied law, and rose to be assessor of the highest court of law. He was of good family, and had both will and talent. Attaching himself to Court life, he was appointed *Kammer-junker*, and joined his fortunes to those of the splendid Struensee, who was then far-shining, 'like a blazing tar-barrel.' Struensee, in his capacity of physician, undertook the training of the little Crown Prince, and subjected the unfortunate child to a most Spartan regimen. He was afterwards accused of having designed to put an end to the life of the heir to the Crown. The child was three years old, and was of weak constitution. He was subjected to a cold diet only, consisting of vegetables, rice, and milk; he was lightly clothed, was allowed no fire in winter, and went about with bare feet. At length Berger, another Court physician, interfered strongly, and introduced such ameliorations in the child's treatment as might be consistent with the prolongation of his existence. Friedrich VI. died ultimately of physical exhaustion.

It is a proof of the influence which Struensee had acquired over the Queen that she should allow such unnatural treatment of the boy who, though he was Christian's son, was also her own child. The King was supine in the matter.

At this period her Majesty excited some scandal and offence in Copenhagen by frequently appearing in public on horseback, in masculine costume. The attention which this conduct excited is proved by the number of pictures still to be seen in the Royal Library, in Copenhagen, of the fair young Queen in this dashing and piquant attire. May it not be that Caroline Mathilde was then losing something of her delicacy, was deteriorating in modesty and self-respect, in consequence of her defiant life and coarsening manners?

The King himself was the true ally of any lover of the Queen. Outraged as a woman, insulted as a wife; with a husband who could leave a celestial bed to prey on garbage, her woman's joy in revenge led her to lend an ear to the suit of the unscrupulous man whose power could yield her support, whose love could afford her the means of vengeance. Caroline Mathilde, not lofty enough for patience, was woman enough to repay conjugal wrong with connubial infidelity. Her long revolt of indignation broke forth in a *liaison* which yielded her a feeling of triumph, a sense of requital. The volcano of her excited feeling had to be snowed over by the forms and ceremonies of her high station, by external duties performed in the fierce light that beats upon a throne. Whatever sense of wrong might exasperate her heart, she had to be careful of appearances. What hypocrite like lawless love? Emboldened by time, and by the blindness of the besotted King, she gradually forgot her caution; and all Denmark, except its monarch, became cognisant of her guilty amour. Christian VII., with a heart hardened, a soul coarsened, the will weakened, and the mind confused by excess in riotous debauchery, was wholly blind to the conduct of his fair young wife. He had become a puppet and a tool, and was glad to be relieved by clearer wills of the burden of State affairs. He lived languidly for pleasure, and the Landgraf Karl records that his physician injured the King's health yet further by giving him stimulants to increase his amatory enjoyments. Christian had never been taught, and had never wished to learn, the duties of an absolute monarch. His life-theorem was indulgence in sensuality. It was over an unfenced precipice that Caroline Mathilde, pushed by a vicious and worthless husband, fell into the abyss of crime. She had no standard by which, in her debauched Court, she could judge of nobleness in man. But, whatever excuse there may be for her guilt, there can be none for the conduct of the base and underbred man, who, for his own vanity and interest, could employ all his influence and all his arts to make a victim of the wronged and angry Queen. She sinned; but she was more sinned against than sinning.

Struensee, a true beggar on horseback, took an ever more active and audacious part in public affairs. He became insolent to opponents, arrogant to dependents, despotic to the Crown. Bernsdorff and other high functionaries were dismissed in disgrace. The Kammerjunker v. Köppern, the Kammerherr v. Warnstedt, were both deprived of all offices and position, merely for having spoken against the favourite. A successful courtier may be a gross failure as a statesman; but no favourite failed more completely than did Struensee. '*Das Regierungsgeschäft ist ein sehr grosses Metier*'—'The business of government is a very great undertaking,' says Goethe. Not many men, trained only to medicine, could develop in two years into successful, absolute, irresponsible rulers of the State; and Struensee, who was a mere windbag, possessed none of the great qualities necessary for his high office. His reforms were not successes. Good was to be done in order that good might be done to Struensee; but he had not the capacity for State reforms.

He expedited the administration of law, and in so far did good. He instituted a Foundling Hospital and gambling hells. He introduced freedom of the press. This step was taken with a view to popularity; but as Struensee's unpopularity was growing at the time, the freedom was 'abused,' and had to be withdrawn. One result was the growth of *Schmutzblättern*; surely then, as now, an undesirable thing.

A Copenhagen journal asked the pregnant question—'Can the paramour of a married woman be the sincere friend and true adviser of that woman's husband?' Nor was the Queen spared. The most shameless reports about her unlawful relations with Struensee were circulated, until the 'excesses' of the press were bridled.

Beyond his general condition of weak understanding, the King had occasional attacks of positive insanity; but his Majesty, who could speak Danish, rose in the love of the Danes, because they believed him to be the puppet and the prisoner of the minister. Struensee *gab sich alle ersinnliche Mühe dem König das Leben angenehm zu machen*—gave himself all conceivable trouble to render the King's life pleasant; nor was he neglectful of the favour of the Queen.

On July 7, 1771, the Queen was delivered of a daughter, christened Louise Auguste. Concerning the paternity of this child, history has its perplexities. It is improbable that Christian was its father. Horace Walpole, writing to Sir H. Mann, says that the amour of the Queen with her 'medical Prime Minister,' was a theme of current gossip in London; and he expresses, in his light way, his doubts about the paternity of this infant—doubts which were, as it would seem, generally entertained in England and in Denmark.

The Queen cared nothing for political reforms; but her woman's heart, empty and sore, did need passionate personal devotion, and he who would give her even the show of love might take the reality of power as his payment. Struensee could not give her love; but he could and did dishonour her with a simulacrum of love, disguised in base passion, and he took advantage of his opportunities to profit by her weakness and her desolate position. Struensee said afterwards of himself that his demon was sensuality; but one devil seldom reigns alone. He makes place for others, and Struensee did not reckon the demons of vanity, of self-seeking, of ambition that knows no touch of greatness or of conscience. Whirled aloft by singular circumstances, he was yet in very essence vulgar of soul; was not equal to his fortune, and remained always a coward and an upstart. In the day, in the society, and in the Court of Caroline Mathilde, the tie of wedlock was but a slip-knot, and she had example, as well as provocation, to lead her into sin and shame.

Struensee's reforms, even when they contained some good, did yet more evil than good: they were the offspring of his own caprice, and were carried out without consideration as they were devised without wisdom. He knew nothing of Denmark, of men, of laws, of institutions, of government. Sudden changes, violently introduced, and carried into effect with highhanded despotism, are not true organisms. A defiant Freethinker, with power to make his meaning law, Struensee deeply outraged the religious feeling of the nation; nor could the spectacle of such a man, in possession of despotic power, conciliate any genuine reformer.

One of his early steps was to do away with the Council of State. Henceforth the King was to rule alone and absolutely; but every one knew that that meant only the absolute rule of the Queen and Struensee. The King was to be his own Foreign Minister. Russia so strongly resented the new *régime* in Denmark, that she threatened to send a fleet to bombard Copenhagen. The English ambassador was rudely treated by the insolent favourite, and kept aloof from the Court. A 'Mathilde Order' was created, with which the Queen's partisans and friends were to be decorated; and, of course, Struensee was one of the first recipients. The Queen-Mother and Prince Friedrich were driven from Court. A *cordon* was drawn round His Majesty, and his nobles and officers were excluded from his presence. Brandt, in the absence of Struensee, was always near the person of the monarch, and kept all others from access to Christian. It was generally considered that the *Mathilden-Orden* was intended to lower the value of the old Dannebrog and Elephant Orders. The dismissals of objectionable officials continued. The order for dismissal was, during the sway of Struensee, carried to the victim by a royal groom mounted on a cream-coloured horse; and it became a standing inquiry in Copenhagen, 'With whom has the cream been last?' His army changes and reductions were grossly unwise and greatly unpopular. He dissolved the King's Life Guards. This *corps d'élite* consisted of picked men, and the officers were all nobles. It would seem that the Royal Guards were much loved by the Copenhageners, and the public indignation at this step was extreme. Struensee's real object was—and there was no object to which he clung more tenaciously—to humiliate the nobility; but the dissolution of the body-guards was looked upon by the public as a slight to the King. The Queen loyally supported her paramour in all his measures, and shared his ever-growing unpopularity.

When the order which commanded their dissolution was read to the Guards, they rode into their barracks to deliver up their horses and then to disperse. Struensee happened to meet them when they were so engaged. Probably the corps was in no very pleasant mood, and men and officers may have looked threateningly upon the hated favourite. Struensee's craven heart took fright. He dreaded some strong expression of their discontent and dislike to him—and fairly ran away; but when he ceased running, he tore a leaf out of his pocket-book and wrote on it with pencil a hurried order for the dismissal of Count Ahlefeldt, the King's Cabinet Secretary, whom he connected with the conduct of the Guard. In his day of highest power, when supreme over State and King, Otto von

Falkenskjold, perhaps the noblest and ablest of Struensee's adherents, ventured to warn the despot of the fickleness of fortune and of the dangers that he was incurring—without effect. The besotted adventurer believed that he had chained Fortune to his car.

And he seemed at the time to have judged rightly. To superficial appearance his position was secure and his power increasing. In 1771, he was promoted by the King to be Kabinetsminister, with absolute power; the orders and the signature of the Minister to have the same force and validity as those of the King himself.

This was indeed *Ego et Rex Meus*. Such an appointment was unknown in Denmark; such power had never been conferred upon a subject. The Queen was delighted; but many of Struensee's friends fell from him, partly terrified by the unheard-of audacity of the measure; while national indignation grew deep and dangerous.

In 1771 also, Struensee and his chief adherent, Brandt, were raised to the nobility, each with the title of Count. No such power and position had ever been attained by any man in the Kingdom. Struensee was literally all-powerful. Internal affairs and foreign relations were administered solely according to his will and pleasure. All titles, honours, degrees, and offices were held only by his favour. He invented for himself an ornate and boastful coat of arms. All the world wondered at the upstart's success. With Struensee, as with other men of his class, lowliness had been his young ambition's ladder; but that ladder was kicked down so soon as he achieved success.

The King made presents of 10,000 thalers to the Queen, and of 6000 thalers each to Struensee and Brandt. At his trial it was one of the charges against Struensee that he had altered the figures on the warrant from 6000 to 60,000. It was improbable that the King should give larger sums to Struensee and Brandt, than he did to the Queen. Jenssen-Tusch estimates that Struensee, during his two years of power, obtained quite enormous sums from the Treasury, though it is impossible to ascertain accurately the moneys he had received for himself and for his adherents. He had imported into Denmark his brother, who was made Justiz-rath, and afterwards became the controller of the national finances. After this appointment had been made, Struensee, when he found it right to reward himself by grants of Crown money, could bestow upon himself, without troubling any one—even the King—such sums as he might think a fitting recompense for his own merits and services.

Heartless and haughty, Struensee, in dealing with his own supporters, used tools rather than loved friends. Graf Rantzau-Ascheberg became embittered against the too insolent favourite, and began to coalesce with Colonels von Köller and von Sames, and other friends, in opposition to the Minister. Brandt, warned by anonymous letters, and terrified by the evidences of national disaffection, wrote to Struensee, expressing a wish to retire to Paris, and requesting a yearly allowance of 120,000 francs. Brandt, in his letter, uses the memorable expression,—'*Kein Despot hat sich jemals eine solche Gewalt angemasst oder auf solche Weise sie geübt wie Sie*'— 'No despot has ever acquired such power, or has used it in such a way as you have.' He adds, '*Sie haben jedermann Schrecken eingejagt: alle zittern vor Ihnen . . . . von Schrecken sind Alle ergriffen; man spricht, man trinkt, man isst—alles mit Beben*'—'You have infused terror into every one: all tremble before you . . . . every one is seized with fear; men speak, drink, eat—always in trembling.' 'Even the Queen,' says Brandt, 'has no longer a will of her own.'

Struensee replied in writing and at some length. He will not allow Brandt to fly. He says, 'as regards my conduct towards Her Majesty, I do not permit you to judge it:' and adds, with almost a touch of pathos,—'You are the only person who is in possession of all my secrets; and to whom I have, on all occasions, unfolded myself without any reserve.'

So Brandt stayed and waited—for death.

Meanwhile the air was becoming electrical, and there was danger in it for Struensee. The patriotism of the nation was revolted by the spectacle of a Court favourite—'a man without experience, without honour, without religion, without truth or honesty, or knowledge of the laws'—who was the lord of all, the lover of the Queen; and who was supposed to have designs upon the King's life. Struensee himself became afraid of 'meeting with Concini's fate.' He received threatening letters, and the streets were placarded with denunciations of him. Furious attacks upon him were thrown into the King's carriage. There was a mutiny among the sailors, who brought their grievances to the castle at Hirschholm. The Court fled. Struensee showed his usual cowardice, and yielded to the malcontents. The Minister of Marine, von Rumohr, was, however, summarily dismissed. Next came an uprising of the silkworkers; and they carried their point. Then Struensee surrounded the palace with a cordon of guards; and he appointed at a high rate of pay his own special bodyguard. Keith, the English ambassador, offered Struensee a large sum of money if he would take himself off, and trouble the Commonweal no longer. Such an offer could only have been made to a man whose character and principles were thoroughly despised and despicable. Supported as he was by King and Queen, Struensee could only be dethroned by something in the nature of a plot; though, if his guards were not trustworthy, he might easily fall a victim to popular fury. The nation was resolved upon his destruction, and it only remained to find the persons who were able to carry the national will into effect.

In such cases, the needful persons are seldom wanting.

The conspirators, if they may be so called, at last obtained the co-operation of the Queen-Mother and of her son; and the following persons became leagued together to effect the fall, and even the death, by law, of the arrogant and unprincipled Minister.

The Queen-Mother, Juliane Marie; her son, the Hereditary Prince Friedrich; Graf Rantzau-Ascheberg; Owe Horg Guldberg; Colonel von Eichstedt; Colonel von Köller and Kammerjunker Magnus Beringskjold.

The two colonels answered for the troops; Guldberg, a patriotic Dane, was secretary to Prince Friedrich; Köller was a strong, determined soldier. Whatever other motives may have played a part, it is certain that all the plotters were indignant at the reign of Struensee, and were revolted by the Queen's illicit relations towards him. No one had any purpose to injure the King.

With such plots speedy action is indispensable. Left to ripe and ripe, they rot and rot. The conspirators, who were risking their heads, lost no time.

On the night of January 16-17, 1772, there was a *bal paré en Domino* in the palace. The Queen was radiant: unusually gay and full of coquetry. Struensee was present; he continually danced with Caroline

Mathilde, and the brilliant Court festivity lasted until two in the morning.

Two hours later, when tired revelry had sunk into deep repose, four of the conspirators, headed by the Queen-Mother, stole through the hushed passages of the sleeping castle, and stood round the King's bed. Their object was, they told him, 'to free land and King.'

The King's terror lent him temporary lucidity. He, at first, refused to believe anything that could touch the honour of the Queen; but Juliane Marie and Guldberg soon carried conviction to the mind of the husband and the King.

His Majesty wrote a short note to the Queen: 'Comme vous n'avez pas voulu suivre les bons conseils, ce n'est pas ma faute, si je me trouve obligé de vous faire conduire à Kronenbourg.' He then signed a warrant, authorising Eichstedt and Köller to take the measures necessary to save the King and the Fatherland; and he further signed warrants for the arrest of Struensee, Brandt, and the rest of that faction. These warrants were countersigned by the Prince.

The arrest of Struensee was effected by von Köller. The great Minister submitted patiently and with a trembling depression to his fate. He tried to seize a small étui, but von Köller snatched it from him, and it was found to contain poison. Bound hand and foot, the man, so recently all-powerful, was hurried into a carriage and driven to the citadel, in which he was incarcerated.

Colonel von Sames undertook the more dangerous task of seizing Graf Brandt, who met the colonel and the guard with a drawn sword, a weapon which Brandt well knew how to use. Disarmed by the soldiers, he also was securely bound. He then said, 'Eh bien, Monsieur, je vous suivrai tranquillement.' Brandt also was carried in a coach to the citadel, and there imprisoned. His courage and cheerful fortitude contrasted strongly with Struensee's abject cowardice.

A more delicate task was entrusted to Graf Rantzau-Ascheberg, who undertook the arrest of the Queen. Told by her women that the Count wished to see her by order of the King, the terrified Caroline Mathilde cried out, 'Hasten to send for Struensee. Let him come to me directly!' She was told that Struensee was already in confinement, and she exclaimed, 'Verrathen! verloren! Ewig verloren!' 'Betrayed! lost! For ever lost!' The Count and three officers were then admitted, and he presented to the Queen the King's letter, adding his advice to her to submit to the commands of His Majesty. 'The King's commands!' she said bitterly: 'commands of which he understands nothing; commands extorted from his imbecility by shameful treachery! A Queen does not obey such commands.' Rantzau urged that his orders admitted of no delay in their execution. 'I will obey no order until I shall have seen the King,' replied the passionate Queen. 'Let me go to him; I must—I will speak to him!' This could not be permitted, and Caroline Mathilde gave way to a paroxysm of wild despair. She shrieked for help, until she was told that none could hear her. Then she tried to throw herself out of the window, but one of the officers seized and restrained her. She tore his hair, and struggled with her captors in a desperate fury, until she fainted from exhaustion. Dressed by her women, she melted into tears. 'Je n'ai rien fait; le roi sera juste.' Then she declared that she would not leave without her children. It was explained that she could not be allowed to take the Crown Prince, but that her infant daughter might accompany her. Rantzau offered her his hand to conduct her to the carriage, but she repulsed him with, 'Loin avec vous traître! je vous déteste!' The Hofdame von Mösting, and a lady of the bedchamber, accompanied Caroline Mathilde in the carrriage, and opposite to the Queen sat Major von Castenskjold. Surrounded by thirty dragoons, the carriage moved off, and bore the Queen from the palace which she was never to see again.

After a drive of about four hours, she reached Kronenburg. Alighting in the courtyard, she exclaimed, 'God! I am lost for ever! The King has given me up!' Presently she said, 'Away, away from here! For me there can be no peace more!' Then she burst into tears, and clasped the little child to her bosom. Two days elapsed before the unhappy Queen would consent to go to bed or to take nourishment. And so we leave her, for the present, imprisoned in the Kronenburg.

The minor adherents of Struensee were easily arrested by the inferior officers of the new Government. The success of the plot was complete. Denmark was saved from anarchy and ruin; and the capital was in an ecstasy of joy.

On the following morning the excited people assembled in masses before the palace, and the King came out to them, and shouted with them, 'Hurrah!' He drove through Copenhagen in a State carriage, and the people took out the horses and themselves drew the coach. Prince Friedrich rode with him, and was well received. The enthusiasm of the people was real and was great. 'Man feuerte mit Gewehren Freudenschüsse ab, warf Raketen in die Luft, sang und schrie und geberdete sich vor Freude wie betrunken.'

The whole country was in a ferment of exultation at the fall of the godless cabal which had for so long weighed upon the land. The whole literature of Denmark triumphed in the fall of Struensee; nor was the Queen spared. All the pulpits of the capital thanked Heaven for the downfall of those who had injured and disgraced the Fatherland. The mob wrecked the house of the father of Esther Gabel because she had been the mistress of Struensee; and then, actuated by a singular inspiration of revenge, they pulled down the brothels. The city was illuminated. The King, the Queen-Mother, and Prince Friedrich appeared in the royal box in the Hoftheater, and were received with enthusiasm, the audience shouting, 'Long live King Christian VII.!'

Graf zu Rantzau-Ascheberg, von Eichstedt, von Köller, Beringskjold, received honours and rewards. Guldberg alone refused all recompense. This sturdy Dane had done what he did for the sake of the Fatherland and the common weal; and, as he had acted from no base motive, he despised all reward.

Struensee, meanwhile, as cowardly in adversity as he had been presumptuous in prosperity, fell into a condition of abject despondency. For some time he refused food, and then he attempted suicide. He tried to dash out his brains against the walls of the prison; and he sought to put an end to his life by swallowing some horn buttons. Brandt displayed an equable and cheerful fortitude. The echoes of the popular rapture at his fall penetrated into the dungeon of Struensee.

Juliane Marie and her son were well liked by a grateful press and people. 'Her fame,' it was said, 'would outshine that of Semiramis.'

It was felt in Denmark that the country which could allow the despotism of a Struensee must be held in contempt by other nations; and there was strong national pride in throwing off such a yoke. The next step to be taken was to bring to trial the

Queen, Struensee, and Brandt; and commissions were appointed for this purpose.

The men chosen for this purpose were *einsichtsvolle und rechtschaffene Beamte*—officials of insight and of character. Before the trials there were interrogatories addressed to the prisoners. Struensee was too cowed to think clearly, too ignoble to feel rightly, and he hoped probably to save his worthless life by connecting himself with Her Majesty. He had no chivalry towards the Queen; no honour which could try to shield the fame of the woman whom had been led by his arts into sin.

He confessed with tears *ein unerlaubtes Verhältniss* between the Queen and himself; and, under a second examination, he gave ample details. He signed a protocol which recorded a full confession of adultery.

Counsel were assigned to the accused, and both advocates and judges were released from their oaths as subjects, in order that they might freely discharge their duties. Kammeradvocat Bang represented the King, and the Queen was defended by the Höchstengerichtsadvokat Uldall. Generalfiskal Wiwet conducted the prosecution against Struensee and Brandt, who were defended respectively by Uldall and by Bang. It may fairly be said that the counsel for the accused discharged their duties to their clients with, at least, average advocate ability.

The counsel for the prosecution of the Queen had an easy task. Her Majesty had admitted to the Commissioners who interrogated her that she had broken her marriage-vow. The confession of Struensee himself was full and was explicit; and his statement of details accorded fully with the evidence of the Queen's ladies-in-attendance and of her female servants. These ladies had remonstrated with Her Majesty about her conduct with Struensee. For a short time his nightly visits ceased, but were soon resumed with defiant frequency. To the Kammerfräulein von Eyben the Queen had admitted that 'the thing was unfortunately true;' and had said that there was nothing wrong in a wife being unfaithful to a husband who was old, or who had been forced upon her. The Queen added that she knew what reports were circulated, but that she should not alter her course on that account. The evidence of the ladies and of the female domestics was very full and conclusive. The advocate prayed for a dissolution of the royal marriage, on the ground of adultery, with a divorce which would set the King free to marry again. All punishment rested with His Majesty.

The sentence of the High Court was, that the divorce, as prayed for by the King's advocate, be fully granted; and this decision was communicated to the ex-Queen.

Meanwhile, Sir Robert Keith was not idle. He sent off a courier to George III., and protested energetically against any sentence of death, or of perpetual imprisonment in Denmark. George III. responded by sending to the ambassador the Order of the Bath, and by threatening that, if the Queen's life were endangered, an English fleet should sail at once (it was in readiness) to bombard Copenhagen. With the matter of the divorce, or with the decision of the Court of Law, George III. would not in any way interfere. Twelve days after the news of the divorce reached London, the mother of Caroline Mathilde, the Princess of Wales, died, her end hastened by the afflicting intelligence of such a decision against her daughter.

It was on March 8, 1772, that the Royal Commission presented itself at Kronenburg to examine Caroline Mathilde. They began by informing her of the confession of Struensee. Flushed with indignation, the unfortunate woman exclaimed that it was impossible that Struensee could have compromised her in such a manner. For answer they placed in her hands the protocol which Struensee had signed. When she saw the well-known signature at the foot of such a damning statement, she was seized with horror and with terror. Shack-Rathlau remarked :—
'Si l'aveu de M. Struensee n'est point vrai, Madame la Reine, alors il n'y a pas de mort assez cruelle pour ce monstre qui a encore osé vous compromettre à ce point.'

The struggle in the poor Queen's breast must have been terrible. Changing from white to red, she thought long, and then asked, with a true woman's consideration, even in such an hour, for a base and perfidious lover:—'Mais si j'avouais les mots de Struensee, pourrais-je sauver sa vie par-là?' Shack-Rathlau answered:—'Surement, Madame, cela pourrait adoucir son sort de toute manière.' He then presented to the Queen a paper which contained an admission of the truth of Struensee's confession. 'Eh bien, je signerai!' cried the Queen, and, taking a pen, she signed the document which admitted her guilt and blasted her reputation. So soon as her signature was attached, she realised the consequences of her admission, and, in a paroxysm of despair, the unhappy Queen sank back fainting on the sofa. The Commission returned to Copenhagen with the two fatal confessions duly signed and witnessed.

The indictment against Struensee was a terrible impeachment. All the forms in which he had committed high treason were set forth at length. Wiwet terms Struensee die allerdummdreisteste Person die man sich imaginiren kann; and a patriotic indignation against the unworthy man who had degraded Queen and country glows through the advocate's address. The crimes and offences of Struensee are in essence known to us. Suffice it to say, that the prosecuting counsel summed them up in nine heads, each one of which covered a charge of high treason.

Through the mouth of his advocate, Struensee repeats a full admission of his guilty relations with the Queen, expresses the deepest contrition, and prays the King to forgive his offence. He also pleads that the influence of the Queen was the only support upon which he could rely. Generally, he asserts purity of motive in all that he did.

Brandt's case came next. He was charged with being the assistant and accomplice of Struensee in all the Minister's misdeeds; and that Brandt knew fully the footing on which Struensee stood with the Queen. Brandt was further accused of having subjected His Majesty's royal person to indignities and even to violence.

On April 27, 1772, sentence was pronounced and was signed by the King. Both culprits had been declared guilty of the highest kind, known to the law, of *crimen læsæ Majestatis*; and the sentences on both ran—that they should be degraded from all rank and office; their coats of arms broken by the hangman; that their right hands, and then their heads, should be struck off; the bodies quartered and extended upon the wheel; and the heads and hands exposed upon poles.

So much grace was extended to them that they were not to be broken alive upon the wheel. Both criminals appealed to the mercy of the King; and Owe Guldberg tried passionately to save the lives of both, but specially of Brandt, who was the lesser criminal, and to whom mercy might have been extended. Guldberg's humane efforts remained, however, without result.

After signing the sentences, the King went to the

opera; and on April 26th a masquerade was given in the castle.

On the morning of April 28, 1772, the two ex-Ministers, Struensee and Brandt, were executed in pursuance of their sentences. While in prison, both had become converts to religion. Dr Münter had attended Struensee, and accompanied him to the scaffold; Probst Hee was Brandt's chaplain. At 8.30 A.M., the fatal procession started from the citadel. The two State criminals rode in carriages, that which contained Brandt going first. Both were gaily dressed in Court costumes, and wore fur coats. The huge scaffold, eighteen feet in height, had been erected in a field used as a military exercise ground, to the east of the city. The scaffold was surrounded by soldiers, and the immense mob of people that gathered to see the Ministers die was kept at some distance from the scaffold itself. The carriages stopped at length, and Brandt descended. The carriage which contained Struensee was humanely so turned that the occupants could not see the scaffold. Brandt was serenely brave. Without bravado he was thoroughly calm and composed.

When he had reached the high platform, his sentence was read out, and then the executioner saying, 'Dies geschieht nicht umsonst, sondern nach Verdienst;' 'This is not done without cause, but has been deserved,' broke and defaced the Count's coat of arms. He demanded his profession of faith, and asked if Brandt repented of his treason. The Count professed regret, and asked pardon of the King and the country. He declared his lively faith in the blood of Jesus Christ; and the pastor replied, 'Be of good cheer, for thy sins are forgiven thee.'

The headsman approached. Brandt himself, his courage remaining unshaken, took off his coat and waistcoat. He laid his neck upon one block, and extended his right hand upon another. A single blow upon each, and head and hand were severed from the body.

Struensee's turn came next. In that dread hour his courage forsook him, and it was with difficulty that he ascended the steps of the scaffold. Again the sentence was read out, and again, with the words, 'Dies geschieht nicht umsonst, sondern nach Verdienst,' a coat of arms was broken and defaced. His confession of faith and forgiveness of enemies were satisfactory to Münter.

Here the unhappy man's forces failed him; he could not remove his own clothes, and this had to be done by the hangman's assistants. He tottered a few steps towards the block, but could not reach it or without assistance assume the necessary position. As the right hand was struck off, the whole body of the condemned was seized with strong convulsions. The first blow upon the neck was a failure. Struensee sprang up to his full height, and the assistants had to use force to replace him on the block.

A second blow was not sufficient, and it required a third stroke to sever the head from the body.

The bodies were then quartered and duly exposed and the heads and hands were carried to the Rabenstein, there to be set upon poles. And so the sentences were fulfilled.

The other members of the Struensee faction were treated with remarkable mildness. The Council of State (which had been recalled to existence by Juliane Marie and Prince Friedrich), simply ordered these persons to leave the capital. In some cases pensions were allowed when offices had been confiscated. Struensee's brother, the Finance Minister, was allowed to leave the country after taking an oath not to divulge any State secrets that he might have learned in the Danish service.

It was at first proposed to immure Caroline Mathilde in Aalborg in Jütland; but the energetic Keith obtained as a concession—a concession which the Government was probably not very unwilling to grant—that the ex-Queen should be given up to her brother, George III.

It was impossible to have Caroline Mathilde at the Court of Queen Charlotte, or even at the Court of Hanover; and George III. determined to assign to his younger sister his castle at Celle, as a place of honourable captivity. Celle had been the residence of the Dukes of Lüneburg, and was still a fortified castle with moat and walls.

The ex-Queen had an allowance of 30,000 thalers a year, with a sufficient household, and every comfort. Of course she was separated from her children; but she must have been of an elastic temperament, as she soon had companies of comedians in the castle, and began to enjoy herself.

Her elder sister, the Erbprinzessin Auguste von Braunschweig-Wolfenbüttel, exercised a kind of control over Celle and its royal inmate, and was regarded by Caroline Mathilde as a spy. Auguste would seem to have been convinced of her sister's guilt.

Presently the ex-Queen began to intrigue, taking care to keep the thing a secret from her sister Auguste. Some adherents proposed to make her Regent in Denmark, until her son should attain his majority. Caroline Mathilde listened gladly, but she could do nothing without George III., and Sir N. Wraxall became the go-between. He made several journeys between Celle and London. George III. seems to have given a provisional assent, expressing readiness to recognise the step if it should succeed, but declining to take himself any active part in it. The King of England stipulated that no revenge should be used against Juliane Marie and Friedrich. However a few partisans might flatter her, it seems unlikely that Denmark would have received as Regent a Queen, divorced, convicted of adultery, and once leagued with the hated

Struensee. However, all such projects came to an untimely end, by the death, May 1, 1775, at Celle, of Caroline Mathilde. She had reached the age of twenty-three years and nine months.

The cause of death was scarlet fever. A portrait of Caroline Mathilde is now lying before me. She has not the receding forehead of George III., but is otherwise a very handsome feminine likeness of her royal brother. The figure inclines to a voluptuous *embonpoint;* the lips are full and pouting; the eyes languishing and large. The nose is rather thickly modelled; the face expresses gaiety, good humour, obstinacy, sensuality. She must have been vivacious and pleasure-loving; passionate and light. Altogether a woman of an attractive sexual presence; and essentially a woman of the morals and manners of her place and time. Some of the light conversation recorded by her ladies-in-waiting suggests rather the placid laxity of Emilia than the steadfast purity of Desdemona.

Juliane Marie has been violently attacked by the defenders of Caroline Mathilde, but I cannot find that the Queen-Mother deserved the opprobrium with which she has been assailed. She was no doubt fond of power, and capable of intrigue. Her own son was only about three years younger than Christian VII.; and during the childhood and early youth of the latter, she acquired a love of rule. During the sway of Struensee she was rudely pushed on one side. Speaking to Dr Münter about Struensee, she said,—'I am truly sorry for the unfortunate man. I have examined myself to ascertain whether I have acted out of personal enmity; but my conscience acquits me of the charge.' A Danish Queen might well feel a righteous indignation against such an unprincipled and insolent upstart; nor could Juliane Marie have regarded with indifference Struensee's disgraceful relations with Caroline Mathilde. When, after the fall of the lackey-Minister, the Queen-Mother returned to power, she at once restored the old Council of State. She was kind to the two children of Caroline Mathilde, and resisted the desire of the Council to treat the little girl as if the child were not legitimate. When Friedrich VI. had arrived at a proper age (his demented father being still alive) she made no difficulty in resigning the Regency to him, and retired with her son into private life; abdicating, practically, a throne without any attempt to retain her splendid position. The Queen-Mother must have been a woman of ability and of some force of character.

Germans love Germans, but do not love Danes. Struensee was a German, and has, even yet, German admirers. Jenssen-Tusch admires him; and as a necessary consequence defends Caroline Mathilde.

Anne Boleyn has doubtful defenders; Katharine Howard has hardly any: but Mary Queen of Scots has still champions of her chastity; and has not a book been written to prove the platonic character of Frau von Stein's relations to Goethe? Truly, historical sentimentalism is still an active power.

It is one thing to urge for Caroline Mathilde all the excuses which justice and mercy can fairly plead; but it is another thing to deny facts. There is excuse for the fair Queen's sin; but sin there was. Her husband could only inspire in her breast loathing, contempt, anger. The times were dissolute, and temptation was at hand; but those who feel impelled to pity frailty take a wholly wrong line of argument when they ignore or deny facts.

Friedrich VI. applied to George III. for an English princess to wife, but was sternly refused. He married his cousin, the daughter of the Landgraf Karl von Hessen, and of Louise, the youngest sister of Christian VII. The refusal of the English Monarch embittered the King of Denmark, and threw that country into the arms of Napoleon. Hence the bombardment of Copenhagen, and its capitulation to Nelson in 1801, and the capture of the Danish fleet in 1807 by Gambier.

Of Christian VII., when in London, Horace Walpole writes :—

'He is as diminutive as if he came out of a kernel in the fairy tales—he is not ill made, nor weakly made, though so small; and though his face is pale and delicate, it is not at all ugly. . . . . Well, then, this great king is a very little one. He has the sublime strut of his grandfather (or a cock-sparrow), and the divine white eyes of all his family on the mother's side. . . . . His Court is extremely well ordered, for they bow as low to him at every word as if his name were Sultan Amurath. . . . The very citizens of both sexes, who resorted daily to his apartments at St James' to see him dine in public with his favourites, mistook him more than once for a young girl dressed in man's clothes, whose conversation and deportment commanded neither respect nor attention. His confidants were of the same stamp.'

Sir Robert Murray Keith records that Christian VII. was, at the age of seventeen, of a figure light and compact, under middle height, but well proportioned. His features, if not handsome, were regular; he had a good forehead and aquiline nose, a handsome mouth and fine set of teeth. He was fair, with blue eyes and very light hair. Altogether a slight, but not unattractive figure.

Headstrong and shallow, Struensee had but little of the wisdom of the statesman, or of the patience of the reformer. Reform, in his eyes, was to be a popular drama in which he was to play a showy part. He was unable to estimate the complexities of correlated existing institutions, or to comprehend the forces arrayed against him. Nor was Struensee

'A moral child without the craft to rule.'

He relied upon craft, when violence was dangerous, and he should have commenced his career as a moralist by reforming himself. For a time his success, not as a reformer, but as a courtier, was supreme; but that success was based upon the favour of a morbid Monarch and a wanton Queen. The essence of Struensee's reform meant, in reality, place, power, pleasure, for Struensee himself. He had not the single eye. There was, no doubt, much that was rotten in the state of Denmark; but a man vain, restless, personally ambitious, is naturally more attracted by gain than revolted by evil. He cannot serve liberty who cannot rule himself; and Struensee, without self-restraint or modesty, was not master of his own passions, or capable of serving humanity. He was neither patient to understand, or wise to improve; but he took a masterful delight in the exercise of absolute power, and joyed in subjugating the wills of others to his own.

Struensee had, unquestionably, a power in his personality. He was, when he chose to be so, sympathetic in a high degree; he was fluent, plausible; supple in intrigue, and had the magic of fervent will and strong determination. It would be unfair to assume that he had not some tendency—even if that tendency were a sham, or sentimental one—to reform abuses; and he ardently desired popularity and applause. But he was as selfish as showy, as greedy as insincere. A great man, with great plans, must be greater even than his plans. Struensee, whose glaring path was darkened by self-seeking and self-love, was not capable of following out abstract ideas in purity of aim. Unlike noble, if deeply erring Launcelot, Struensee *was* the sleeker for

'The great and guilty love he bare the Queen;

though his love for her, guilty certainly, was doubtful in its greatness. His plans for reform, his schemes for popularity, all failed; but he remained the despot of a nation, the dictator of a King, the lover of a Queen—and became, at last, the victim of a headsman. His career was successful so long only as it was supported by the imbecility of a King, by the passion of a Queen. With a power based upon hallucination and adultery, Struensee, as a reformer, or would-be great man, remains a solecism incarnate.

An upstart and a *parvenu*, Struensee naturally found the Danish nobility in strong opposition to him and to his plans. He separated the nobility from the throne; he degraded the order, and exasperated its members. Struensee's hatred of aristocracy was not an abstract feeling; for he desired for himself titles, riches, position, and power. It was the feeling of a coarse plebeian, filled with envious hatred of a class which combined the heritage of command with fine manners and with long traditions. It was a joy to him to injure and to humiliate such a body. In order to counterpoise the nobles, he favoured the *bourgeoisie;* but even towards this class he was arrogant and capricious, and from it he won but little gratitude. His attempts to introduce his ill-judged reforms among the sailors led to the revolt at Hirschholm; his efforts to remodel the army resulted in disaffection and disgust. The nobles and the nation—every one, indeed, except the monarch—

knew of his relations to the Queen; and she became involved in the hatred with which the foreign adventurer was regarded in Denmark. Struensee was bent upon outraging the Danish nationality, and he filled all high offices with creatures of his own, imported from Germany. He also displaced the Danish, in favour of the German tongue. Danish he never learned. For a time his position must have been intoxicating in its splendour and success. He could oppress foes, and could exalt friends. His will was law; and his pleasure, government. He was absolute, and the throne itself was only his first subject. The King was subject to the Queen, and she was slave to Struensee. He was long held up on his dazzling eminence by the fair small hand of a devoted and infatuated woman; and he repaid her boundless devotion by dragging the Queen down with him in his fall, and by involving her in the tragedy of her divorce, and of his own death by the headsman's axe.

But, during the seeming security of Struensee's day of unlimited power, there was maturing, silently, a stealthy and a deadly revolt against him, his rule, and his life. Everything depended at last upon the King. When Christian should realise Struensee's relation to the Queen, all would be lost—for both the lovers; but who, during a long period, who should dare to tell the truth to the King? Blind, easy, sickly as he was, Christian was yet known to be sensitive on the point of his conjugal honour ; and the relation of the truth became the signal for an inexorable revenge.

Heinrich Laube has based a tragedy upon the subject ; and the dramatist has chosen well. The story itself, which we have just essayed to tell—with all its dramatic incidents, with its contrasts of character, with its baseness, its weakness and its sorrow, with that full revolution of Fortune's wheel which leads to such a terrible catastrophe—is, indeed, a striking drama of history. A powerful and a most moving tragedy is contained in the sad, the striking story of STRUENSEE.

# ELIZABETH STUART, QUEEN OF BOHEMIA.

ELIZABETH STUART, some time Queen of Bohemia, and still titular Queen of Hearts; daughter of James I. and Anne of Denmark; granddaughter of Mary Queen of Scots, fourth in descent from Margaret Tudor; sister of Prince Henry and of Charles I.; wife of the Winter-König; mother of the Princes Rupert and Maurice, and of the Electress Sophia; friend of Lord Craven—is the Princess who took the blood royal of England and of Scotland to Germany, where it became blended with that of the Guelphs; the result being that Elizabeth's descendants, Stuarts on the spindle side, succeeded to the throne of England, after the last Stuart King had been deprived of the Crown, and after his two daughters had died without leaving issue.

A direct descendant of this mixed strain of royal blood now wears the Crown of Britain. 'The sovereign qualification was restored to the realm (at the accession of the House of Hanover) in its highest purity through the descendants of the Guelphs, passing back through the House of Este to connect themselves with some of the illustrious Roman Gentes. The new dynasty was, indeed, by centuries older in history than the Plantagenets.'—(Burton.) Elizabeth Stuart was born in Falkland Palace, 19th August 1596; she died, 13th February 1662, in Leicester House, London.

Between birth and death, this descendant and ancestress of kings lived through many adventures, saw many men of mark in many foreign lands, experienced bitter sorrows, and passed through a strange life of royal romance. Princess, Electress, Queen, fugitive, and refugee, her career knew pomp and pleasure, penury and pain. After stormy alternations of rule and of reverse, the (titular) ex-Queen of Bohemia returned from the Continent to England to die there, generally neglected and half unknown. The years which elapsed between the period at which she quitted England as Electress Palatine and returned to it a beauty-waning and distressed widow, discrowned and forlorn, embraced the terrible epoch of the Thirty Years' War; and Elizabeth's vivid memory was filled with vital images of the long agony of that most cruel civil and religious struggle. She had actually and intimately known the persons, intrigues, interests, of the great war; had seen many of the heroes, adventurers, tyrants, of that woeful time; had spoken with Gustavus Adolphus, Maurice of Nassau, Mansfeld, Christian of Brunswick, and many other notabilities of that distinctive epoch of history; had shared the somewhat heavy splendours of the German Courts of the seventeenth century, and had experienced the substantial comfort of the hospitable States-General in the great days of Holland. Around her image stand the figures, behind her glooms the sombre background of that dire convulsion. The years over which her active life extended were of singular importance alike to the politics and to the religion of all Europe. A witness of, and an actress in, that supreme struggle between faiths and dynasties, Elizabeth lived in the very midst of the horror, the romance, the woe of that dæmonic strain and anguish of thirty years' duration. She saw the long process of that exhaustion of war-worn nations which dictated the peace of Westphalia: her own brother, after the civil wars of England, perished on the scaffold at Whitehall: she lived through the time of the Protectorate, and she witnessed the restoration of the royal line in England. Her life, and the times through which she lived, are surely subjects of surpassing interest for an historical essay. Of the sources of information about the Thirty Years' War, it may well be said that their name is legion. The number of German authorities, the plethora of continental records are, in truth, almost bewildering; but the writer about that complex time may well bear in mind Professor Masson's modest and pregnant saying, 'I can never pass a sheet of the historical kind for the press without a dread, lest from inadvertance, or from sheer ignorance, some error, some blunder even, may have escaped me.'

The girlhood of Elizabeth, after her father's accession to the throne (1603), was passed chiefly at Combe Abbey, under the wise guardianship of Sir John, afterwards Lord Harrington, and of his wife. There she played, and studied, and became a mighty huntress. The influences which surrounded her youth were noble, kindly, natural. The Gunpowder Plot conspirators designed to seize her person, and to proclaim her Queen after the murder of her father. They hoped to mould her tender youth to the religion of the Romish Church, and to obtain from such a sovereign Catholic supremacy in England. During the danger arising from the plot, the young Princess was removed, temporarily, from Combe Abbey to Coventry; but after the execution of the conspirators, she returned to the beloved home of her childhood. The great delight of her years of girlhood consisted in the tender affection which subsisted between Elizabeth and her noble brother, the young Prince Henry; a Prince of rare promise, 'the expectancy and rose of the fair State,' who evinced in his early years a true sympathy with all that was noblest in English life and thought. Henry, had he lived, would probably have been, like the last great Tudor monarch, an England-loving ruler, 'more English than the English themselves,' and in intimate and instinctive union with the essence of the national life. Both Henry and Elizabeth were convinced and ardent Protestants. Between the royal children and their parents there was not—there could not be— much intimacy or close sympathy. Anne of Denmark was gay, pleasure-loving, cheerful, frivolous. James, fittest, by nature, to squabble with another mind of like calibre with his own about the trivialities of theology, was a monarch besotted with his own fatuous conception of the divine right of kings; and was unstable, pedantic, undignified, and unvirile. That he had a coward's cruelty, the fates of Arabella Stuart and of Sir Walter Raleigh amply prove. Ungainly in person, he was yet more unlovely in mind. Entering upon the noble inheritance of a reign which succeeded to that of Elizabeth, he alienated the nation from his dynasty, he prepared the great rebellion, he lowered England in the councils of Europe; and, while a most exasperating tyrant to people and to Parliament, he remained long the abject slave of Spain and of unworthy favourites. The best excuse, perhaps, for the pusillanimous King of England, who dared not look upon a drawn sword, consists in the fatal event which occurred while he was yet in his mother's womb. James and his daughter never came very near together; James and his son

Henry drifted even farther and farther apart. It was inevitable that it should be so.

As the years rolled on, the question of the marriages of such a hopeful Prince and Princess began to press. 'I would rather espouse a Protestant Count than a Catholic Emperor,' said Elizabeth. In this, as in other things, she took her tone from her knightly Prince brother, who opposed heartily a scheme for marrying him to the Infanta Anna of Spain, sister to that Infanta Maria whom his brother Charles afterwards pursued in Madrid with bootless courtship. Henry, indeed, proposed to accompany his sister to Germany in order there to be able to remain purely Protestant, and to select and marry some Protestant Princess.

At the suggestion of Maurice of Nassau, a suitor for the hand of Elizabeth presented himself in the person of Frederick, Pfalzgraf of the Rhine, and son of the Kurfürst, or Elector, of the Palatinate, Frederick IV. Frederick IV., who was born in 1574, and married, 1593, Luise Juliane, daughter of William the Silent, a noble daughter of a noble father, was the most considerable Protestant Prince of Germany. His territory did not equal in importance that of Saxony, but the talents, the character, and the zeal of Frederick IV. soon placed him at the head of Protestant Germany. He took a leading part in founding the famous Protestant Union in 1608; and was, indeed, the Chief of the Union, which included among its members the Duke of Würtemberg, the Landgraf of Hessen-Kassel, and the Markgrafs of Anspach and of Baden Durlach. Frederick IV. died 18th September 1610. The Protestant Union called into being the Catholic Liga, founded 10th of July 1609. The Union had many heads; the Liga only one; but that one was Maximilian of Bavaria, while its general was Tilly. Maximilian was unscrupulous, eager, crafty, energetic. A pupil of the Jesuits, and a bigoted Catholic, Maximilian knew well what he wanted, and he hesitated at no means that would serve his ends. He had the advantage, to a partisan, of a clear will, a ruthless cruelty, and a cunning audacity.

The youth of Frederick V. was passed chiefly at Sedan, under the guidance of the Duke of Bouillon, though his guardian was the Herzog Johann von Zweibrücken, to whom Frederick IV. left the Government of the Palatinate while Frederick V. should remain a minor.

At Sedan the young Kurfürst was in a court, but never in a camp. He learned politics, and not war; he was taught accomplishments, but not warfare; he acquired arts without learning arms. His education was political, and was peaceful. The son of the Chief of the Union, he remained ignorant of the art of war. Such knowledge as he attained to in the use of arms, fitted him rather for the holiday tilt-yard than for the terrors of the battlefield. He was but a poor soldier, and he was no general. For the needs of his day, and of his own future life, he was but imperfectly trained. He was a cavalier, but not a warrior. Frederick was graceful, and was gentle; courteous, tender, and true. He was capable of a constant and noble love. His person was fine, though not stalwart; he shone more at the ball than in the school of arms. His father had passed from Lutheranism to Calvinism, and the young Kurpfalz was a convinced and zealous Calvinist. As a suitor for the hand of Elizabeth Stuart, he was acceptable to James, and was highly popular with the English nation, which ardently desired a Protestant Prince as a husband for the daughter of the throne.

The match was distasteful to the Catholic party, and to the gay and sprightly Anne of Denmark. Her ambition desired a king as the husband of her daughter, and Anne's sneer at 'Goody Palsgrave' damped the present joy, and influenced the future career of Elizabeth, who inherited much of her mother's light and frivolous temperament.

The race of the renowned Otto of Wittelsbach split itself into two branches—the Bavarian and the Palatine. The original stock obtained the Duchy of Bavaria, in 1180, from the Emperor Frederick I.; and, afterwards, from Frederick II., the Palatinate of the Rhine. The treaty of Pavia, in 1329, divided the two countries under two reigning houses springing from the parent root, and in the early years of the seventeenth century, Bavaria was ruled by the strong and wily Maximilian (born 17th of April 1573), while his cousin, the weak and gentle Frederick V., inherited the Government of the Palatinate.

Prince Henry, the gallant-springing young Stuart, died November 6, 1612; but, amid the actual mourning for her well-loved brother, Elizabeth married Frederick on the 14th of February 1613. The nuptials were celebrated with great rejoicings and with extraordinary pomp and expense. The honeymoon over, the married lovers sailed from Margate to Flushing, where they were received by Maurice, and whence they passed, in a sort of triumphal procession, to Heidelberg—Elizabeth's new home.

Born in the same year, 1596, Frederick and Elizabeth were alike seventeen years of age at the date of their marriage. Frederick was still a minor when they reached Heidelberg; nor did he assume the reins of Government until the next year, 1614; but his territory had been well administered by his mother and his guardian. In 1614, Elizabeth's first child, Heinrich Friedrich, was born in the Palace of Heidelberg.

The early time of their marriage was one of singular happiness; of a happiness so great that it contrasts painfully with the sorrows of the coming years. Elizabeth exercised an unlimited empire over an uxorious young husband, who found his chief delight in her affection. She had all the things for which she vitally cared—pomp, pleasure, dominion, and hunting; though the crumpled rose-leaf in her lot was, perhaps, the rankle of her mother's sneer at ' Goody Palsgrave.' The years of peace and of pleasure in Heidelberg were but few. Frederick and his wife could not remain contented with their own Palatinate. Light and trivial natures both, they were not too light or too trivial to remain untouched by ambition during the intoxication and the ferment of their day of strain and storm :

> 'Tis dangerous when the lesser nature comes
> Between the fell pass and incensed points
> Of mighty opposites.

To his own utter undoing, and to the great injury of the Protestant cause, Frederick plunged into those troubled waters in order to encircle the round hat of an Elector with a golden crown. The primary cause of the Thirty Years' War in Germany was the determination of the Austro-Spanish Monarchies, aided by the Catholic Princes—and notably by Bavaria—to establish the ecclesiastical dominion of the Pope in all Germany, in Holland, and afterwards, if possible, in the northern kingdoms of Scandinavia, and in all the other 'Heretic States' of Europe. The Treaty of Augsburg (1555) was to be torn up, and the Reformation suppressed by force as well as fraud. The House of Hapsburg, as vassal of the Pope, was to rule and reign throughout the land of Luther.

Religion furnished the impulse; political ambition the secondary cause; while bigotry lent ferocity to the conduct of the merciless and devastating struggle.

The Austrian branch of Hapsburg sought absolute imperial power and universal monarchy. The war was a battlefield for princes and for captains who desired either to acquire or to defend territories and inheritances. It was an arena for the plots of schemers and for the ambition of heroes. It fostered the trade of mercenary soldier, and developed to gigantic dimensions the place, the profit, and the pride of the able warrior of fortune. Through valour, cruelty, treachery, it marched over a country rendered wretched, desolate, and waste. By the process of utter exhaustion, it left the chief combatants in the situation, in which, as regards principles, if not position, they were at the treaty of Augsburg in 1555. It confirmed a religious toleration which it ought never to have disturbed. It returned practically to the point from which it started. In result it was a triumph for Protestantism and for religious liberty; its issue repelled the fierce onslaught of Catholicism; but the war was, on the part of those who provoked it, a wicked war: and such success as was attained was purchased by oceans of blood and by years of misery.

The preliminary indications of the long war were the violent seizure by Maximilian of Bavaria of Donauwörth, and the intricate tangle of the question of the inheritance of the Duchies of Cleve and Jülich. The weakness of Protestantism in Germany was caused in part by the fatal split between Lutheran and Calvinist, and by the contemptible character of the leading Protestant Princes—of such men as Johann Georg, of Saxony, and Georg Wilhelm, tenth Elector of Brandenburg. Both Electors honoured and dreaded the Emperor more than they loved their religion; neither would peril aught for that cause. Carlyle says, 'In fact, had there been no better Protestantism than that of Germany, all was over with Protestantism. . . . Over seas there dwelt and reigned a certain King in Sweden; there farmed and walked musing by the shores of the Ouse, in Huntingdonshire, a certain man; there was a Gustav Adolf over seas, an Oliver Cromwell over seas.' Selfish and sensual, a lover of the wine-cup and the boar hunt, *Kur-Sachsen* was an 'unspeakable curse to Germany. A man of no strength, devoutness, or adequate human worth;' and the Elector of Brandenburg was led by him of Saxony. At the outbreak of the great war Protestantism in Germany had but little to hope from its natural leaders.

Then came the irresistible temptation for Frederick and Elizabeth. The great prize of a crown— that of Bohemia—was dangled before their eager eyes.

When, in 1612, Matthias succeeded Rudolph II. as Emperor, he managed, by practice, to impose

upon Bohemia, as his successor to the crown of
Bohemia, Ferdinand, son of the Archduke Charles,
Prince of Styria. Both Rudolf and Matthias were
childless men. Charles was brother to the Emperor
Maximilian; and both Charles and Maximilian were
the sons of the Emperor Ferdinand I., and of Anne,
heiress of Bohemia and Hungary. Bohemia resisted
the nomination of Ferdinand as King, but could
not shake off the yoke. The country was essentially
Protestant, but saw its liberties invaded and its religion proscribed by the fanatic, Jesuit-led monarch
who was so ruthlessly forced upon the country.
When, in 1619, Ferdinand was elected Emperor, as
Ferdinand II., and ruled the Empire, being himself
ruled by Father Lämmerlein and Father Hyacinth,
the Bohemians hastened to depose him as King of
Bohemia, and to offer the crown to the best Protestant Prince who could be induced to accept the
dangerous dignity. It was promptly refused by
Saxony and by Brandenburg, nor was it accepted even
by the Prince of Transylvania; and then, as a last
resource, the crown of Bohemia was offered to Frederick. Anne of Denmark died (1619) before a crown
was placed within the reach of 'Goody Palsgrave;'
but there can be no doubt that the chance of becoming Queen was welcomed by Elizabeth with
light-hearted rapture.

To Frederick every project was easy; every action
difficult. However he might secretly hesitate about

accepting so perilous a crown, he was yet elated by the prospect, and he had his wife to lean upon. She chastised him with the valour of her tongue; and she wrote to her father, asking James I. for his approval and advice. Charles I. said, later, of the Palatine pair, that 'the grey mare was the better horse;' and Elizabeth's exultation overcame their sense of dread of danger. Meanwhile Frederick sought advice from various quarters. Saxony besought Frederick to remember that, in accepting the Bohemian crown, he hazarded the loss of his hereditary dominions. Max of Bavaria wrote in a frank, even cousinly way, and warned Frederick earnestly against acceptance. Max told his cousin how fickle the Bohemians were : ' You want subjects ; they want a servant :' and added that motives of interest alone impelled them to choose Frederick. Maurice of Nassau would not help, but did not dissuade. Had Maurice himself desired the Bohemian crown, he would, probably, have won and have worn it; but Frederick was not Maurice. Luise Juliane, the mother of Frederick, addressed her son in a letter of singular ability (*Mémoires sur la vie et la mort de la Princesse Louise Juliane.* Leyden, 1644), and this remarkable State paper is worth producing here. She said that 'the affairs of the Empire might soon be retrieved, and that the Pope would convoke all Catholics to defend the Emperor. The King of France, however inimical to Austria, is not in a state to oppose its power; the King of Spain will eagerly sustain it. As to the King of Great Britain, believe me, you little understand him if you persuade yourself he will break with Spain for your interests. On my brother Maurice, there is more reliance to be placed; but the States will not sacrifice Holland to the Palatinate. What aid can you expect from the King of Denmark? He is too far distant. The houses of Saxony and of Bavaria are already jealous of yours, and will heartily concur in driving you from Bohemia. Trust not too much to the Protestant Union. . . . Distrust still more the Bohemians. If they offer you the crown, it is not that they love you better than another prince, but that they have no other resource. Do not flatter yourself they will be more constant to you than they have been to Ferdinand; but, even though you could depend upon your kinsmen, your allies, your friends, and your subjects, you have neither troops nor treasures adequate to the charges of war.' Surely wise advice. Every prophecy of Luise Juliane was fulfilled by the bitter event. Frederick was not the man, nor had he the means, to obtain success in such a desperate venture. He was well known to the men of his own day and land; no man would help because no man believed in him. Frederick could not oppose Ferdinand. Bohemian Protestantism could only be helped by German Protestantism; but that, in 1619, was selfish and supine, and would by no means stir for Frederick. If Frederick could not maintain himself in Bohemia, and defend the Bohemians, his enterprise sank into a mere usurpation, which would give grounds for reprisals, and for the further oppression of Protestantism. Nowhere in all Germany was there any enthusiasm for, any belief in, Frederick.

Half deceiving themselves, Frederick and Elizabeth attempted to sanctify their decision with the name of religion, and veiled ambition under the pretext of piety. The Kaiser himself deigned to warn Frederick, though Ferdinand steadfastly refused to believe that *Kurpfalz* could contemplate a seizure of 'Austrian territory.' Meanwhile, Bohemia was pressing for Frederick's answer. His council in Heidelberg advised him to come to no decision until he should have heard from England; but Elizabeth was not inclined to wait for anything. After declaring that the chance was a call from God, she writes to Frederick,—'Nor shall I repine whatever consequences may ensue; not even though I should be forced to part with my last jewel, and to suffer actual hardship.' Söltl quotes another letter of hers in which she reminds Frederick that he has married the daughter of a King, and should not want courage to make his wife a Queen. Elizabeth concludes by saying,—'Rather *Sauerkraut* with a king than luxury with a prince.' This sentence expresses her real motives for decision, and exhibits her character; which was ambitious, shallow, and fond of splendour.

Without waiting for her husband's final decision, she made all preparations for starting for Bohemia. Another pressing mission came from Prague, and Frederick was ultimately pushed over the edge of treason. As he rode away from Heidelberg, his weeping mother cried out, 'Ach! Du trägst die Pfalz nach Böhmen!'—'Thou art carrying the Palatinate into Bohemia!'

The Palatinate itself was left under the Government of Zweibrücken; but Frederick, who, in his incapacity, seemed to forget that he was burning his ships behind him, made no provision for the defence of his native territory.

Frederick and Elizabeth entered Prague amid great rejoicings, on 31st October 1619. His coronation took place on November 4th.

He immediately issued an address to his new kingdom. This manifesto was large and loose and liberal as a modern hustings declaration. It promised everything to everybody, and was so framed as, if possible, to please all his subjects.

Acting with the nervous hurry of small natures bent impatiently upon a darling project, Frederick and Elizabeth accepted the Bohemian crown without having waited for the reply of James I.

James was, according to Clarendon, 'very quick-sighted in discerning difficulties, very slow in mastering them.' His confused love of peace and poverty of spirit threw him into a perplexed astonishment when he heard of the serious step taken by his son-in-law without his royal concurrence; nor did he ever approve Frederick's Bohemian usurpation. It may well be contended that a King of England should not have wasted English blood and gold in the mere attempt to win a crown for a son-in-law; but it may be a question whether, in the larger sense of European politics, a great English King, the natural antagonist of Hapsburg ascendency, and natural defender of Protestantism, might not have enlarged the question into such an action of combined Protestantism as that which Gustavus Adolphus afterwards led. James might have wielded the strength of England, and such a war would have been highly popular. Frederick personally was liked, though he was not known in connection with great affairs, in England; and his cause and that of Elizabeth would have merged into the greater cause of European civil and religious liberty. But James, a laggard in love and a dastard in war, was not the man for great causes. He might have ruined Austria and have served Protestantism; but he was led by Gondomar, and was, probably, in reality a crypto-Catholic. Diego Sarmiento de Acuña, Count of Gondomar, reached London as Ambassador from Spain in 1613; and soon acquired complete dominion over the lean-souled King. Marc Antonio, Archbishop of Spalatro, was made Dean of Windsor in 1618: and Goodman, yet more Catholic than Laud, sat upon the bench of bishops. Rightly had Luise Juliane said that James would not break with Spain. The Spanish marriage was dangled before his eyes by the astute Gondomar. On 4th of November 1616, the rickety Duke of York (afterwards Charles I.), had been created Prince of Wales; and James burned to match his son with the blood of Hapsburg. James hastened to disavow his unfortunate son-in-law; he would not recognise Frederick as King of Bohemia, and he apologised to Ferdinand for Frederick's 'usurpation' of Austrian territory. The Spanish leanings of James were, until the Spanish match was broken off in failure and contempt, very pronounced; and were as stable as anything in his unvirile nature could be stable or strong. The first Stuart Kings, who robbed the English Nation of the Church of Elizabeth Tudor, drove the force and passion of the National religious character into Puritanism; into the 'sectaries'—Presbyterians, Independents, Anabaptists—into those intense, if gloomy convictions which animated the Ironsides, and rode in victory through the red fields of Naseby and of Marston Moor.

The German title of 'Winter-König' is, being interpreted rather than translated, to be rendered into English as a mockery 'King of Snow.' An estimable country gentleman may be a very poor monarch; and incapable, fatuous Frederick, whose very amiability increases the contempt felt for him by history as a King, soon began to melt away. Anxieties commenced early to surround the new royalties of the hapless King and Queen of fickle Bohemia; and yet their first time in the palace of Prague was one of unalloyed triumph and exultation, especially to the sanguine, pomp-loving Elizabeth. Feast succeeded feast; ceremony followed ceremony; she was, at last, a Queen, and Elizabeth was royally happy. Despite the tolerant tone of poor Frederick's 'hustings' manifesto,' he too, as a Calvinist, was priest-ridden. He took with him to Prague his narrow and bigoted chaplain, Schulze (*Scultetus*), and the interfering minister soon embittered both Catholics and Lutherans against his royal master.

Bohemia became gradually dissatisfied with its new King. It was found that Frederick could neither help Bohemia nor himself; and that he could bring no help from outside. Elizabeth, who in the flush of her triumph was extremely gracious, and was always graceful, was, for a time, popular; but Bohemia found that there was but little behind that superficial gracefulness. Neither Frederick nor Elizabeth could speak, nor could understand, the Bohemian language. The split between Court and Nation widened, until Frederick found himself in the position of a timid and unskilful rider mounted, without saddle or bridle, on an unbroken, vicious horse.

> They that stand high, have many blasts to shake them;
> And if they fall they dash themselves to pieces;

and none stand in greater danger than those who, impelled by their own vanity, and assisted by accident, have attained to an elevation for which they are incompetent. He who, in the seventeenth century, would usurp a possession of the House of Austria must have been a warrior who could hold what he had seized in the tenacious grip of an iron gauntlet.

The dangers thickened round them; and Frederick, with his want of insight, and confused vision, was like a short-sighted man before the invention of spectacles. A miner does not notice the lengthening or shortening of the days. Frederick, in the darkness of his incapacity, seemed unconscious of the fate that was surely drawing near. The Pope Paul said: 'That young man has got himself entangled in a nice labyrinth.' Ferdinand absolutely refused at first to give credence to the report of Frederick's coronation. Such blind audacity seemed to the Emperor incredible. The Protestant Princes, meeting at Mülhausen, under the guidance of Saxony, wrote to Frederick, urging him to relinquish the crown, and not to involve the cause of Protestantism with 'his rebellion.' The Emperor curtly summoned Frederick to vacate the throne by the 1st June; failing which—ban of the Empire and war. Spinola and his Spaniards were gathering to march on the Palatinate; the *Kriegsvolk*, the war-folk of the *Liga*, were assembling for the Empire. Spinola led one army—Tilly and Bucquoy the other. The Palatinate had been left defenceless; what would Frederick do to defend his new kingdom? The Bohemians were tired of Frederick, and were in dread of Ferdinand. Frederick's army was indifferent in point of quality, and had no heart in the cause; there was no discipline and but little pay. The troops had to live by plunder; and, indeed, they seized Elizabeth's private jewels, as they were being conveyed to Prague, and confiscated their own Queen's gems. Frederick was not the man to teach drill, to enforce discipline, to lend a soul to an army, or to inspire it with confidence in its King and leader. His affairs were ready to tumble to ruin. Elizabeth refused to quit Prague, and held on to the last to the seat of her brief Queenship.

The smaller fight of Rakonitz was lost for Frederick; and, on Sunday, November 8, 1620, the Imperialists attacked Prague; and the battle of the White Mountain—a battle which lasted only one hour—completed the defeat and ruin of the wretched Frederick. Most characteristically, Frederick was at dinner, at a stately dinner which he gave to the Ambassadors, during this crowning fight for his own crown and interests. 'After dinner, the King resolved to go to horse to see the army; but before the King could get out of the gate, the news came of the loss of the Bohemian and the royal cause.' The fact is, Frederick was driven back through the city gate by his own troops, who, in full rout, crying out, 'The battle is lost!' were tumbling pell-mell into the city, to gain the protection of its walls.

It was intended to defend Prague, in order to secure the retreat of Elizabeth, but she herself opposed the measure. Cousin Max granted an armistice of eight hours; during which the King and Queen fled wildly, and in such haste that they left behind them crown, papers, jewels—almost everything that they had. Prague, with terror in its heart, did trembling homage to the incensed Emperor. Frederick *had* taken the Palatinate to Bohemia; had lost crown, Elector's hat, his new kingdom, and his ancient inheritance. He was to become a penniless, discrowned fugitive, and under the terrible ban of the Empire.

The hardships which Elizabeth had been willing to incur for the sake of a crown had come upon her, as, with husband and with child, but reft of all else, she fled through the snow of a severe winter to Breslau in Silesia. The Markgraf Georg Wilhelm of Brandenburg had married (in 1616) Frederick's sister, Elizabetha Karolina; but the timid brother-in-law hesitated, at first, to grant to the hapless couple refuge in Cüstrin; where, on December 25, 1620, Elizabeth's son, Maurice, was born. Rupert, the 'Rupert of the Rhine,' of our Civil Wars, was born in Prague, December 20, 1619. In 1617, Karl Ludwig; in 1618, Elizabeth was born; indeed, the first dozen years of Elizabeth's life abroad are all speckled with confinements.

Frederick preached resistance, and called loudly upon every one to help him. Meantime the Upper and Lower Palatinates were overrun by Spinola; and Heidelberg was taken by Tilly. Without consulting the Electors, the high-handed Ferdinand gave the Palatinate Electorship to Max of Bavaria, who also got the Upper Palatinate, while the Lower was, for the moment, given to Archduke Albert. The Archduke died July 13, 1621, and then the Lower Palatinate fell also to Maximilian. Max 'had done more than any Emperor could expect,' and deserved reward from a grateful *Kaiser*. On December 13, 1621, all Protestant preachers and teachers were rejected from Bohemia. On February 28, 1621, Tilly put to death, in Prague, some eight-and-forty of the best and noblest citizens, on a large public scaffold, similar to those used by Alba, for similar purposes, in the Netherlands. The tongues of some were torn out by the roots; the right hands of others were hacked off. Confiscation, persecution, death and misery succeeded Frederick in Bohemia.

On January 22, 1621, the Ban was pronounced against Frederick. On April 12, 1621, the Protestant Union dissolved itself. The whole Palatinate was subjected, compulsorily, to the Romish religion, and the Pope wrote to the Emperor to congratulate him upon the triumph of Catholicism. Truly,

Frederick's zeal for religion had done but little for the Protestant cause.

Frederick and Elizabeth took refuge in Holland, and were received with great kindness by the generous States-General. Even James, stung by the violent seizure of the Palatinate, awoke to a certain passionate activity—of words. On January 30, 1621, the King told the Parliament, 'Now shall I labour to preserve the rest; wherein I declare that, if by fair means I cannot get it, my crown, my blood, and all, shall be spent, with my son's blood also, but I will get it for him (Frederick). And this is the cause of all, that the cause of religion is involved in it; for they will alter religion when they conquer, and so, perhaps, my grandchild also may suffer, who hath committed no fault at all.'

Brave words! But James 'dared not strike one blow for the inheritance of his daughter's children, and was dallying with the oppressors of the people and of the Church of God.' Of James' negotiations Nani (quoted by Mr Samuel Rawson Gardiner) says, 'His first proposals to Vienna might have been listened to, but they were so impracticable and absurd that the subtle Spaniards soon saw what sort of person they had to deal with, and availed themselves accordingly of his improbable schemes and delays; they knew, likewise, that James trembled at war, and abominated a rebellion.'

The polite evasion of contempt was the only answer obtained by James.

On January 30th, James, seeking for popularity, told the Parliament that religion 'was the cause of all;' and yet Gondomar reports to Philip (Simancas MSS.)—also quoted by Mr Gardiner—on February 18th, the pith of a memorable conversation between James and himself, held on February 2d, in which James admitted that he was 'ready to acknowledge his readiness to recognise the Pope as the head of the Church in matters spiritual, and to allow appeals to lie to him from English Bishops, provided the Pope would refrain from meddling with temporal jurisdiction in his (James') kingdoms, and would renounce his claim to depose kings at pleasure. If in his writings he (James) had spoken of the Pope as Antichrist, it was because of his usurped power over kings, and not because he called himself the head of the Church;' and, in testimony to the truth of this statement, the King gave his hand to the delighted ambassador. The Pope might have the diviner right, but yet was not to interfere with the 'divine right' of kings.

Elizabeth implored her father to take action for the recovery of Bohemia as well as the Palatinate, and, by her advice, Frederick refused to lay aside the title of King of Bohemia. In this dark hour of her fortunes, Elizabeth, a true Stuart, with a nature satisfied with the pleasures of the present, writes to

Sir Thomas Roe, the English ambassador (she always addressed him as 'Honest Thom'), 'yett I am still of my wilde humour, to be as merrie as I can in spite of fortune.' The gentler Frederick felt his misfortunes, and especially the loss of his hereditary possessions, more keenly. 'The Winter King's account was soon settled;' but the Elector's loss was harder to bear, and this loss he owed partly to Elizabeth, partly to his own imbecility.

German political sympathy was, to a great extent, with Frederick so far as the Palatinate was concerned; but it was also felt that Frederick, in taking Bohemia, had done to Ferdinand the same thing which the Emperor, in savage reprisal, had done to the Elector. The sentiment of the sacredness of hereditary possession was then strong among the German Powers. The monarchy of Bohemia was not, in a practical sense, an elective monarchy. In default of an hereditary succession, the crown of Bohemia was seizable by him who could take and hold it. The crown had on various occasions been the prey of violence and fraud, and had been mainly at the mercy of the *Kaiser*. Thus, Matthias compelled the weak Rudolf to cede Bohemia to him; and Matthias, when he was elected Emperor, compelled the Bohemians to accept Ferdinand. The unfortunate, if fickle, Bohemians constantly saw their religion and their liberties outraged by Catholics and by tyrants. They sought freedom by means of a Protestant Prince, and, failing in obtaining one of power and mark, they had the misfortune to see their ruin consummated by their last resource, Frederick. Their hope that the Union, that the German Protestant Powers, that England, would support Frederick was soon shown to be the shadow of a shade.

Two defenders sprang up for the lost cause of Frederick and Elizabeth. One was a partisan of policy; the other a champion of chivalry. The first was Count Mansfeld; the second was Christian of Brunswick.

Mansfeld was the ablest adventurer, the most successful soldier of fortune of his land and day. He had strong reasons for hating Austria, and hated her accordingly.

Christian was a man of a very different stamp. He was *Geschwisterkind* (first cousin) of Elizabeth (Söltl), and was born Sept. 10, 1599. He was, therefore, three years younger than Elizabeth. Christian's mother, also an Elizabeth, was the daughter of Frederick II. of Denmark. Christian first met Elizabeth Stuart when, after the disastrous day of the White Mountain, she had taken refuge in Holland. He was charmed with his cousin; he felt knightly sympathy for a Queen's misfortunes: a passionate Protestant, he glowed with true zeal for Elizabeth's religion. Burning for military glory, a fanatic of chivalry, a knight-errant of romantic devotion; high-flown, sombre, and intense, Christian eagerly devoted life and fortune to his cousin and her cause. He wore her glove in his helmet; he adopted as his motto, 'Alles für Ruhm und ihr'—'All for glory and for her.' He called himself 'Gottes Freund, der Pfaffen Feind'—'The friend of God, the foe of priests.' When, after a wound at the siege of Breda, his arm had to be amputated, he caused the trumpets to sound while the operation was performed, and said that 'the arm he had left would be enough for revenge upon his enemies.' Heroic as a knightly champion, Christian was yet unsuccessful as a general. Intrepid, rash, and headstrong, he was easily beaten by the wily Tilly. Mansfeld was abler and more successful; but their joint help had really availed but little when Frederick saw himself compelled (partly by pressure put upon him by his father-in-law) to dismiss the two generals who—the one from hatred of Austria, the other from love to Elizabeth—bravely maintained and kept alive a falling cause.

After the bitter step of such a dismissal, Frederick would seem to have begun to suffer from life-weariness. He stood apart, and left his affairs mainly to his sprightly wife, and to the Secretary Russdorf.

It is impossible in this short essay to narrate all the battles, sieges, fortunes which occurred in the great war, even in so far as such events may have indirectly affected the fortunes of the Palatine House.

Much must necessarily be passed over, and I am compelled to restrict myself to those leading occurrences which were most clearly determinate of the fortunes of Germany, and by consequence of those of Elizabeth Stuart.

The next great event which was of vital moment for Europe and for Elizabeth was the advent, from over-seas, of the great *Schwedenkönig*, Gustavus Adolphus. In July 1630, the Swedish deliverer landed on German soil. He had completed his conquest over Poland. He knew well that the Polish war had been fomented, he knew that Sigismund had been supported, by Austria ; he knew that, if Wallenstein could create a fleet, the House of Hapsburg, eager for universal dominion, and then in the zenith of its power and success, would attack him in Sweden itself ; and he defended his kingdom by attacking her enemies. The very successes of Ferdinand drew down Gustavus Adolphus upon him ; the supineness of the German Protestant Princes called forth the great Swedish defender of Protestantism. 'Universal monarchy must be repressed by neighbouring nations at great hazard and inconceivable expense, provided such nations are only protected by a small interposition of ocean.' Wallenstein and Spain were preparing a fleet to attack the navy of Sweden when that navy bore Gustav Adolf and his army to German soil.

Nor was it by any means the safety of Sweden alone which called Gustavus into the field. 'Mich treibt ein anderer Geist,' 'I am actuated by other motives,' said the King. It was the cause, the great cause, of Protestantism and of true religion that weighed most heavily upon his soul. Hear him for a moment; his voice still seems to speak vitally to us across the abyss of two hundred and fifty years. 'I embark in a war, far from my own dominions, and seem to court those dangers and difficulties which another man might labour to decline; but the Searcher of the human heart will see and know that it was neither ambition that tempted me, nor the avarice of extending my dominions, nor the appetite of fighting, nor the mischievous temper of loving to interfere in my neighbours' concerns. Other object I have none than to support the afflicted and oppressed, to maintain the religious and civil liberty of society, and to bear my testimony against a tyranny over the whole human race.'

And Gustavus described his lofty motives truly. If the Protestant princes of Germany were supine, her Protestant people were worthy; nor could the King endure the spectacle of Jesuit rule, through Kaiser and through Pope, carried out by means of blood and fire, of force and fraud; of infra-human persecution by the priest. Gustavus is a singular historical apparition, in respect that he combined the earnestness of a Cromwell with the grace of a cavalier.

He was not *Gott-betrunken*, or God-intoxicated, as Novalis said of Spinoza, but he was God-inspired. A hero of conscience, he was also a hero of charm. He could not only command the reverence, but also win the love of men. In him force was tempered by sweetness. Intense as clear, there was nothing gloomy or morbid about the strong bright Gustavus. No cause ever had a nobler champion; but his kingly and knightly mind was expressed through his broad, lofty forehead; through his well-opened, blue, and steadfast eyes; through a figure and bearing which approach to an ideal of great manhood. His religion was that of a royal man, his politics those of a manly king. Fervent, and even rash in fight, generous in victory, the first captain of his time, he fought for an abstract cause, and defended oppressed humanity. Stern where sternness was necessary, he was full of 'flowing courtesy' and princely manners. His army was well paid, and restrained within the limits of strict discipline. It was a moral force, which paid, and did not plunder its way through the territory of friend and foe. In this respect the Swedo-German army differed from those of the Liga, of the Empire, and even from the troops of Mansfeld. 'Der Krieg müsse den Krieg ernähren,' 'War must support itself,' said Wallenstein; and the armies of Tilly, of Wallenstein, of Mansfeld, simply devastated any territories that they had to occupy.

In earlier years Gustavus had been a half suitor for the hand of Elizabeth Stuart, and was therefore likely, being of noble mould, to have a kindly feeling toward an olden love. The light of the North, the Aurora Borealis of the Baltic, was now happily married to Maria Eleanora, sister of the Kurfürst Johann Georg. Gustav was born on December 9, 1594.

James I. died in 1625, and had been succeeded by his son, Charles I. Charles was her brother, and Elizabeth might, perhaps, hope more from a brother than even from a father.

Charles was very willing to do anything to help his sister—so long as the doing involved no action. So soon as Gustavus appeared victoriously upon the scene, Charles tried to delegate to him the task of restoring Elizabeth to the Palatinate.

On November 7, 1632, Sir Henry Vane, successor to Roe, met the Swedish King at Würzburg, and Vane thus reports Gustavus' answer: 'If Charles wished sincerely to bring about the restitution of the Palatinate (no question more of Bohemia) and wished it in good faith, he must afford such assistance as justly merited the appellation of royal.' If Charles contributed money and an English army of 12,000 men, he, Gustavus, 'would never sheath his sword until the Palatinate should be recovered.' Vainly did Gustav expect anything royal (except, perhaps, the portraits of Vandyke) from Charles, who was negotiating with Vienna when he should have been fighting side by side with Sweden. If he had really wished well to his sister's cause, there was no way to help her but by fighting. Spannheim records that James I. felt, in his last days and hours, some compunction and remorse with respect to the Palatinate. Forty-eight hours before his death, James charged his son Charles, 'as he hoped for a parent's benediction and that of Heaven,' to exert all his powers in order to reinstate his sister and her children into their hereditary dominions; for (said James) *it was my mistake to seek the Palatinate in Spain.* The italics are ours.

Charles was as incapable as had been his father of clear and noble action.

'My God, Sire!' exclaimed Sir Richard Glendale, to the Pretender, when that Prince landed 'for a hunting expedition,' in *Redgauntlet*—'of what great and inexpiable crime can your Majesty's ancestors have been guilty that they have been punished by the infliction of judicial blindness on their whole generation!' In this indignant burst of Sir Richard Glendale, Walter Scott summarised the essence of the career of the Stuarts.

Ferdinand never refused to negotiate. Negotiations, as for instance that for the restoration of the Palatinate, amused others and did not hurt him. Besides, while people were negotiating, they were not likely to act; and this was true of Charles, as it had been of James. Conscious of his violent aggression in the Palatinate, the Emperor was ready to restore that—if any one could or would compel him to do so—but he would never give it up to mere negotiation. Charles's ambassador at Vienna, Sir Robert Anstruther, had been instructed to say to Ferdinand (22d of July 1630) that 'the King, his master (Charles I.), acknowledged with grief and shame that his brother-in-law, the Elector Palatine, disregarding *his* opinion and concurrence, had acted formerly in reference to the crown of Bohemia, not only rashly, but unadvisedly, which imprudent measures ought chiefly to be attributed to the ambition and inattention of youth; and that it would highly become the Emperor, consistently with his accustomed clemency, to receive Frederick's submission, and reinstate him in his own dominions, inasmuch as such an act of free and gratuitous favour would oblige the kings of England to all posterity.'

To amuse Charles, a counter proposition was made from Vienna, to the effect that Frederick should resign the Upper Palatinate for ever to Bavaria; that he, Frederick, should receive a small pension for his own life; that his eldest son should be bred a Catholic at Vienna, and then, having espoused an Austrian Archduchess, be reinstated, at his father's death, in the Lower Palatinate. Further, that Frederick should, on his knees, ask pardon of the Emperor.

It was clear that Charles, who was incapable of

royal or other decisive action, desired to lean upon Gustavus for the reinstatement of his sister.

Charles urged Elizabeth to allow her son to be educated as a Catholic in Vienna, but the ex-Queen, whose character was much more positive than that of her unstable brother, replied with noble anger, that, 'sooner than see her children brought up as Catholics, she would kill them with her own hand.' Both Elizabeth and Frederick remained always steadfast in their religion, nor could any prospect of advantage ever lure them from it.

All that Charles could do was to permit—but not as King—English volunteers to fight for the Palatinate; and the Marquis of Hamilton led some 6000 volunteers, who did not do very much, to Germany. These were speedily reduced to one English and one Scottish regiment, and, after a quarrel with Banier, Hamilton resigned and his force melted away.

We cannot spare space to follow the great Swedish King through his glorious campaign. He would have recovered the Palatinate in due time, as he did recover for his kinsmen the Duchy of Mecklenburg which Wallenstein had seized; but Gustavus could not turn aside from his main purpose, which was to prevent the extirpation of Protestants and Protestantism in Germany, in order merely to recover the Palatinate without help from Charles. Making it a condition that Frederick, if reinstated, should tolerate Lutheranism in his dominions, Gustavus sent to Holland for

Frederick to join his armies. Frederick was unfit for any command in the warlike monarch's forces, but he was 'present' at Nürnberg, and at that memorable passage of the Lech, at which Gustavus's valour and strategy so completely defeated the veteran Tilly. After Breitenfield, the King thought that the Palatinate cause was hopeful, and wrote to that effect to Charles, requiring from the English King 'magnanimous resolution,' an assistance in men and money and the despatch of a fleet to cope with the fleet that Spain was sending to the Baltic.

Charles refused the necessary co-operation, but explained that he was ready to negotiate.

And now Gustavus and Wallenstein, the two great captains of the age, each at the head of an hitherto unconquered army, met, for the first time, as opponents in actual war on the fatal plain of Lützen. The battle was indecisive in result, though victory leaned to the Swedes, as the imperialists vacated the field and retreated on Leipzig; but the battle involved the most terrible loss that could have happened to the Protestant cause—Gustavus Adolphus fell in the arms of victory.

With the fall of Gustavus the cause of the Palatinate seemed to be hopelessly lost. What other champion could replace the 'Lion of the North?'

After Lützen, Frederick became a prey to deep dejection. He died of a broken heart, of utter despondency, away from wife and children, at Mentz, on November 17, 1636. His coffined corpse, after many wanderings, found its final resting-place in Sedan.

His son and heir, Henry Frederick, a prince of promise, had predeceased his father. On January 17, 1629, father and son went to see the trophies of Peter Hein as they floated in Dutch waters at Rotterdam. The small boat in which they sailed was run into by another craft, and speedily sank. Frederick was saved, but his heir was drowned. The son's last vain cry was, 'Save me, father!' That last despairing cry of the sinking prince rings still pathetically through history. Thus Karl Ludwig, the second son, became the representative of the banished Palatine family.

Elizabeth and Frederick were united by a sincere affection and by a numerous progeny. Misfortune borne in common, a faith thoroughly shared, strengthened their union. Frederick's nature was capable of a deeper tenderness than was that of his wife. His fondness for her was unquestionably great. Many of his letters to her (see Bromley's Royal Letters) are still extant. In one he writes:—'Would to God that we owned some little corner of the earth in which we could live together happily and in peace!' It were to be wished that his prayer could have been answered. As private persons, they would have been most estimable, most happy; but they were elevated into positions high above their capacities. Frederick constantly addressed his wife, 'Mon très cher Cœur.'

Elizabeth passed her widowhood at the Hague or at Rhenen, in the province of Utrecht, secure under Dutch shelter. She was fond of hunting and of gardening. Her children grew up around her, and the still lively lady became the centre of a small but cultured circle of friends. Elizabeth's little court was a model of social gaiety, and flatterers called it the 'home of all the muses and of all the graces.' Her elastic temperament was cheerful under misfortune. She could always enjoy any pleasure that the present moment offered. Once, when hunting, she was nearly seized by some Spanish soldiery, but escaped owing to a fleet horse and her good riding. Henrietta Maria had been a bitter opponent at the Court of England of the interests of Elizabeth; but when Henrietta Maria, herself a fugitive, came to Holland, Elizabeth received and comforted her. Both were Stuarts, the one by birth, the other by marriage; and their interests in Great Britain were imperilled by the same foes. There may have been policy in Elizabeth's kindness. Her eldest surviving son, Karl Ludwig, who had been educated by Frederick's brother, grew up headstrong, selfish, and avaricious. When in England he sided with the Parliament, and even sat in the Westminster Assembly of Divines.

He ultimately obtained from the English Parliament a yearly grant of £10,000—£8000 for himself, £2000 for his mother; but Elizabeth was deeply grieved at her son's departure from the traditional and even natural politics of the house of Stuart. Her next sons, Rupert and Maurice, fought, as is well known, and with distinction, on the royal side, and this was some comfort to the daughter of James and sister of Charles. Ever after the execution of her brother, Elizabeth wore a mourning ring (a picture of which is now before me) on which a crown surmounts a skull and cross-bones, while both are encircled by a lock of Charles's hair.

Cousin Max, who thought that all misfortunes arose from tolerance to Protestants, was getting on with the conversion to Catholicism of the upper and lower Palatinates. His plan was simple and direct. Every person who would not become a Catholic was driven out of the territory. Max was fully determined to root out heresy.

The 'counter-Reformation' in Germany was being carried out with incredible cruelty and ruthless persistency. The hopeless and hapless 'peasants' war' was extirpated with terrible inhumanity. Protestant parents were expelled, and their children detained to be brought up as Catholics. Söltl, speaking of the oppression then exercised upon the unhappy Protestants, says, 'davon schweigt die Geschichte,' on that subject history is silent. In Bavaria the popular threat to an enemy remains to this day, 'Ich will dich schon Katholisch machen!'—'I will force you to become a Catholic!' and this threat to tame and to compel dates from the counter-reformation under the

House of Hapsburg. The Jesuit view was, that heretics should be subjected to a yoke intolerable, but yet not to be shaken off. The Papal Ambassador, Caraffa, agreed with the Emperor that heretics should be rooted out without pity and without scruple.

On February 12, 1637, Ferdinand II. died, and was succeeded by his son, Ferdinand III., who carried on the lines of his father's policy. 'Mi Fili, parvo mundus regitur intellectu,' said the wise Oxenstierna.

The great war dragged its slow length along, but we cannot spare space to follow its fortunes.

Among the partisans who were attracted, in part by her personality, to the cause of Elizabeth, the most distinguished and the most constant was William, Lord Craven, afterwards Earl Craven. Christian of Brunswick died May 6, 1626, and Prince Maurice of Nassau had passed away on April 23, 1625. Craven first met Elizabeth when she was already a refugee in Holland, and he quitted the Dutch service in order to devote himself to that of the ex-Queen of Bohemia. History contains few instances of a more chivalrous, romantic, self-sacrificing friendship. His purse and person (Craven was rashly brave) were both zealously devoted to the service of his royal mistress. Munificent in outlay, indefatigable in military activity, reckless in contempt of danger, Craven might well have adopted Christian's motto, 'All for glory and for her;' the only difference being that Craven thought more of her than he did of glory. In Christian the passions had been mixed. Gustavus himself paid a compliment to Craven's valour; and of all the volunteers—Reay, Hepburn, and others—who fought for her, and for the Palatinate, Craven was animated by the purest devotion. He was entrusted by Elizabeth with the care of the fiery young Rupert, when both were taken prisoners by the Emperor. Craven paid for his freedom a ransom of £20,000. Rupert was detained for three years in mild captivity, the object being to convert him to the Church of Rome. During the dark days—days dark for the Stuarts—of the Protectorate, Craven's estates were sequestrated; though they were restored to him at the Restoration; but he found means still to help his mistress. In Elizabeth's saddest hour, when she seemed to be abandoned of all men, the faithful Craven remained by her side, and he returned with her to England. There is no evidence of such a fact (indeed evidence on the subject would be very hard to procure), but history whispers that the pair were privately married. Certain it is that nothing could detach Craven from her side, and that his life and fortune—all that he had—were unceasingly and loyally devoted to her comfort and her service. In 1661, Pepys saw Elizabeth in London, 'brought by my Lord Craven' to the Duke's Theatre. A Paladin of Romance, Craven remains one of the noblest instances in history of a knightly, generous, unswerving devotion to a woman and her cause.

Let us now glance for a moment at the domestic relations of Elizabeth.

She had around her, in Holland, four daughters—Elizabeth, born 1618; Luise, born 1622; Henrietta Maria, born 1626; Sophia, born 1630; and her two younger sons, Edward and Philipp, were also for a time with her.

Elizabeth, the eldest daughter, was the plainest of the sisters. She was quiet, melancholy, absorbed in study. In 1636, Ladislaus of Poland proposed for Elizabeth, but she peremptorily refused to marry a Catholic Prince. Des Cartes (born 1596) was the friend, the tutor, the correspondent of this learned daughter of Frederick and of Elizabeth, who remained unmarried, and ultimately became Abbess of the Protestant *Stift* of Herford, in Westphalia. She died in 1680.

Of Henrietta Maria there is no vivid record, but she married, 1651, Prince Ragoczy von Siebenbürgen.

Luise was pretty, and was lively. She was a paintress of repute in her own little circle, and seems to have loved gaiety and society.

Sophia—the ablest and most beautiful of the daughters—'one of the handsomest, the most cheerful, sensible, shrewd, accomplished of women,' says Thackeray—married, 1658, Ernst August, Bishop of Osnabrück, and brother of the Duke of Brunswick. This lady, called in our history books 'the Electress Sophia,' is the direct ancestress of our present Royal

Family. In 1672 her husband succeeded to the possession of Hanover and to the Electoral dignity. In 1714, a few weeks after his mother's death, her son, George Ludwig, succeeded Anne on the throne of Great Britain as George I. This boorish, ungraceful prince recalled no suggestion of his bright mother, but seemed to have absorbed a terribly large infusion of the characteristics of his ungainly father. The English nation specially settled the succession on Sophia and her Protestant descendants, while passing over the claims of all her brothers and sisters.

Her brother Edward, and his brother Philipp, were sent to Paris to 'finish their education,' a plan which was not attended with happy results. They were probably glad enough to go, and to escape from the weary routine, from the intrigues, littlenesses, spites, of their mother's mock Court in Holland.

Elizabeth does not seem to have been very successful in educating or in securing the love of her children. Her daughters, Elizabeth and Sophia, voluntarily left their mother to go to Kassel or to Heidelberg. In 1645, her son Edward married Anna, daughter of the Duke of Nevers, and turned Catholic, his apostacy being doubtless a serious sorrow to his mother. Karl Ludwig wrote very angrily to his recusant brother; but the life of Edward was thereafter lived apart from the main current of the career of his family. It is certain that Edward married in Paris, where he found favour and countenance, without his mother's knowledge or consent, and that this step and his perversion were a sore surprise to her. Philipp had a quarrel in the Hague with a certain debauched Sieur d'Epinay; and on the day following, January 20, 1646, Philipp, assisted by his myrmidons, killed d'Epinay, for which offence he had to fly Holland. In 1655, Philipp was killed at the siege of Rethel.

In 1644, the noble Luise Juliane, the generous mother-in-law of Elizabeth, died.

The conduct of Rupert and of Maurice in the Civil Wars had alienated the English Government from Elizabeth Stuart, and, to some extent, she had become an object of dislike to the nation. During the late years of the Protectorate her allowance from England seems to have been withheld.

One child only, her daughter Luise, remained to cheer the solitary mother. After some shadow of scandal, into the details of which history now vainly tries to pierce, Luise, one morning, was found to have left—to have fled from her lonely mother; but a few lines informed the distracted Elizabeth—' I have gone to France, there to be reconciled to the true Church, and to enter a cloister.' This was a heavy blow to the still fervently Protestant widow of Frederick. Luise became Abbess of Maubuisson; but hers was no austere, cloistered seclusion. She lived gaily, went to Court in Paris, and had, as Söltl tells us, 'many children.' Her conversion brought with it no retirement from the world, no asceticism of the cloister.

Her last child having thus left her, Elizabeth could turn for comfort only to Lord Craven. We must now pass at a leap, and without regard to the tangle of petty events, to the Peace of Westphalia, which, in 1648, virtually concluded the Thirty Years' War, and settled, among so many other things, the question of the Palatinate.

The primary cause of that memorable peace was the thorough exhaustion of the combatants, and especially of the Catholic Powers. Exhaustion only, inability to continue the conflict, could have constrained Rome, Spain, Austria to grant toleration to German Protestants. The result of thirty years of wastefully wicked war—of a war in which oceans of blood were unnecessarily shed, and in which unspeakable human misery was caused—gave to Protestantism that for which it had contended at the beginning ; and Catholic, Lutheran, Calvinist had to live together in mutual toleration, each belief holding its own as best it could in Germany. Henceforth the disciples of Loyola could not kill, oppress, or extirpate the followers of Luther or of Calvin ; and worn and wasted Germany, which had been for so long the scene of civil war, the battlefield of ruin, was no more subject to the lust of Hapsburg universal dominion or to the bloody tyranny of priestly rule.

Despite of angry protests and of much 'negotiation,' Karl Ludwig could obtain no more than this— the restoration of the Lower Palatinate ; while the

Upper Palatinate remained annexed to Bavaria. Both Max and Karl Ludwig were Electors; Bavaria being the eighth Electorate, and ranking above *Kurpfalz*. The spirit of Gustavus had been at work up to the close of the sad, long war. It is noticeable that the Swedes were the strongest force then left in the field with power to fight. Wrangel (with whom was associated in command Turenne) was the last Swedish general. He entirely overran Bavaria, and, that done, no barrier stood between his victorious army and the gates of Vienna. This crowning success induced Maximilian, and compelled the Emperor, to agree, on equitable terms, to a peace. When Max demanded an armistice, he was, at first, held at Vienna as a *Majestätsverbrecher*, or traitor guilty of high-treason; but it was soon seen that Max had not capitulated without very sufficient cause. He wished to stipulate that the Lower Palatinate, if he had to cede it, should remain Catholic; but to this the victors would not agree. To the last, Sweden did good service to Protestantism. When the terms of peace became known, the Catholics were furious; the Reformers were obstinate; but maugre all objections, necessity had dictated an enduring treaty. Maximilian of Bavaria died at Ingolstadt the 27th of September 1651.

And so, as *Kurpfalz*, though with sadly shorn territory, Karl Ludwig, the son of the *Winter-König* returned to Heidelberg, and to his desolated, wasted, miserable land. Even the great library of Heidelberg had been transported to the Vatican. Karl Ludwig married, 22d February 1650, Karoline, daughter of the Landgraf Wilhelm V., of Hessen. On 10th of April 1651, a son, Karl, was born to Karl Ludwig; and in 1652 he became the father of a daughter, Elizabetha Charlotta. When first he resumed residence in the Old Palace of the Palatinate, his sisters Sophia and Elizabeth were with him in Heidelberg. The new Palatine's marriage was not a success. He entered into an undisguised intrigue with the *Hof-fräulein*, or Maid of Honour, Degenfeld, and his wife left him in indignation, and returned to her father in Kassel.

Karl Ludwig was the most hateful of the children of Frederick and Elizabeth. He withheld from his brother Rupert Rupert's inheritance. He would not allow his mother to come to Heidelberg, nor would he pay to her the money that was justly hers. He refused her her jointure, and would not give her her dower of Frankenthal. He was *karg und geizig*— mean and avaricious. There is something pathetic in Elizabeth's letters to Karl Ludwig. They express a mother's indignation at having to apply for her own to her own son, and then the sense of her necessities lends poignancy to her piteous appeals. It seems that she received 1000 guilders a month from Holland. She writes to Karl Ludwig, August 23, 1655,

'I do not ask you much. I pray do this for me; you will much comfort me by it, who am in so ill condition as it takes all my contentment from me. I am making my house as little as I can so that I may subsist by the little I have, till I shall be able to come to you; which since I cannot do because of my debts, which I am not able to pay, neither the new nor the old, if you do not as I desire, I am sure I shall not increase. As you love me, I do conjure you to give an answer.'

In writing from the Hague to Prince Rupert on April 29th, year not given, she says (Bromley's Royal Letters), 'The next week I hope to hear Louysa's justification against all her calumnies.'

The years just preceding 1660, were times of trial for the poor ex-Queen, who found herself in sore straits and without much hope of better times. The battle of Worcester was a very real fact; the Restoration was very uncertain. The Stuarts were much dispersed over Europe. Rupert and Maurice were pursuing their adventurous careers as corsairs; and she was soon to lose Maurice, who was drowned at sea. Elizabeth's debts increased; and creditors became pressing. She was too poor to visit Rhenen. Widowed, childless, friendless (but for Craven), and hopeless, her last years before the Restoration must have been, even to her, sorrowful and lonely.

But the Restoration came, and her nephew sat upon the throne of Great Britain. Elizabeth desired at once to return to her native land, but Charles II. urged her not to think of coming to England. His comprehensive tenderness for women did not include any fondness for an aged aunt, impecunious, unfortutunate, importunate. The money that he wanted to spend upon the female sex was required for Mrs Palmer and others of that sort. But Elizabeth was not to be deterred. She had determined to return to England, and on May 17, 1661, she landed at Margate, and travelled on to London. Her arrival was little noticed. Her old friends were all gone, and her popularity had vanished also. She had outlived the contemporaries of her youth, and a generation had arisen that knew her not. She was slightly regarded, with an indolent curiosity, as the titular Queen of a remote country, which was all but unknown to Whitehall.

The England to which she returned was for Elizabeth a changed England. Between her youth and her age stood the great shadow of the Protectorate, and the mighty image of Cromwell separated her brother and her nephew. Craven alone remained ever tender, ever true. She lived in Drury House, Drury Lane. From that mansion she moved to Leicester House, Leicester Square, and there, five days after her removal to the new dwelling, on February 13, 1662, Elizabeth Stuart, Dowager-Electress Palatine and titular Queen of Bohemia, died.

German literature contains very many works of

authority and research about the great Thirty Years' War, but no one historian has set his mark upon the subject. Germany separates in such matters more carefully than we do. She keeps poet and historian as things apart; we mix the two qualities and functions.

The great historian, resembling in that respect the poet or the dramatist, must, when depicting a personage, create a character. The hints of history are the equivalents of the suggestions of imagination. The historian must see clearly both outside and inside the person that he would portray, and must combine into an art-whole the complete portraiture, round and finished, of the hero or heroine of history. This task is the duty of every true historian, but it can, necessarily, be discharged but by few, since, to fulfil it satisfactorily, requires qualities which nearly rival those of the poet or creator. Carlyle is the one man in the domain of history who, through many absolute creations, really fulfils the ideal requirement; but yet another instance may be cited in Froude's picture of Mary Queen of Scots. In its higher aspects, history needs an imagination only just below that required by a great poet.

To piece out the imperfections of evidence; to read, by insight, the motives of action and the depths of character; to feel, by instinct, the passions that once fired a man or woman, long since dead, and but imperfectly depicted by the chronicler—

these are difficulties which can only be overcome by a man of high and penetrating imagination, who possesses also a judicial power of criticism. It is given but to a few to realise, with any objective force, the body, form, and presence; the true and living images of human beings that once existed; of times that are past. The great historian must possess a touch, at least, of the poet; and we, in England, have been most successful in developing this ideal historian.

Elizabeth can never have been beautiful. Pepys, who may be credited with some critical judgment of female charms, saw her in Holland when he went with his patron to bring over Charles II., and records of the Queen of Bohemia, that 'she seems a very debonair, but a plain lady.' Mr Pepys hits the mark. Her pleasant, lively manner would last into her age, and the loss of youth would only render the fact plainer. Four portraits of her are known to me. The one by Honthorst, in the National Portrait Gallery, is a performance of little mark or likelihood. There are two at Hampton Court; one (No. 128) is a full length, also by Honthorst, in which she is depicted in a dark dress with a large ruff; the hair red, the face rather pointedly oval, with an expression of some shrewishness, caused, apparently, by sorrow. The mouth is thin and tightly compressed, and the expression is scarcely loveable. The other Hampton Court work (No. 765) is by Derick, a good painting, badly hung, and the *youngest* portrait of Elizabeth that is extant. The face is round, like that of James in youth, and the expression is happy. It is the Princess Elizabeth, with all life opening in hope, when the young Count Palatine has crossed the sea to woo her for his bride. Honthorst was teacher of painting to the Princess Louisa.

To the Royal Academy we owe those recent exhibitions of the works of the 'Old Masters,' which are the delight alike of the art critic and of the historical student. In the winter exhibition of 1880 appeared a portrait of Elizabeth (No. 127) by Mierevelt, which belongs to the highest class of portrait art, and which is the best existing portrait of the Queen of Bohemia. It was painted in Holland, and represents Elizabeth at about the middle of her career. Beneath the veneer of femininity we recognise the ignoble features of James. The modelling of every feature resembles that of her father's face. He had very protruding eyes; they are seen, softened, in this portrait. The aspect is serious; the face is painted in repose, but is full of character, and the spectator feels that he stands in the presence of the true Elizabeth. Her hair is red, and the complexion is opaquely white. The lips are ugly, thin, and are closely compressed. The forehead is poor and narrow. Obstinacy, rather than firmness, is expressed. The shape of the face is oval, with a somewhat pointed chin. The dress is a study of a royal costume of the period. The portrait is full length, and gives the physiognomy of the whole figure. The bearing is that of a woman accustomed to play the Queen; the hands are fine; and the totality of the being expressed agrees fully with all that we know, or can divine, of the superficial, though amiable character of the pleasure-loving but unfortunate daughter of the House of Stuart. This portrait is quite admirable and masterly. The face, in its still gravity, is not altogether loveable or attractive. You retain an impression of shrewdness and vivacity, coupled with a mean intellect, and with a calculating heart.

Elizabeth and Frederick were light, trivial characters, and were, it must be admitted, somewhat shallow weaklings; but the romance of history may still regard with a certain tender interest their lives, their loves, and their misfortunes. Behind and around their careers stands the great portent of the Thirty Years' War, with all its crowd of historical figures, with all the turmoil of its important events.

To the general public in England, the Bohemian royal couple have subsided almost into mere names, vaguely realised through the mists of a by-flown time. They were set to sink or swim in a period, and among conflicting powers, that were too terrible and too powerful for their small idiosyncrasies. Hence, in part, the pathos of their story. In India, in the country in which deadly snakes do most abound, the natives walk about with bare legs; and Frederick and

Elizabeth had no armour that saved them from being easily bitten by the poison of ambition and the venom of vanity. Aggression, to be successful, must be backed by mental power and by warrior prowess—they had neither. Ambition should be made of sterner stuff than that of which they were composed. Vanity impelled them into ambition, impotence reduced them to misfortune; but they bitterly expiated their faults, and their miscalculation of their own means or of the help of others.

James, owing to weak legs, had to lean upon the shoulders of men; Frederick and Elizabeth, owing to their want of mental and physical force for great enterprises, were compelled to depend upon the help of others, and they leant upon broken reeds—as on the German Protestant Princes, the Union, James and Charles. Heavy losses and serious sorrows punished their errors and their deficient judgment; but neither duplicity nor treachery, even in such a distracted and immoral day, can be charged against them, nor can they be accused of cruelty or found guilty of tyranny. The impression that they leave, if thin, is pure. His nature, if weak, was tender; her character, though shallow, was clear. They were nobly steadfast in the faith, and they resisted the temptations of interest to deny their religion.

Frederick was, at least, a gallant, gentle, and accomplished carpet-knight. Elizabeth was graceful and gracious as Princess and as Queen. Their conjugal fidelity and true attachment render them models, as royal married lovers, in their dissolute century. They had vanity without ability, ambition without success. Their capacity, though but small, was equal to that of Ferdinand; was certainly superior to that of Philip II. Circumstance made the difference of success, and caused the revolution of their wheel of fortune. For many reasons I have thought it good to try to snatch them from a submerging oblivion, and to place on record a brief, if imperfect, picture of that English Princess who was once Queen of Hearts and Queen of Bohemia.

# EPPELEIN VON GAILINGEN.

> Heisa aufgeschaut!
> Wem graut vor Strauss',
> Der bleib' zu Haus;
> Eppela-Gaila zieht zu vierzehnt aus,
> Eppela-Gaila von Dramaus!—*Old Ballad.*

THE scene of our present sketch is laid in Germany; the action of our romantic drama—which is based partly on living legend, partly on the records of old chronicles and archives—plays itself chiefly in and around Nürnberg. The date is the fourteenth century.

The state of Germany in that age was anarchic, chaotic. The Church, the Kaisers, the Fürsten, nay, even the Imperial Free Cities—whereof there were then some hundred and six—were all, in a rage of strain and storm, struggling together, each force opposed to the other in a wild welter of disordered conflict. Out of the collision of these warring elements was pressed into life the order of *Raubritter*, or Robber-Knights: men of birth who elected to live, in a lawless age, by saddle and by sword; who sought gain by masterful spoliation, and strove for glory by despiteful deeds of arms. The *Raubritter* was a natural product of his land and time. The younger and wilder nobles pressed into the career—for such it then was—with joyous eagerness, and without much sense of shame or wrong. They may almost be called crusaders of crime; and indeed they very often sublimated their wild life with a strain of knightly daring and warrior enterprise. Many of them were, naturally, mere coarse common robbers, greedy and cruel; but there were some who surrounded the perilous avocation with chivalry, and ennobled it with romance. That one of the *Raubritter*, who is the best type of the nobler sort—Eppelein von Gailingen—forms the subject of the present narrative.

England has her Robin Hood, Scotland her Rob Roy, and Germany her Eppelein. The last named, too, is still a name and a fame. I was the other day in his Franconian country, and found his memory still very full of life. At Nürnberg they show you the site of his famous leap for life, though the city wall is now much higher than it was in Eppelein's olden day; in Rothenburg on the Tauber his name is still a household word, while at Muggendorf, in the fair Franconian Switzerland, they point out to you the ruins of Eppelein's ancient castle. You can hear from peasants an account of some of his many exploits; and the reputation of Eppelein remains a popular romance.

Herr Franz Trautmann has brought together, out of ballad, legend, and chronicle, a pleasant volume which presents some picture of its hero; and to Herr Trautmann and his book I owe acknowledgment and thanks.

Eppelein von Gailingen was no mere robber. If he had been only that, the popular interest in him would not survive as it does.

You see in Germany many a ghostly ruin of an olden castle which still retains feeble hold of a name of its own, but enshrines no memory of a now forgotten owner. The rough robber is forgotten so soon as the life is beneficently knocked out of him; but the mixed characters of men like Robin Hood or Eppelein live yet in story and in song.

It is difficult for us to realise the actual, tangible law of might which ruled in the fourteenth century; a might which had to be encountered or died under; and yet we must try to conceive this sway of force if we would understand the Middle Ages and the robber-knight. The 'Kings of the Romans,' the Emperors, were far too busy with their own concerns to think of protecting the life or property of the trader travelling on the highway; indeed, some Kaisers—such ones as Ludwig the Baier, Karl IV., Günther von Schwarzburg—were really Raubritters on an imperial scale. It is clear that Eppelein did not think his profession any disgrace. He was indignant at the misdeeds of Church and State, of Kaiser

and of Pope. He always held himself to be an
'honourable knight;' he never broke his knightly
word; he was furious against the 'slanderous
tongues' that called his followers 'Staudenhechte'
and 'Schnapphähne'—'pikes-in-the-weed,' or 'snatch-
cocks.'

Bravest among the brave, he had a wisdom that
could guide his valour to act in safety; he was
capable of courtesy, generosity, chivalry; he was
always gentle to women; he had a keen wit and a
humorous power of strong sarcasm. There was also
'the grace and versatility of the man.' He loved
adventure, and courted danger for its own fierce sake.

Had Eppelein found an honourable career in noble
wars, or in national politics, his singular qualities and
his distinguished prowess would have won for him a
royal name; but his times were against him, and they
drove him to become—the thing that he was.

Thus much premised, I pass on to show you something of our tarnished hero as he lived and died. I
shall try to place before you some vital picture of the
best and greatest of the *Raubritter*. His own deeds
—and misdeeds—will depict Eppelein best.

Early in the fourteenth century, the good knight
Arnold von Gailingen was lord of the Castles of
Illesheim near Windsheim, of Wald near Gunzen-
hausen, of Trameysl (or Dramaus) near Muggendorf,
and of Gailingen, his Stammschloss, which latter was
situated near Rothenburg on the Tauber. His wife

was named Apollonia, and he had two sons, one of whom was a monk at Würzburg, while the other pursued the Kriegshandel, or trade of war, in far lands. The soldier-son, following his trade of war, procured himself to be effectually killed in some one of those far lands; so that Arnold's two first-born sons did not yield him an heir to his name, his honours, and his castles. Out of this dilemma he was helped by woman's wit, when, in or about the year 1311, the Frau Apollonia proposed to make her husband once more a father. 'If,' said the good lady, 'my coming child be a girl, it shall be a nun; if a boy, he shall be a monk.' Father Isidorus, the resident castle chaplain, warmly approved the pious resolution; and Arnold, his wife being weak, did not dissent. In deep winter, in the Castle of Illesheim, Apollonia was safely delivered of a son. They called his name Apollonius, which means, being interpreted, Eppelein; and this infant became Eppelein of Gailingen and his father's heir. The mother had a bad time, and the infant was, at first, to all appearance, rather weakly. 'He will make a good monk,' they thought; but when they said this in the child's hearing, he (as chronicles record) raised a great cry, kicked and threatened as if he were angry at the very idea of becoming a monk. When Eppelein was christened, he, so soon as he felt the touch of water, uplifted a terrible shout that frightened all that heard it; he nearly upset the christening vessel, and behaved so violently that all were astonished. In this line of conduct, however, Eppelein resembled the infant who afterwards became the Emperor Wenzel, and who, when baptised in the St Sebaldus Church in Nürnberg, comported himself in the like uproarious manner. Arnold remarked, as he watched his child's behaviour, 'I should almost doubt whether this boy will ever make a monk.' The little Eppelein soon ripened into a strong and sturdy boy. When he was about six years old, his great delight was to take down from the wall his father's sword, and to swing it about. He tried to draw on his father's heavy riding-boots and spurs; and when Arnold rode out on 'Black Adam,' the boy insisted upon riding in front of his father on the great war-horse. At ten, Eppelein could ride 'Black Adam' almost better than his father. The boy never knew fear. He would catch wild, unbroken colts by the mane, swing himself on to them, and gallop furiously round the meadows; nor could the fiercest horse ever throw the boy. He sat as if he had been molten on to a horse. Arnold did not wish to pain his wife, and therefore held his tongue before her, but he was often heard to mutter, as he watched Eppelein, 'They will never make a monk of that boy.' Himself an old Haudegen, the knight had a secret joy in his son's strength and daring and unruliness.

Frau Apollonia was a weak and pious woman. Given such a lady of it, and the castle is like to be ruled by a priest ; as indeed was the case with all Arnold's many castles, in which the Father Isidorus, while maintaining a decent show of respect for the good knight, was practically almost supreme. The education and control of the young Eppelein were confided to the priest, but without good results. Eppelein soon detected that the Father was selfish and a hypocrite ; and the boy rose in revolt against the priestly rule. Eppelein would obey only Arnold, who seldom interfered between priest and scholar ; but, with a smile, let them fight it out between them, though Isidorus was always complaining of the boy, and urging Arnold to punish him. The quarrels between Isidorus and Eppelein became fierce and frequent ; and the lad played his reverend tutor many evil tricks. One day, after some mischievous prank, the incensed father, after calling Eppelein a 'heilloser Gesell,' pulled the boy's ears, receiving in return a blow which nearly knocked him down. 'How can you honour my father and mother,' asked Eppelein, 'when you take their son by the ears?' 'A pretty monk you'll make!' roared the enraged chaplain. Eppelein, who generalised too rapidly, conceived an unhappy dislike to the whole body of the clergy. If monks or priests were coming to the castle, he took away the plank or tree by which they had to cross the river ; when they reached the courtyard, he let loose all the great dogs of the castle, and fastened all the doors. Twice, when Isidorus went to the cellar, for purposes no doubt innocent in themselves and certainly conducive to his comfort, Eppelein locked him in, and the father could only get let out by frantic knockings and callings. On another occasion the boy glued together the leaves of the Father's breviary. Isidorus did not find out this trick for some days, and the boy pointed out that the priest must have neglected his duties for at least that period.

Arnold and Apollonia were induced to scold Eppelein, who, in consequence, resolved to be further revenged upon Isidorus, and accomplished his purpose in this wise.

Eppelein began by upbraiding the father for setting his parents against him.

'Verruchter Gesell!' shouted the angry priest; 'if I did not know you to be the son of your pious mother, I should hold you to be an imp of Satan!'

'Ah!' returned Eppelein, 'you abuse my mother, do you? Very well, you shall pay for that. I have a mind to line your cap with pitch—'

'I'll take care,' roared the father, 'that you shall have no chance. You sha'n't get my cap into your mischievous hands. See, I'll put it on at once.'

And he hastily did so. But Eppelein had been beforehand with him, and the cap was already lined with pitch. Isidorus could put it on, but he could not get it off again. He roared for help, and they tried to pull off the cap, but it stuck fast, and the Father's howls were so piteous that they had to leave it where it was; and, indeed, it remained there for many a long day. Isidorus carried his woes to the Lady Apollonia, and she urged her husband to interfere. Arnold was really angry; he had just put his foot into the stirrup of 'Black Adam,' but he turned back, moved by his wife's tears, and called to a Knecht to bring a stick. Eppelein wrenched the stick out of the man's hand, ran downstairs, sprang upon 'Black Adam,' and rode away. He was then twelve or thirteen years old. When he reached the great wood near Trameysl, he dismounted, and began (for he was a boy still) to pick and eat bilberries. 'Black Adam,' who was like a dog with Eppelein, waited by and grazed contentedly.

Presently Eppelein heard voices, and creeping through the brushwood, he saw a large band of riders, headed by his father's chiefest enemy. He listened, and found that they were lying in wait for his father, intending to kill Arnold, and then to seize his castle. Noiselessly did Eppelein return to his noble horse. He led 'Black Adam' over the sand, in order that the horse's hoofs might make no noise; then he remounted, and rode swiftly back. On his road he met Arnold, mounted upon the chesnut, and told him all.

Now, when Isidorus saw father and son ride into the courtyard, the good man's heart swelled with joy, for he thought that Eppelein had been caught, and was brought home for condign punishment. However, it was another matter that had brought the pair home, though Isidorus did not yet know it.

'Gottvergessener Gauch!' he cried out to Eppelein. 'Now you shall learn what it is to maltreat a holy man! You shall be locked up for days; you shall be—'

'Silence!' cried Arnold, who had to think of more serious matters. 'There is other game afoot!' and it was boot and saddle in the castleyard, where all the riders were soon mounting, under arms, while the castle prepared for a defence.

Eppelein suggested that a Knecht should be sent out, disguised as a peasant, should let himself be caught by the enemy, and should then tell them that Arnold was away from Trameysl, and would not come home for many days.

This was done. Arnold's foes were overjoyed. They postponed their attack until evening, and detained the sullen peasant to lead them in the dark to the castle, which he unwillingly did.

Things did not, however, fall out quite as they had expected. Just as they reached Trameysl, Arnold, Eppelein, and all the riders fell upon them from behind, and defeated the foe with such slaughter that only five remained alive.

This was Eppelein's first knightly deed of arms, but he did well and worshipfully, himself unhorsing and wounding two Lanzknechts. When the fight was over, said Arnold, as he wiped his sword on the mane of Black Adam—and he said it proudly too,—

'That boy will never be a monk!'

Some ten years rolled on, and Eppelein developed rapidly. He could keep his own counsel, and carry out his own will. He was feared and liked by the soldiers and the tenants. All said, 'The lad has as much character as courage, and will come to be a puissant knight; but a monk—never!' One day his father Arnold died; and shortly after, Frau Apollonia prepared to follow her husband. Es fehlte ihr im Magen und im Kopfe—she suffered in the head and in the stomach—and the simple leechcraft of Isidorus could not avail. He mixed, and administered to the good lady, all the draughts that he knew of; but even this treatment did not help, and Apollonia died.

So Eppelein became lord, and this was his first act of mastery. He sent for Isidorus, and said,—

'You have caused me many a bitter hour; you set enmity between my parents and me; and more than all' (here Eppelein's anger rose high) 'you would have made a monk of me. All is ended between us. I am now master here, and you shall not remain another hour in my halls. Go!'

Now you may think that this was not pleasant for Isidorus, who, as priest and *protégé* of the lady of so many castles, had for long years borne sway and influence, had had an easy life, with free run of cellar and buttery, and who saw himself turned out by the young lord, and relegated to meagre fare and to some sort of work. So he pleaded, and offered to pray for Eppelein, who, however, remained inexorable. Then Isidorus, who was of a heavenly temper, gave way to it, and emitted an impromptu commination service, brief but intense, which contained prophecies of evil and malignant denunciations. This, also, did not help, and the discomfited priest left the halls of the young Knight of Gailingen.

Eppelein's next step was this. He sent out his trumpeters to all the castles round about to invite the knights and Junkers to a great banquet. Some stayed away; but the noble, swelling spirits, the young and wild springalds of nobility all came, and were royally entertained by Eppelein at Trameysl.

Eppelein's position was this:— He was young, strong, proud, brave, eager for adventure, desirous of glory. He had a hearty hatred of priests and Jews; he loathed hypocrisy; he had a knightly scorn of traders, of usurers, of money-changers; and he held in contempt Bürgermeisters and town councils. Hence he determined to live by the saddle and the sword, *i.e.*, to become a *Raubritter*, or robber-knight. An Eppelein had not much of a career open to him in Eppelein's land and time. Of the sea he could know nothing. In the distracted anarchic condition of Germany there were no political causes that could present a field for his energy and enterprise. He believed—or believed that he believed—that his pursuit was not unworthy of a knight fired by love of glory, and he embraced it with a serious joy. There was, in Eppelein's complex nature, a strong love of romance, of daring for its own sake; and he loved the right—as he understood the right. Among the wild spirits who came to Trameysl we find the names of Ruban von Neuerstein, Fritz von Gattendorf, Hans von Krähenheim, Götz von Jachsberg, Albrecht der Eisenhut, Hermann von Nest, Kress von Peillstein, the two Kammerers, Fritz der Walch, Ditmar von Roth, two Bachensteins, and the two von Bernheimer. Last and worst, fiercest and fellest of all the company, was Wolf von Wurmstein, already known as 'The Wild Wolf;' and these reckless young nobles formed themselves into a band of knightly robbers, with Eppelein von Gailingen as their chief. They were strong enough to set the cities at defiance; and they had no imperial opposition to fear.

The new band soon made itself felt and known. No highway in Franconia could be travelled in safety, nor did it help that the traders engaged escorts of mercenaries. When a merchant rode out of any city gate, the mob chanted—

> Komm g'sund nach Haus,
> Der Nürnberger Feind reit' aus,
> Eppela-Gaila von Dramaus.

It soon appeared that the free Imperial city of Nürnberg was the object of Eppelein's peculiar detestation. It was full of priests, Jews, traders, usurers, town councillors—the people that most he hated—and the city was very rich. What woe he wrought to Nürnberg, what scoffs and mocks he put upon it, we shall soon see. Above all his contemporaries of the sword, Eppelein soon made himself a distinctive name in the land. His daring, craft, generosity, romance, became the theme of general talk and popular rumour. Hated by the classes that *he* hated, Eppelein was well loved of the common people. Never did he any harm or wrong to poor or simple folk; indeed, he often did good to them.

Now, of Eppelein's many exploits I can only relate a very few. It would need a book, and not a mere article, to tell you all the wild, daring deeds of this fearless *Raubritter* of the fourteenth century. Eppelein had, as I think you will soon see, a strain of fierce, practical humour, as of misdirected chivalry, in the ardent nature driven by disjointed times to such a lawless life. If 'ower bad for blessing,' he was, at times, certainly 'ower good for banning.' He never broke his knightly word; he conceived that he was doing wild right and rough justice; he often helped true love; he was not murderous or cruel, even to prisoners; and though fell in fight, he killed only in hot blood. First, I will tell you of a pleasant adventure. *Es ist zu wissen,* as the quaint old chronicles say, that there was then in Nürnberg a very wealthy burgher, Tetzel by name, who had one fair daughter that he loved passing well. Agnes was proud of her beauty and her wealth, scorned all her suitors, and declared that she would only marry a nobleman. Thereupon Eppelein wrote to the *Rath* offering through them to Agnes his 'ritterlich höchsteigene Hand.' He added that if Agnes should marry any Nürnberger he should levy a fine of 8000 gold gulden upon the city, and would, moreover, have a kiss from the bride. Nürnberg answered angrily, but feared to let Agnes marry anyone. When her father had wished her to marry, Agnes would not; but when he wished her not to marry, the wilful beauty decided to marry, and proceeded to fix her affections strongly upon one Ulrich Mendel, a proper young fellow, though scarcely quite attaining to Agnes's original standard of nobility. However, from dread of Eppelein, the marriage of Agnes and Ulrich was postponed. Suddenly the news came to Nürnberg that Eppelein was sick unto death. He sent to the city for Doctor Rehm, the great physician, to whom Eppelein promised a large fee and a safe conduct. The *Rath* gladly sent the doctor to Trameysl, but intimated to Rehm, before he started, that he need not go out of his way to cure Eppelein.

Dr Rehm found his patient very weak and very red in the face. This latter symptom, however, Eppelein had brought about by taking a mighty draught of strong wine. The doctor felt the sick man's pulse, shook his head, and said: 'You have the burning fever, and will probably die. You must repent of all your sins and prepare for death. Still I will see what I can do;' and he prepared a draught for the sick man. 'Drink, Eppelein!' said Dr Rehm. 'Rascal!' cried the patient, springing out of bed; 'do you think I don't know what you mean? How little you know! I am quite well. You shall drink that draught yourself; if it be poison, you will be served right; if it be harmless it will do you no harm!'

No help for it. The doctor made a wry face, but he drank. Then it occurred to Eppelein to make further experiments in medicine, and he mixed all Rehm's drugs into one draught, and made the doctor drink *that*. This nearly finished the wretched physician, who was removed in a very uncomfortable condition.

As Rehm had been sent to him, the news of Eppelein's death was easily believed. A black flag floated over the castle, and traders began to crawl out of Nürnberg. Tetzel and Menzel sent away a large cargo of valuable goods, but the caravan was waylaid, and a person, recognised by his comrades as the dead Eppelein, said gaily, 'We have the 8000 gulden and more; now I go for my kiss. Hide about here and wait my return, in case I should bring friends from Nürnberg with me.'

The wedding feast of Agnes and of Ulrich was merry and was splendid. Ulrich said it was a double festival, and celebrated both his marriage and Eppelein's death. 'Do not be too sure of that,' said a venerable old man among the guests. 'I hear that Eppelein has been seen again.'

Now the bride, who was curious and anxious, went to the venerable old man to inquire further, when suddenly, to her surprise, she was passionately embraced and heartily kissed. Off went white wig and beard, and the rest of the disguise; out flamed a bright, keen sword, and the guest, no longer old, cried: 'I have had my money, I have had my kiss! I am Eppelein! After me who lists to follow.' He sprang upon his horse, and rode thundering over the bridge at the *Frauenthor*. Then there was mounting in hot haste, and the enraged Ulrich and the Nürnbergers rode, as they might, after the bride-kisser. Eppelein kept ahead, but did not ride so fast as usual. Presently he whistled, and from copse and shaw came forth the Wolf and the riders of Dramaus. Eppelein tied Ulrich to his horse, gave him in charge to two *Knechts*, and said: 'Sir Bridegroom, we shall soon meet at Trameysl. I always keep my word. You will know Eppelein again!' Then Eppelein returned to the joy of fierce fight. The Nürnbergers retired sorely discomfited, but Ulrich remained Eppelein's prisoner.

The next day Eppelein wrote, as he always did, in stately and ceremonious fashion, to the *Rath* of the praiseworthy free city of Nürnberg. He said two friends of theirs, Dr Rehm and Ulrich Mendel, were on a visit to him; but, though the air at Dramaus was good, both seemed rather to pine for Nürnberg, and would gladly return home, which they could do so soon as the praiseworthy free city aforesaid should have paid for them a little ransom of 4000 gold gulden. This ransom Nürnberg paid forthwith, and recovered her citizens; but Eppelein had his kiss, his glory, and his gain.

It is to be noticed that neither Dr Rehm nor Ulrich had been at all ill-treated while they were prisoners; though the doctor had—perhaps deservedly—been subjected at first to some rather tempestuous playfulness.

And now you shall hear the story of Eppelein's great leap for life; a leap such as, perhaps, no other horse and rider ever took.

There was a certain Jew in Nürnberg, called Elias, who, like Isaac of York, dealt, among other things, in armour and in horses. Now this Jew had for sale a certain matchless horse, said to be the best in all Germany; but there was one objection to the peerless grey—that is, he was so wild and fierce that no man could mount and ride him. The *Burggraf* wanted the horse, and Eppelein, you may be sure, who could ride any horse, wanted such an one sorely.

Elias sold the horse to the Burggraf for twenty gold gulden, but when Eppelein made offers for the steed, a plan of treachery occurred to the cunning Jew, and he offered, for 2000 gulden, to deliver Eppelein into the hands of the Nürnbergers. The Jew reasoned well, because Eppelein was so fond of a good horse, that he forgot his usual caution. So

Elias said he would bring the gallant grey to Forchheim, that Eppelein might see the horse; and Eppelein went there eagerly aud unattended. At Forchheim, Eppelein did not find the horse, but he found an ambush of Nürnberg *Lanzknechts*, who succeeded in seizing Eppelein, and in carrying the great *Raubritter*, securely bound, into Nürnberg; that is, to certain death. He was borne into the city on the shoulders of the spearmen, and the mob, which had always pictured Eppelein as a kind of terrible devil, was surprised to see a handsome cavalier, gay, confident, bold. Eppelein knew his danger well; but he kept his wits about him, looked round him (specially at the city walls), and maintained a cheerful debonair demeanour.

Eppelein was taken before the Burggraf, who, with Bürgermeister, Rath, patricians, soldiers, and much people about him, sat on horseback in the great wide *Schlossplatz*, or open ground below the *Burg* of Nürnberg.

'Eppelein of Gailingen,' said the Burggraf sternly, 'we have caught you at last; and for your many misdeeds you must prepare to die the death!'

'Burggraf,' replied Eppelein gaily, 'I love life as well as any man, and I don't think that I shall die to-day.'

Then Elias, the Jew, stood forward. With spiteful glee and deep malice, he told the story of his treachery; he claimed the 2000 gulden and the payment for his horse.

'Burggraf,' said Eppelein, 'may I see this horse before I die? I am accounted a good rider, as you know, and it may chance that I could tame a horse that none other can ride!'

'Agreed!' cried the Burggraf. 'And you, Eppelein, shall decide whether I am to pay this Jew for a devil's horse that no man can ride. Bring forth the horse!'

And the horse was brought, snorting, and stamping, and foaming, into the open space. Several grooms led him, and they were all afraid of him.

Eppelein looked at the grey with a born horseman's joy. Never had he seen such force and fire; such spirit, strength, and speed; and then the creature was so beautiful! 'The very horse for me!' thought Eppelein, 'and I will have him, too!'

'Mount, if thou darest, Eppelein!' said the Burggraf. 'Unbind him, *Knechts*, and lead him to the horse!'

And then they saw a marvellous thing. Eppelein showed no fear; he patted and stroked the horse, which seemed to know his master, and suffered Eppelein to approach and touch him. In a moment Eppelein had hold of bridle and of mane, and with one vault, he sat firmly in the saddle. The horse neighed, and plunged, and kicked, but Eppelein sat as if the two had been moulded in one casting. Erect and fair, the cavalier kept his seat; and the wild horse, leaping high into the air, in furious bounds, flew round and round in circles, which Eppelein took care to widen. The people drew back, and suddenly Eppelein, seeing the way clear, headed the horse for the city wall, struck him with the spurs, and at one wild leap cleared wall and moat, and stood safe outside Nürnberg!

The Burggraf could not restrain his admiration; but the astonished soldiers soon rushed to the wall, threw spears and discharged cross-bows at the mocking horseman, who sat, laughing and jeering at them, on the horse that he alone could ride. 'I can throw a spear better than you!' cried Eppelein, as he snatched one out of the ground and hurled it through the arm of the Jew Elias. 'Burggraf, you need not pay for the horse. I alone can ride him! And you need not pay the Jew for my capture, for I am not captured—I am Eppelein! Adé!'

And he turned and fled like the wind. Never had he felt such a horse beneath him. It was not long before he was safe in Dramaus; having acquired a matchless horse that he alone could master and could use.

And that wild horse became as celebrated throughout Franconia as was his yet wilder rider, Eppelein von Gailingen.

But the traitor Jew came badly off. He was not paid for Eppelein, nor for the horse, but he was banished from Nürnberg on pain of death, and fell into the hands of Eppelein.

'You have well deserved death at my hands!' said

Eppelein, with a dark scowl, 'but fear not, Elias, I will be merciful. You shall have a safe conduct, and a ride into Nürnberg as my messenger. Bring out the wild boar!'

And Eppelein wrote a letter to the Burggraf and tied it to Elias, and the Knechts tied Elias to the wild boar. They prodded the beast with their spears, and drove it towards Nürnberg; and so, amid the fierce laughter of the wild followers of the *Raubritter*, Elias, who had caused Eppelein such a desperate ride, began an unpleasant ride on his own account. Arrived in the city, more dead than alive, Elias yet duly delivered Eppelein's letter. The knight of Gailingen stipulated for the Jew's life, but added, that he had more generosity and was a better Christian than the Nürnbergers were, for he had spared the life of a man who had sold *his* life for a price. The letter ended, 'You shall soon hear more from Eppelein.'

The Rath was sorely perplexed at this threat, but they spared the life of Elias, and the Jew escaped safely to his own people, in Poland, Hungary, or Bohemia. And so Elias vanishes from this history, and the fame of Eppelein von Gailingen, and of his wonderful horse, waxed ever greater in the land.

Love came to Eppelein, as it does to all men. He loved Kunigunde von Wurmstein, the sister of his friend 'The Wolf.' Kunigunde was of noble birth, was beautiful and high-hearted; but at first she refused Eppelein, saying that his way of life was too dangerous, that she should always be anxious, and might be left an untimely widow. All is fair in love, and Eppelein planned, without changing his way of life, to convince her of his reformation by extracting a marriage-gift from Nürnberg. He wrote his request to the Free City, but the reply was that Nürnberg would not give him a *Spatz*—a sparrow. He replied that if they would not give him a sparrow, he would take their singing-birds. He rode disguised into Nürnberg, entered the Treasury, put their portable gold cups and the like into a sack, which he shook and rattled 'to make the birds sing,' and rode safely off. When Kunigunde received her wedding present, she understood the whole thing, and she told Eppelein that if he had yielded to her request she would never have accepted him, that she loved his fame, and admired his life of wild adventure. 'Henceforth,' said the lady, 'your friends are my friends, and your foes are my foes.' So they twain married, in great splendour, at Dramaus. They were well suited to each other, and lived very happily. Kunigunde died in a few years, leaving one son, Johannes, who promised to become a second Eppelein, but was killed in fight when quite young, falling with his face to the foe, and with all his wounds in front.

The favourite horse did another great feat. Eppelein was in Nürnberg on some private business connected with a merry mock at the Rath, when, as he rode out, he was recognised. Seventy-two *Lanz-*

*Knechts,* under their captain, sat ready mounted in the market-place, and were sent in hot pursuit after Eppelein. Then there was galloping! Eppelein rushed by the St Lorenz Church, and out of the *Frauenthor*, with the Nürnberg riders in full chase after him. Many a Nürnberg horse broke down and dropped out of the race, but Eppelein's grey flew as if he would never tire. Before Eppelein lay the Main, wide and swollen, in flood. He did not hesitate, but leaped the grey into the fierce current. Never heavier man and horse stemmed a swollen river's course; but while the spearmen stood watching on the one bank, Eppelein reached the other bank safely, dismounted, lay down on his back, and mocked the baffled Nürnbergers with many a merry jibe. Eppelein was so pleased with the noble horse to which he owed this escape that he had a gold bridle made for the steed, and washed its hoofs daily in wine.

I could—but cannot for want of space—tell you many more exploits of this famous knight. I could tell you how he saved the life of Father Damian, who, being accused of being 'too bold of tongue,' was to have been walled up alive in the Church of St Lorenz by the priests; I could tell you how he confessed in the St Sebaldus Church; I could tell you how he once actually preached at Nürnberg; and how, after lashing the vices of the Nürnbergers, he concluded a powerful discourse by mentioning the fact that he was Eppelein. When he arrived at this point there arose a most unseemly disturbance in the congregation. Women screamed and crossed themselves, while the men, rising up tumultuously, made as though they would have embraced their pastor. But Eppelein then disappeared suddenly; and when his excited hearers sought to follow him, they found all doors locked; and while they strove to obtain egress, they heard the rapid beat of a horse's hoofs dying away further and further into the distance, in the direction of the *Frauenthor*. It is, however, painful to have to contemplate such evidences of a want of proper reverence on the part of a hater of monks. Once Nürnberg, when Eppelein was away, turned out with all its force and tried to burn Trameysl. Eppelein returned in time, though with but a small force, and beat back the Nürnbergers with great bloodshed. They had, however, burned down a part of the castle, and but for the peasants who loved 'Eppa-Gaila,' would have wholly destroyed Dramaus. Eppelein threatened revenge, and he always kept his word. During a mighty tempest of great wind he set fire to Nürnberg, and burned down 400 houses. It happened, in 1343, that Nürnberg was visited with the 'Black Death,' and with a terrible dearth and famine. The people were dying miserably of sickness and of starvation, so that it was piteous to see and hear of. Now there was a certain usurer who had bought great stores of corn, which he held back that he might sell his stock at an enormous profit when the poor people should be driven by hunger to pay any price. Had Eppelein known anything of political economy he would have recognised that such dealing was a natural and beautiful transaction; but he was ignorant of the 'dismal science,' and what he did was this:—First he himself warned the usurer, who denied having any corn, but when, a few days later, the usurer thought it safe to drive his corn to Nürnberg to market, Eppelein's riders seized the cargo and gave it away to the poor, starving people; who, indeed, loved 'Eppa-Gaila' well—better than they loved Burggraf, or Bürgermeister, or Rath. He interfered once to make the course of true love run smooth. An old man, one Muffel, who was very rich, had got the consent of the parents of a pretty girl, and the marriage was being forced on. Now this girl loved, and was loved by, a nice young fellow, and Eppelein interfered to help the lovers. He so frightened old Muffel that the hunks gave up the girl, and the young lovers were happily married.

Once when Eppelein was in Nürnberg, a rumour got abroad that he was in the city. All the gates were closed, and a mounted band was got ready in hot haste to pursue. While they were preparing, Eppelein went and took one of those peculiar baths which were then held to be good for the liver. As the riders went forth Eppelein rode with them, and when they got sufficiently far away, he turned to them and said, 'Oh, you dullards! Why don't you catch the poor soul? The bath has done me good, and I am minded to gallop. Do you know him when you see him? No? Well, I am Eppelein!' and he turned and fled like the wind. '"They'll have fleet steeds that follow," quoth young Lochinvar.' And the riders did *not* catch Eppelein, who arrived, laughing, at Dramaus, after a healthy gallop, which, no doubt, assisted the action of the bath.

When the troubles in Nürnberg were at their height, the poor people, maddened by misery and wasting with sickness, got hold of the idea that the Jews had poisoned the wells, and then began a cruel persecution of the unhappy Israelites. Eppelein, I grieve to say, inflamed popular passions against his old enemies the Jews, and he is partly to be blamed for the ill-treatment to which they were subjected. One day, riding near the city, Eppelein saw an unhappy Jew, one Jäcklein, followed by some citizens who wished to ill-use, or perhaps kill the Hebrew. Moved by some impulse of pity, Eppelein interfered. 'Now that I have saved you, what will you do?' asked Eppelein, and Jäcklein begged frantically to be allowed to enter into the knight's service, and to live and die there. Something in the man's manner touched Eppelein, who trusted in the Jew and granted his request. Jäcklein was found astute and active; he was always eager and bitter whenever anything was to be done to injure or insult Nürnberg.

Ah! there is so much to tell—and yet I must leave

so much untold. It is pain and grief to me to have to pass over so many things in silence; but I must just tell you of the meeting between the Kaiser and Eppelein.

On the occasion of the Burggraf's marriage, Karl IV. honoured the nuptials with his presence, and there were great feastings, and mummings, and maskings, and Eppelein, you may be sure, in good disguise, was one of the gayest there. He rode in the cavalcade, and rode so well, 'witching the world with noble horsemanship,' that people cried, 'Why, that cavalier rides like Eppelein!' And the bride said to him, 'How I should like to see that brave Eppelein!' and he replied, 'Fair lady, you shall see Eppelein, that I promise you. But you may see him and yet not know that it is Eppelein. Remember what I have said to you!'

The bride dropped her glove, and Eppelein, returning it to her with knightly grace, asked her to ask the Emperor to grant him two favours. She consented, and she asked the Emperor to do what the courteous stranger demanded, and Karl readily promised to do as the bride wished. Thereupon Eppelein and the Emperor talked long together, and Karl was charmed with Eppelein's bright, bold wit. Then Eppelein preferred his first request; it was that Karl would give a gold gulden to Hans von Lobenstein.

The Emperor laughed loud and long.

'Thou art a nobleman, though, it may be, a poor

one,' said Karl. 'The gold gulden shall be paid; but yet I have a mind to lay thee in the tower for thine audacious talk and bold request.'

But the Emperor could not do this, because he had given his royal word for the stranger's safety. So Eppelein bowed and vanished, and shortly after the Chamberlain handed to the Kaiser a letter. It was from Eppelein, who said that a good *Knecht* should always, so far as possible, imitate his master; that he did, so far as he could, imitate his Emperor, who pawned and pledged cities and towns, took spoil, and sack and plunder, wherever he could seize them. The writer did the same thing also. He had pawned Nürnberg to Hans von Lobenstein for a gold gulden, and was, for the information of the Kaiser and the bride—EPPELEIN. Karl laughed rather grimly, but the fair lady knew that she had seen Eppelein without knowing that he was Eppelein, and she thought with pleasure of the stately figure and bright face of the renowned robber-knight.

This Jäcklein was a Jew, who was consumed with a fierce hatred of the oppressors of his race. He used Eppelein to obtain vengeance upon the Nürnbergers, and he meant then to use Nürnberg to be revenged upon Eppelein. He was the second Jew —Elias was the first—who treacherously sought to betray the *Raubritter*.

One day Jäcklein stabbed Eppelein's favourite horse, took another from the stables, and on it rode into Nürnberg, and proposed a plan for Eppelein's capture. The Rath listened to him and trusted him, so great was Nürnberg's hatred and dread of Eppelein.

Jäcklein denounced all Eppelein's adherents in the city, and these unfortunate persons disappeared into the *Froschthurm*. At the cold feet of the Iron Virgin yawned a deep and dark *oubliette*. . . .

Eppelein was beside himself with rage, and swore to have the life of the traitor Jäcklein. The Jew meanwhile vanished from the city, and the Rath began to suspect his honesty.

One day a man rushed into Nürnberg calling out that Eppelein was taken! What had really happened was this. Jäcklein caused it to be intimated to Eppelein that he, the Jew, was hidden in a certain village. Eppelein called for his horse, and with the two Bernheimers and four *Knechts*, rode off at once, bent blindly upon vengeance.

Arrived at the village, Eppelein and his followers rode straight to the inn in which they expected to find Jäcklein. The landlord, who was in the plot, asked them to hide themselves in the house till Jäcklein, who was looked for every minute, should arrive.

So Eppelein fell into the wily Jew's snare.

While the Bernheimers and Eppelein sat drinking in the inn, crowds of armed men gathered round the house, and they drew up nine waggons across the front of the door.

Eppelein heard the sound and hum of a mass of

men, and he soon became aware of the trap laid for him. The Bernheimers and the four Knechts tried to escape by the back of the house, but they were surrounded by numbers and made prisoners.

Eppelein mounted his horse—not, alas! *the* grey —and issued forth alone by the front gateway of the inn. The great crowd, which bristled with spears and swords, raised a shout when they saw the terrible Eppelein appear mounted before them. He saw his danger at a glance. Crying out, 'Freedom or death! You shall not easily take Eppelein!' he put his horse at the waggons, hoping to cut his way through his foes. The horse sprang over eight of the waggons, but could not clear the ninth, and crashed down upon the pile. Then Eppelein on foot, with only his sword, stood facing that host of enemies. They wanted to take him alive; he wished to die if he could not escape.

The fight — Eppelein's last fight — began. This man, alone amongst that crowd of enemies, did prodigies of valour. He is said to have killed or mortally wounded twenty of his foes, but the fight was a fight of utter desperation; he fought, not for life, but for death, and the odds against him were too terrible. He was borne down, seized and bound, and carried away to Neumarkt.

In the fight Eppelein had cloven Jäcklein through the skull. The fanatic of revenge perished by the sword of the master he had betrayed.

The long career of success had come to a violent end. The *Raubritter* were condemned to die; and on a fair summer morning, Eppelein and the two Bernheimers stood upon the high scaffold in the market-place of Neumarkt. An enormous crowd raised upturned faces to the lofty platform. Nürnberg was defrauded of its show, and Neumarkt rejoiced in the horrible spectacle.

The Bernheimers perished first by the shearing sweep of the headsman's broad blade, and then Eppelein was broken alive on or by the wheel. He refused the services of a priest. In his day of pride and power he had always been wont to say that 'a man should live as a free and mighty hero, and should die without fear.' He had laboured to live up to his theorem of life, and he certainly bore his death of slow agony with the calmest courage.

When the head was gone, the members were no longer dangerous. Wolf von Wurmstein succeeded to the command, but the dreaded band, which Eppelein had led so long and so successfully, soon melted away. Some perished by the sword of the foeman, others by the sword of the headsman. Many disappeared, and the highways of Franconia were freed from the terror of the great robber band.

So ended the wild life of the chivalrous criminal, of the most renowned robber-knight, EPPELEIN VON GAILINGEN.

# FACTS AND FANCIES ABOUT FAUST.

## I.—The Legend and the Stage.

' Der Faust ist doch etwas Incommensurables, und alle Versuche, ihn dem Verstande näher zu bringen, sind vergeblich. Auch muss man bedenken, dass der erste Theil aus einem etwas dunkeln Zustande des Individuums hervorgegangen. Aber eben dieses Dunkel reizt die Menschen, und sie mühen sich daran ab, wie an allen unauflösbaren Problemen.—GOETHE *to* ECKERMANN.'—3*d January* 1830.

BIOGRAPHY, basing itself mainly upon tradition, and largely impregnated by fable, records the existence, in the second half of the fifteenth, and in the early years of the sixteenth century, of a Dr Johann Faust, philosopher, scholar, magician, conjuror. This Dr Faust was born, it is supposed, in Kundlingen, now called Knittlingen, in Würtemberg; left ordinary studies for that of the black science, which he mastered in Krakau, and there instructed in unlawful arts his *Famulus* (or servitor) and disciple, Wagner. Faust is said to have exercised his power of summoning to his aid the Evil One, and to have made a compact with the devil, in virtue of which the soul of the magician should become the property of the fiend in consideration of a period of twenty-four years of enjoyment of all desires, and of all the pleasures that the senses, that the lust of the eye and the pride of life, can yield. Faust was to have, for the fulfilment of his purposes, a certain devil (Mephistopheles by name) attached to his person and service, and always at his command. The doctor travelled far and wide in Germany, with his attendant fiend; enjoyed himself to the uttermost, and set the world wondering at the feats that he could perform. At the end of the covenanted time, the inexorable Evil One claimed his bargain, and the unhappy doctor was robbed of life, under circumstances of gross cruelty, at the village of Rimlich, between the hours (these are very precisely given) of twelve at night and one in the morning. Meantime his fame for wonder-working and for the diabolic art had become great, and widely spread throughout all Germany, and even in other countries of Europe.

The priests were glad of so pregnant an example of the danger of meddling with those unholy arts which, though forbidden, were yet then generally believed in; the vulgar love of the wonderful and the horrible was deeply excited by the life, death, and adventures of this potent magician; and hence it came to pass that Dr Faust became the property of popular credulity and awe; and that, within some few years after his terrible death, his name and fame were bruited through all the land. Narrative and drama, the book and the stage, laid hold of the dark doctor ; and such reputations speedily became the subjects of exaggeration. The life of Faust penetrated into the life of the people, and from many sides was found to be attractive, awful, and suggestive. The flames of hell light up a huge fire upon earth. The sense of that dim unholy power which can command the services of demons, and which can, by such aid, enjoy years of the enjoyment of every earthly lust, lays hold of superstitious fancy ; and the tragic end of such a man has an appalling grandeur which impresses and stirs the popular imagination. Poems, pantomimes, puppet-plays, tragedies upon the subject of the great conjuror appeared in numbers. In 1599 Wiedemann published, in Hamburg, his 'Wahrhaftige Historien von denen greulichen Sünden Dr Joh. Faustens.' Printed at once in Cologne and in Nürnberg, but without date on the title-page, comes next 'Des durch die ganze Welt verrufenen Erzschwarz Künstler's und Zauberer's Dr Faust mit dem Teufel aufgerichtetes Bündniss, abenteuerlicher Lebenswandel, und schreckliches Ende.'

Nay, the legend of Dr Faust spread beyond Germany to other countries of Europe, and, before the end of the sixteenth century, Marlowe had produced in England his 'Tragicall Historie of Dr Faustus.' It would be impossible to enumerate here all the shapes which this most popular, though intensely German legend, has taken in literature and in the drama. A direct product of its time, the tradition is yet full of vital, of perennial essence, whether of wonder only, or of wonder blent with superstitious fear. We no longer believe in the gods of Greece, but we still love the beauty of the myths that they represent, and the sculpturesque glory of the forms in which they were incarnated by human imagination, and in which they still exist in the ideality of the pure marble. Goethe found a most moving and picturesque tradition, a story known, at least, to every German, and susceptible, as he soon saw, of great art-treatment as the vehicle of the very deepest meanings. It attracted him in his poet youth; unhasting, but unresting, he worked out of it gradually during the long years of manhood his own dramatic version, and the completed work crowned his sovereign age with its brightest glory. Seldom in the history of literature has a great poet so wisely or so happily selected a subject which would exert his powers to the very top of their bent. The idea of *Faust* is now inseparably and distinctively associated with the name of Goethe; and he has made the old, old story immortal by enclosing its rude outline and essence in all the higher meanings, in all the deeper beauty that *he* could add to it. Goethe, himself a magician in the divine sort, found noble material for his art in the mediæval legend of the black wizard, Faust.

The first part of Goethe's *Faust* was begun, probably, in or even before 1774. The execution of the poem spread itself slowly over some thirty years. It was worked upon gradually, in the intervals of much other work, at many times and in many places—one scene was written in the Borghese Gardens in Rome —and was first printed, in its complete form, in 1806; a perilous and distracted time, in which the French victory of Jena exposed Weimar to occupation by French troops, and caused the destruction of many German manuscripts — as, for instance, Herder's posthumous manuscripts and Meyer's works. Goethe's own house was filled with soldiers, and, inspired by a dread of the possible destruction of the completed manuscript of his masterpiece, he at once sheltered it in the security of print.

This first part of *Faust* was first produced upon the stage on 19th January 1829. The theatre to which this honour belongs is the Hoftheater, of Brunswick; and Herr Eduard Devrient, in his 'Geschichte der Deutschen Schauspielkunst,' tells the story of the original adaptation of Goethe's infinite, but dramatic poem, for acting; and of its first presentation on the boards of a German theatre.

August Klingemann had long been the successful director of the Hoftheater in Brunswick; but when, in 1826, the young Duke Karl (he was then eighteen years of age) came to the ducal throne, he evinced a lively interest in the drama. The æsthetic Duke's interference was not of unmixed advantage to the theatre. He paralysed the beneficial working of Klingemann, and he then appointed his Master of the Horse, Herr von Oeynhausen, to be *Intendant* of the theatre. Klingemann was not dismissed, but his excellent theatrical discipline was destroyed, and his efforts in the cause of true dramatic art were seriously let and hindered. The young prince interfered personally with the management of the theatre; he attended rehearsals; he set aside Klingemann's excellent rules, and thwarted Klingemann's strenuous aims and objects. The result of princely interference was not productive of good. Many of the best actors left the theatre, and those who remained were demoralised by a system of capricious favouritism. Young princes who meddle with the management of theatres have a tendency to take an almost disproportionate interest in the representatives of female characters, and Duke Karl's theatrical activity was, in this, as in other respects, very injurious to the Brunswick Hoftheater.

One caprice, however, of the young duke led to a most important result—to the production on the Brunswick stage of Goethe's *Faust*. Klingemann was himself the author of a dramatic version of the old *Faust* legend; and this version, which seems to have had, in its day, a moderate stage success, Klingemann was fond of producing in the theatre which he so ably managed.

On some occasion on which Klingemann's *Faust* was presented, Duke Karl, who loved to tease and to thwart the great manager, asked Klingemann why he did not produce the *Faust* of Goethe; and the Duke intimated that Klingemann dreaded the rivalry of Goethe. Klingemann replied that he would not venture to compare his play with that of Goethe; but that Goethe had not written his poem for the stage, and that it might be difficult to adapt it for representation. This was surely a not unnatural idea, as things then stood, or were held to stand, on the part of the director. The Duke persisted; he had, he said, looked through Goethe's play, and found it intrinsically dramatic and very possible for acting. The Duke, naturally enough, carried his point. Klingemann himself adapted, for the first time, Goethe's poem for actual representation; and the piece was performed, with enormous success, on 19th January 1829.*

\* The following is a copy of the playbill of the first performance, on any public stage, of Goethe's *Faust*:—

BRAUNSCHWEIG-HOFTHEATER.
MONTAG, DEN 19 JANUAR, 1829.
Zum Erstenmal :
FAUST.
Tragödie in sechs Abtheilungen von Goethe, für die Bühne redigirt.
PERSONEM.

| | | | | |
|---|---|---|---|---|
| Faust . . . . . . | Hr. Schütz. | Erster ⎫ Handerwerks- | ⎧ Hr. Feuerflacke. |
| Wagner, sein Famulus | Hr. Senk. | Zweiter ⎬ bursche . | ⎨ Hr. Küster. |
| Mephistopheles . . | Hr. Marr. | Dritter ⎭ | ⎩ Hr. Fischer. |
| Der Erdgeist . . . | Hr. Dessoir. | Erster ⎫ Schüler . . | ⎧ Hr. Berger. |
| Böser Geist. . . . | Hr. Gossmann. | Zweiter ⎭ | ⎩ Hr. Fitzenhagen. |
| Ein Schüler . . . | Hr. Hübsch. | Erstes ⎫ Dienstmäd-. | ⎧ Dem. Solbrig. |
| Frosch ⎫ | Hr. Eggers. | Zweites ⎭ chen . . | ⎩ Elise Hambath. |
| Brander ⎪ . . . | Hr. Günther. | Erstes ⎫ Bürgermäd- | ⎧ Mad Grösser. |
| Siebel ⎬ . . . | Hr. Moller. | Zweites ⎭ chen . . | ⎩ Dem. Höpfner. |
| Altmayer ⎭ . . . | Hr. Scholz. | Erster ⎫ | ⎧ Hr. Gerard. |
| Eine Hexe . . . | Mad. Lay. | Zweiter ⎬ Bürger . . | ⎨ Hr. Clarpius. |
| Margarethe, ein Bür- | | Dritter ⎭ | ⎩ Hr. Haars. |
| germädchen . . | Mad. Berger. | Eine alte Wahrsagerin | Mad. Heeser. |
| Valentin, ihr Bruder, | | Soldaten, Volk, Erscheinungen und Geister. | |
| Soldat . . . . | Hr. Kettel. | | |
| Frau Marthe, ihre | | | |
| Nachbarin . . . | Mad. Klingemann. | | |

Der Anfang ist um 6 Uhr, und das Ende nach halb 10 Uhr.
Die Casse wird um 5 Uhr geöffnet,

Klingemann, to whom the credit of the first dramatic rendering of *Faust* is to be ascribed, died in 1831.

The next appearance of Goethe's *Faust* on the German stage occurred on 27th August 1829, at Dresden. The Dresden Theatre was then under the brilliant and intellectual management of Ludwig Tieck, who naturally desired to add the German masterpiece to his long and glorious *répertoire*. Tieck hesitated, at first, from some fear that Goethe's wonderful poem would suffer when brought into contact with the realism of the scene ; but the Dresden public demanded its production, and Tieck was not willing to remain behind when Klingemann had shown the way. It seems tolerably clear that the version then played at Dresden was arranged by Tieck himself. Indeed, it is highly probable that at least slight differences exist even yet between the various versions of *Faust* played in the different leading theatres of Germany. Each director takes his own view ; and has power, within his own province, to translate his view into action. Each leading theatre in Germany possesses certainly its own acting copy of Goethe's *Faust ;* though some slight modification may possibly be allowed when a great star—as Seydelmann or Emil Devrient—travels about with his *Gastrollen*, and plays Mephistopheles or Faust with the arrangement which, as the actor thinks, best suits his own style, or his own means of producing effect in the play.

The star-actor is, in Germany, as great and as dogmatic a potenate as he is elsewhere in Europe. The actor is the despot of the stage.

Of all parts in the drama, Goethe's Mephistopheles would seem to be almost the most difficult character that an actor could undertake; difficult to conceive, almost more difficult to execute: for Goethe's fiend is an unearthly being. At times we shudder at and shrink from, this mystic being, who is not of our order, who cannot be touched with a sympathy with our feelings or with our infirmities. It will be of interest to us to consider the actor—Seydelmann—who is renowned in Germany as the most notable Mephistopheles, and to analyse a little his conception and his rendering of the great part: but it should be borne in mind that, apart from the character to be represented, apart from the due relations of that character to the play, apart even from the reverence due to the poet's conception, there is a great art of abstract acting; an art which, by tones, looks, gestures, by living dramatically a powerful situation, by embodying moving passion, may be most highly effective, as acting; and which may yet be wanting in consideration for the dramatist's intentions. This abstract art of acting may produce a vital effect out of a poor play; or may find its opportunity of displaying itself without a scrupulous regard to the ideas of the author of the drama.

Mephistopheles is mainly modern in conception;

nay, it may be said that Goethe's fiend could only exist in a world which had known Voltaire. Goethe tells Eckermann of the great influence which Voltaire exercised upon his youthful thinkings; and, long after any teaching of Voltaire had ceased to impel Goethe, this influence survived into his age in the form of his knowledge of the tone of thought which he attributes to Mephisto. In taking human form, in mingling with human action, the fiend loses much of the grandiose mystery with which the pious abhorrence of earlier and of simpler ages had surrounded him. Goethe evidently does not believe—at least, in the ruder and more objective sense—in the fiend; nor does he tremble before Lucifer. If he had believed, he would have had more reverence for Satan; but Goethe shows *persiflage* in his very treatment of the mocking spirit. The sneer of Mephistopheles is as the sneer of Voltaire; as bitter and as barren: for Voltaire's withering mockery was rendered intense by his close contact with *L'Infame;* and Mephistopheles, in his futile activity, in his negative knowledge, and in his frustrated malignity, suggests to us a spirit which has outlived the times in which men believed in him. The dramatic usefulness of Mephisto as the symbol of a spirit of evil is, nevertheless, as great, or perhaps greater, than it would have been in days of infernal faith. That earnestness of ideal belief in a personal Evil Spirit which inspires Milton's vision of Satan was wanting in a day which still tingled with cold laughter at the irony of Voltaire, and at the scepticism of the eighteenth century. Goethe was too unconsciously genuine to depict a demon of much more ideal elevation than one who should combine the costume of the Middle Ages with the tone of the modern master of mockery.

Shakspeare does not genuinely believe in the supernatural. His intellect denies that in which his imagination revels. Note the immense difference between his real awe of death and his half-assumed awe of the supernatural. He uses the supernatural—or men's belief in it—with the grandest art; but his day was so much nobler than the eighteenth century, that no man of Elizabeth's spacious times would have embodied the arch-fiend in a spurious human shape of mocking, and mocked at, irony. In the very play in which Shakspeare introduces a ghost, he speaks of death as a bourne from which no traveller returns. His ghost is forbidden to reveal to Hamlet the secrets of a purgatorial prison-house : the apparition of the dead king appears chiefly to impel human action in a tragic tangle of murder and of incest. The spirit of dead Cæsar appears to warn Brutus at Philippi ; the ghosts of Richard's victims cheer Richmond, and sit heavy on the soul of Richard. The witches, dæmonic agents of Hecate, translate Macbeth's ambitious imaginings into the fulfilment of fatal prophecy ; and a popular, superstitious belief in these debased agents of the Evil One is used for high and subtle art purposes, as a lure to tempt the Thane of Glamis to those crimes which lead him to his ruin. The difference of the ages in which they lived is as great as the difference between the men themselves; and this truth appears clearly when we consider and compare the uses which Shakspeare and which Goethe make of the supernatural in art.

It is a point of some difficulty for the actor playing Mephistopheles to determine how far he shall hide, or seem to hide, from the other persons of the drama, the fact that he is really embodying the devil. It is clear that the author did not intend Mephisto to be recognised for what he is by other characters. Gretchen, it is true, instinctively, dislikes and distrusts him; his countenance is repellant to her—and then he takes no joy in anything—but, on the other hand, Marthe is willing to marry him; and the revellers of Auerbach's Keller, though exasperated by his mocking *persiflage*, do not know that it is the devil himself who has them by the collar. Gretchen herself dislikes him only as a hateful man. The poet could not allow a recognised fiend to mix visibly with human beings in the tragic, or the common-place, affairs of mortal life. For the actor who 'plays the devil' ostensibly, it may be urged that the audience know well who Mephisto is; and they also know that the other persons of the drama must not know. The audience are not careful to see the other characters well deceived in this particular. Seydelmann cared much more for his audience than he did for his poet, or for the other characters. He wanted to display Seydelmann, through Mephisto, and to get the utmost possible amount of effect out of so doing. The genius of the stern and spectral North—differing therein widely from Greek feeling—has always represented the fiend through an objective form of grotesque, repulsive horror. The vulgar idea of horns and tail expresses this tone of sentiment vulgarly. That art which is Representation has evolved out of itself a law, in virtue of which the fiend cannot be embodied in a beautiful human form. Goethe developed the traditions of the Middle Ages, and employed, with a happy result, the red doublet and hose, the short red cloak, the long rapier, and the single cock's feather in the cap, when he depicted his Evil Spirit in human shape. Milton stood in no relation to the mediæval spirit; his high and shaping imagination distended his conception of Satan to the vague vastness of a colossal ideal.

Karl Seydelmann, born in 1793, was the son of a grocer and coffee-house keeper in Glatz. His father's business included a billiard-room, which was much resorted to by the officers of the garrison. These officers were in the habit of getting up amateur theatrical performances, and young Karl Seydelmann, who evinced an early and decided talent for acting, made his *début* at the amateur representations of the officers at Glatz. In 1810, the young Seydelmann elected the profession of arms. Helped, probably, by officers whom he had met in his father's billiard-room, he entered the Prussian artillery; but he soon acquired a disgust for soldiering, and in 1811 he deserted, escaping by means of a forged passport, authenticated by a well-imitated signature of his major. The army succeeded in reclaiming Seydelmann's services, but, on account of his beautiful handwriting, he was exclusively employed in office work. He knew, indeed, so little of his military duties that, as he himself relates with great amusement, he once, on the occasion of an inspection, was wholly unable to fire off a cannon. In 1815 (the year of Waterloo) we find him playing at Count Herberstein's theatre in Grafenort. From Grafenort he transferred his services to the Breslau Theatre, from which he drew a salary of ten dollars a-week.

In Breslau he replaced an actor named Kettel, and had there to perform the young-lover parts. For such characters Seydelmann was but little fitted. He was of middle height, and had bow legs. His features were neither striking nor pleasing; his hair was red. The glance of his blue eyes was full of fire, and yet was cold in expression. But his most serious drawback lay in his speech. His tongue was thick, and was long, and his enunciation was, in consequence, indistinct, awkward and hissing in tone. His voice was rough and thick, had but a limited compass, and was incapable of tenderness or of modulation. In passionate passages it acquired a tone which suggested the growling of wild animals.

Furnished thus slenderly by Nature with the graces or the powers of an actor, Seydelmann's singular determination and fierce, strong will managed at length to conquer the defects which hindered the display of his undoubted genius. Director Professor Rhode urged him to abandon the stage; but no discouragement could repress Seydelmann, who, strong in his conviction of his own powers, announced, through tears of disappointment, but with passionate gnashing of teeth and stampings of foot, 'You shall see; I will be an actor yet!'

Where genuine power exists, such strong unconquerable resolution always leads in time to success.

Seydelmann set to work to subdue his tongue to become the organ of his purpose. With incredible assiduity he practised declamation with a flat stone in his mouth. 'What Demosthenes—who was only a man—was able to do, I must also be able to do,' said Seydelmann, characteristically and defiantly. His proud determination was successful, and he made his intractable voice his slave.

In 1819 he got his first real opening, in the theatre at Grätz, in Steuermark. His artistic insight, his burning zeal, his boundless ambition, his desire to surpass others, were assisted by an acquired skill in dealing with men; and at Grätz he rose rapidly in the profession of his choice. He played all sorts of things; even comic characters, for which, indeed, he had no aptitude; though he endeavoured to supply the want of comic power by a close study and artistic imitation of nature.

The theatre at Grätz fell under the direction of a cab-master, and the haughty Seydelmann at once quitted the company. He strolled about for some time from place to place, and learned thoroughly, in poverty and distress, the miseries of the literally poor player's life. The proud, hard man deduced from his time of sore struggle the bitter lesson that the actor must place his chief dependence upon egotism and self-assertion. Sorrows had hardened, and not softened, his harsh, domineering, and arrogant character.

At the Court Theatre, in Cassel, Seydelmann first obtained the undisputed possession of 'leading business,' and could play the great parts in which his artistic ambition really revelled.

Like a torch, which burns itself away while giving light, Seydelmann consumed his own health in a fiery attempt to attain to the utmost possible amount of *effect* in his performances. Away from the stage he did not drink, but, when acting, he used spirits freely with a view to stimulate his nervous system to its very highest pitch and strain of effort. This practice told, in the long run, very seriously upon Seydelmann's health. Cooke and Edmund Kean both drank spirits freely as stimulants to acting; but then they also drank them when they were not exerting themselves professionally.

Seydelmann must be ranked as a realistic tragedian. He did not belong to the declamatory and ideal school of Quin, or of the Kembles. Garrick, probably the actor who restored most nearly the school of the contemporaries of Shakspeare, the school of Taylor and of Burbage, included in his style both realism and ideality. He remained firmly based upon the truth of Nature, and yet presented ideal characters ideally. Macready, again, belonged to this mixed school, which presents forcibly and naturally profound passion and pathos, and yet maintains a lofty ideal art aim.

Seydelmann aimed at producing strength of effect. He preferred the terrible, the striking, the sensational, the surprising. He loved villainous rather than noble characters. He loved Richard III. better than King Lear. He did not care for the *ensemble* of a performance, and never showed a loyal consideration for the author. He was selfish as an actor, and sought chiefly to unfold and to display his own great powers. He was inconsiderate and unfair towards his brother artists. He himself has said that 'the stage is a field of battle on which one must conquer or must die. Whoever stands in the way of my success is an enemy that I will strike down.' He admits that his object is to produce out of every character the greatest possible amount of effect. He made of every part a subjective property, and developed through it the energy of his own personality. One curious habit in studying he early adopted and always adhered to: he copied out, in his own beautiful handwriting, every part that he played. He could not learn a part from the handwriting of other men. Nothing in life came easily to Seydelmann, and he was always slow of study. He noted on the margin of his copy the details of his 'business.' With inventive insight, he easily detected those great moments in a character out of which he could produce his most splendid effects; and to effect he always looked. His art aims were complected with his personal objects. He burned to surpass all his comrades, and to make of his acting a victory and a glory. The triumph of his own acting—not that of the thing acted—was the result for which he strove. He cared for truth to Nature in her strength rather than for adherence to her modesty. The Weimar school of acting, under the direction of Goethe and of Schiller, had somewhat resembled that of our Kembles: Seydelmann was the fiery Kean who despised art when it hampered the success of strong and working effect.

Fanny Kemble says:—Kean *is* a man of decided genius, no matter how he abuses Nature's good gift. He has it. He has the first element of all genius— Power. . . . Let his deficiences be what they may, his faults however obvious, his conceptions however erroneous, and his characters, each considered as a whole, however imperfect, he has the one atoning faculty that compensates for everything else—that seizes, rivets, electrifies all who see and hear him, and stirs, down to their very springs, the passionate elements of our nature. Genius alone can do this. Kean may not be an actor, he may not be an artist, but he *is* a man of genius, and instinctively, with a word, a look, a gesture, tears away the veil from the heart of our common humanity, lays it bare as it beats in every human heart and as it throbs in his own. Kean speaks with his whole living frame to us, and every fibre of ours answers to his appeal. I do not know that I ever saw him in any character which impressed me as *whole work of art;* he never seems to me to intend to be any one of his parts, but I think he intends that all his parts should be *him.* So it is not Othello, Shylock, Sir Giles; it is Kean, and in every one of his characters there is an intense personality of *his own* that, while one is under its influence, defies all criticism—moments of such overpowering passion, accents of such tremendous power, looks and gestures of such thrilling, piercing meaning, that the excellence of those parts of his performance more than atones for his want of greater unity in conception and smoothness in the entire execution of them.'

Mrs Kemble's fine criticism on Kean would apply,

to a very great extent, to Seydelmann also. They were players whose powers were not dissimilar, and whose aims in acting were based upon the same force of personality and fervour of genius.

Seydelmann took but little interest in the abstract drama. He desired eagerly to startle an audience and to surpass all competitors; and he early saw that 'he who will rule the world must not try to better it.' He accepted everything that he found existing in any theatre, and strove only to find fit opportunities for the display of Seydelmann himself.

I may, perhaps, be permitted to reproduce here a short extract from a previous essay,* in which I said of Seydelmann:—

*Vis-à-vis* poet and public, Seydelmann thought chiefly of himself—of the effect which he could produce, of the applause he could obtain. He is accused of having often sacrificed his part and his author to some startling reading, to some surprising point. On the other hand, he was wholly original; he followed no other actor; he was full of fire and of force, and his own strong, clear will shone through all his performances. When he is compared, as he often is, with his great rival Ludwig Devrient, you always find that Devrient's performance is spoken of as a whole, while Seydelmann is remembered for his points. Devrient sank his personality in modest devotion to his art; Seydelmann asserted himself through and above his art: he was an intense and most moving actor, of strong points, and of electric effects. He always excited his audiences to enthusiasm; and he attracted more, perhaps, than any other German actor has done before or since. He disliked playing with great or even good actors; and he would conceal his most startling points at rehearsal in order to prevent his fellow-artists from divining the effects he intended.

---

\* 'A Glance at the German Stage.'

He was a great, a powerful, a moving, an original actor; but was self-seeking and vain. He was the first and the greatest of the matadors, or staf-actors in Germany.

Seydelmann died in 1843. Herr Eduard Devrient cites many instances of Seydelmann's violations of the poet's text; violations introduced solely with a view to producing new and startling effects as an actor; and Herr Devrient refers particularly for instances of this vice in conception to Seydelmann's Shylock, Marinelli (Emilia Galotti), Alba (in Egmont), Don Carlos (Clavigo), Antonio (Tasso), Ossip (Isidor and Olga), Brandon (Eugene Aram), and Mephistopheles. Thus Seydelmann's Shylock was not the despised and humble Jew of Venice, but was a raging fury, who appeared as a despot, who dominated Doge and Senate, and stood above all other persons. He distorted the relation of Shylock to the drama, and to the other characters; his denunciation of Antonio was so violent that spectators expected to see Shylock assault the merchant, and cut the throat of Antonio. As Alba he received Egmont with such indicated meaning of fell intention, that the *insouciance* of Egmont, as that is depicted by Goethe, seemed the merest folly. He was fond, for the purposes of strong effect, of splitting up a speech into 'asides,' which were never contemplated by the author. When, in the fourth act, Clavigo confesses his intention to marry, Don Carlos has to exclaim,—'Hell, death, and the devil! and thou wilt marry her?'

Seydelmann said the first part of the sentence as an aside, and then said, coldly and scornfully, to Clavigo, 'And thou wilt marry her?' Into the part of Antonio, in Tasso, he imported a suggestion of suspicious relations with the Countess Sanvitale. But Seydelmann has for us most interest in connexion with Mephistopheles.

In Germany, generally, Seydelmann ranks as the great Mephisto. Old playgoers, who accompany you to see some other representative of the arch-fiend of the drama, say, sorrowfully, 'Ah, if you could only have seen Seydelmann in the character!' His biographer, Rötscher, speaks with boundless, if with undiscriminating, enthusiasm of this unquestionably powerful performance, while Eduard Devrient, on the other hand, speaks of it with discrimination, but with a tempered enthusiasm. The part requires the utmost intensity of meaning, but cannot bear the merest suggestion of passion, of warmth of feeling, or of human, earthly force.

Seydelmann maintained that he depicted the devil of the old Faust legend, and that Goethe would have been astonished if he could have seen the terrible attributes and the force that could be thrown by an actor into this fiend that the poet had raised, but had only sketched in words. Seydelmann said,—'He who draws the devil on the wall must not faint with fear if the original should grin at him through the sketch.' Apart from the broad, general consentience of popular admiration, that most powerful, that most awful presentation of Seydelmann in Mephisto is a standing subject of critical controversy in Germany. Seydelmann indulged his realistic tendencies to the top of their bent in Mephistopheles. He was always the fiend as he appears on the Blocksberg, where he is recognised as the devil. Seydelmann destroyed the position of Mephisto *vis-à-vis* the other characters and the drama itself. His 'make up' was dreadfully impressive. He was fierce, coarse, repulsive, dreadful; he excited wild laughter; though that laughter of spectators was, as I imagine, that relief to overstrained feeling which echoes hollowly through the morbid merriment which greets Iago's murder of Roderigo. Seydelmann would not descend, in irony, to the travelling cavalier, to the possible comrade of humanity. 'Where,' asks Immermann, 'where is the Marinelli of hell that Goethe intended?' But, whatever injury Seydelmann may have done to the meaning of the poet, his Mephistopheles, *i.e.*, himself in Mephistopheles, was most terribly real, was most awfully powerful; the nerves, as the imaginations, of spectators were wholly subdued and dominated, and full theatres emptied themselves, after the performance, of excited, deeply moved men and women, upon whose lives was stamped a permanent image of great horror, who had been in dramatic contact with an infra-human being, and who (as I have learned by experience of them) would never wholly forget the impression made upon them by Seydelmann's weird Mephistopheles. The effect that he then produced resembled that which Kean, Macready, Rachel have also made on the feelings and on the imaginations of men. It is the effect produced by mighty abstract acting; and may exist in some cases apart from the design or the creation of the poet whose work has been presented on the stage. The stage itself, as an entity, has something dæmonic in its abstract essence and working.

Kühne, of Darmstadt, is the best Mephistopheles that I have seen. At proper times he raised a shudder in the spectator at imaginary contact with an evil spirit; and he always suggested, subtly, the infranatural, while his relations with mortals were sufficiently probable. He could express the cold, cynical, inhuman fiend. Döring was too human—too full of *bonhomie*. You could not enough realise the devil. Dawison is held to have been too forcible and fierce. I think that Macready would have been as fine and subtle a fiend as the stage could wish for; his intellect would have added to the human devilry of Iago the unearthly devilry of the very fiend himself. He who could so well play Shakspeare would also have interpreted Goethe.

Through Seydelmann the poet had raised a devil that he could not control; the actor played, literally, the very devil. His Mephisto must have been recognised as the fiend by the other characters, and such recognition would have been fatal to Mephisto's plans; but, while acting the part, Seydelmann paralysed criticism. Men do not laugh when they are under water; they do not criticise while their judgments are submerged by the genius of abstract acting. In Mephistopheles there is nothing human but the assumption of humanity; but that assumption should be sufficiently depicted. The incarnate Evil Spirit is seen to act visibly, as he does act occultly, in his attempts to lead men to their harm; but to one man only in the play is the fiend really known. Seydelmann forgot, perhaps, too much the modesty of his art in his lust for her power.

Frau Niemann-Seebach is the best Gretchen that I have seen; indeed, it would be impossible to conceive, or to desire, a better representative of the part; nor could a more perfect Marthe than Frau Frieb-Blumauer be imagined. Emil Devrient was a great Faust; though he failed, before the magic change to youth came, to depict clearly enough the bowed, worn, prematurely-aged student. After the change, he was an ideal cavalier. Hendrichs, as Faust, was too declamatory, robust, loud; he opened the play with a voice of rolling thunder. He began in virile middle age, and did not grow younger after drinking the witch's draught.

Faust is held, by German actors, to be what players call a 'thankless part.' They consider that the character, in stage representation, is overshadowed, is obscured by that of Mephistopheles. German star-actors prefer the fiend to the philosopher ; nor is it to be wondered at that the greater effect should be produced in the most unique part in the drama—in a part which embodies a transcendental apparition seen through the mask of a human form. Faust strives, strains, inquires, acts, sins—suffers ; Mephisto is the embodiment of denial, of blindness to goodness, truth, nobleness, beauty ; he represents, through the terribly grotesque, irony, sneering, scorn, filth, evil, mockery. His very appearance on the stage, among human actors, is a sensation, a terror, a wonder, a portent of incarnate *diablerie*. Intrinsically, Mephistopheles is more a puppet than is Faust ; but, on the stage, this does not seem to be so. This wonderful and terrible drama of two souls apparently hopelessly enmeshed by the devil, places Mephisto, to all appearance, in the position of motor, ruler ; but he is so to appearance only, since his fruitless activity in reality only subserves the high, inscrutable designs of omnipotent wisdom. The devil, according to Goethe's views and showing, is the mere puppet and factor of the Deity. Faust is certainly one of the most exhausting parts for an actor. It is very long, and is always to be played throughout at a high pitch of passion. There is, in the first part, the tragedy of thought and of the soul ; there is, in the later parts of the play, the tragedy of passion, love, conscience, remorse. In the early parts, Faust's impatient, defiant soul, weighted with cares about its relation to the Unseen, feeling (as Goethe himself had felt) the vanity of knowledge, is driven, in haughty desperation, to the black art and to the eager fiend; and this part requires from the actor most difficult and passionate art. Later, after the magic transformation, after the return to youth, the part culminates in passion, though it is passion of a more human sort. Indeed, it has been suggested ('Werel's Goethe's Faust, in Bezug auf Scenerie und Bühnendarstellung') that the part of Faust should be played by two actors, one sustaining it up to the scene in the witch's kitchen, the other assuming it at that point and continuing it to the end. German actors, in my opinion, fail to render in the earlier scenes the comparative age of the over-worn student; they make the Faust of the opening too vigorous and robust; there is not contrast enough between the sage and the cavalier. They trust too much to the philosopher's long beard. Both Emil Devrient and Hendrichs seem to me to have failed in this respect. German actresses, on the other hand, often make Marthe too ugly and too old. A very eminent Mephistopheles said,—' The play is called Faust, not Mephisto; and the greatest difficulty in the latter part is, perhaps, to avoid putting it too strongly forward at the expense of the title-part. My rendering of Mephisto will never be properly appreciated from all sides until I play it with a Faust who can play me down.'

In Shakspeare's treatment of historical characters, history is enclosed and included in a thing more glorious than itself; he did not merely teach the letter of history, but he exalted it to an imaginative ideal, and raised it to the measure of his art. He did not violate, but he did elevate truth. Rapt up to the heaven of imagination in a chariot of the fire of his own genius, he saw the characters of history in larger relations, and he depicted them as abstract poetical conceptions. Take Queen Katharine, Henry V., Richard II., as illustrations; he did not falsify, but he overrode history, and used it as a basis upon which his insight and his imaginatively creative power could raise types of a wider and more glorious truth than was comprised in the actual, limited fact. Goethe dealt with the Faust of the old miracle-play in something of the same spirit. No popular legend could present a human soul so complex, so many-sided, so tried and tempted, as that which Goethe evolved out of the rough lumber of legend and tradition.

To deal with the old Faust legend according to the highest modern ideas; to use the *naïveté* of the still vital old popular story as a vehicle for the highest abstract thought, and as an enclosure for the most moving tragedy—this was a problem for distinctive genius; this is the problem which has been solved to a marvel by Goethe. The idea that the Evil One should directly bargain with man for man's soul, should satisfy all the desires of the heart, the desire for pomp, pleasure, power, at the price of the soul of the bargainer, is a direct product of the objectivity of conception, of the *naïveté*, of the superstition, of the very piety itself, of the Middle Ages. The story is essentially German; it is full of the *diablerie* which is inherent in German imagination. No other country could have so well evolved from its moral consciousness the legend of Faust. No other country could so well have developed the poet who could subordinate the olden story to the highest purposes of thoughtful and imaginative art. The fancy, the half-divine mythus of devil and angel contending for man's soul, is a more direct objective conception; the bargain between man and demon is the distinctive essence of the Faust story.

The peculiar characteristic of Faust as the subject of a drama is the circumstance that the Spirit of Evil must appear embodied and incarnate among the merely human characters. The incarnate dæmonic mingles visibly and tangibly with the human action. The infra-human influence is to be watched and traced in its working, and in the result of that working. Take the simple human story of Faust —without visible dæmonic interference—and it resolves itself into a very ordinary drama of seduction, of murder, of sorrow, and of most tragic issue. Place the Evil One ostensibly in action among the mortals, and the drama acquires a weird and deeper meaning—a strange, supernatural influence. How shall the poet conceive and depict this mysterious, this terrible Spirit of Evil? That which the poet's imagination can body forth must be received through the imagination of reader or of spectator. It is difficult to conceive a more difficult imaginative task than that of placing Satan on the stage. How shall the dramatist make such a being speak?—how shall he depict the dark Spirit of Evil, the antagonist of goodness and of God, assuming human conditions and mortal limits? Were not this high problem so nobly solved by Goethe, we should be inclined to hold it to be impossible. In Goethe's *Faust* the fiend does not appear, as he does in Marlowe's *Faustus*, as a mere conjuror, a slave of the ring, who can be called upon at any moment to perform wonderful, if sometimes childish, tasks. No; the Mephistopheles creation of great Goethe is touched to finer issues, and appears for quite other purposes. The mystery of the great—the perhaps apparent only, but yet immortal—conflict between Good and Evil has to be indicated, not dogmatically or doctrinally, but imaginatively, and as it can be conceived by the free and holy spirit of man. In that fine air of spiritual thought which outsoars all the churches, and extends above all the steeples, must the poet work who will deal adequately and nobly with the Faust legend. There was but one poet who, qualified by very many concurrent circumstances, could discharge the high task; and that poet was Goethe.

Small wonder that the completion of a drama on this infinite subject should spread over years, long as well as very many, of the great poet's life. He was not in any hurry to complete a work which even he could scarcely exhaust.

A little careful analysis will show how wonderfully Goethe has managed the apparently insuperable difficulty of making Mephistopheles fitly talk. The poet must indicate that the unearthly talker knows more than man can know of the deepest secrets of the universe; and yet Mephistopheles does not need, or wish, to tell all that he knows; he unfolds only so much as is necessary to lead and to mislead Faust and the other characters; though at times the fiend speaks as if half thinking his own thought aloud, while on other occasions—as, for instance, with Marthe and with the student—he speaks in order to indulge his irrepressible, grim, hellish, gross, cynical, bitter humour. Goethe had, of necessity, to make his Devil very like a man. If the fiend were absent from the drama, the action would have the same issue; but with the very fiend upon the scene, the spectator is subjected to the weird fascination of seeing the process by means of which the end is to be brought about. Goethe believed in 'the shows of evil;' he conceived that the good, that the Deity, was omnipotent and supreme; and that evil, instead of being a rival power, was only an influence tolerated and used by divinity to work out divine ends. Hence, he draws Mephisto as a *Geist der stets verneint;* as a spirit working vainly, always labouring for evil, and yet controlled by a higher power, and always involuntarily working for good— a conception which may be theologically wrong, but is yet possibly divinely true.

Goethe's *Faust*, as he wrote it, is more than a drama; not less than a drama; it is never undramatic. The dramatic poem, which deals with such great argument, includes a drama within its larger limit. No great Regisseur—no Tieck or Klingemann — would find any difficulty in compressing action, poetry, and event into the practical stage scope of an acting drama. A work purely or merely a dramatic poem is not necessarily a drama. It may contain no moral conflict, no tragic collision with fate, no action, and no event which springs from dramatic attrition; but Goethe's *Faust* contains all dramatic elements, and, as a tragedy half supernatural, half human, it remains 'sad, high, and working.'

# FACTS AND FANCIES ABOUT FAUST—*Continued.*

## II.—The Poem and the Poet.

CARLYLE says, finely, 'Goethe's poetry is no separate faculty, no mental handicraft; but the voice of the whole harmonious manhood; nay, it is the very harmony, the living and life-giving harmony of that rich manhood which forms his poetry.' This saying applies strongly to his *Faust*. With Goethe the ideal is always based upon the real; the bases of his imaginings are his life experiences. We know, happily, so much about Goëthe, that we can trace, through his creations, his profoundest convictions and views of life. A knowledge of Goethe's biography, correspondence, and, especially, of his autobiography, enables us to follow, through *Faust*, his changing and growing opinions—to study some of his life events and his mental progress. Would that we could know as much of Shakspeare! But the personality of our great poet is shrouded in his works. Of Goethe we may say, 'His thoughts are very deep.' Apart even from poetry, and from drama, there is, in *Faust*, always a spiritual atmosphere of the very loftiest thought that is within the reaches of the soul of man; a deep criticism of life which does not disturb, but which does elevate alike poetical creation and dramatic vitality. In Goethe's work there is nothing strenuous; no evidence of effort or of labour; all seems to have grown as a result of god-like ease and spontaneity of production. His bold, high, sometimes wild, but always regally dominated imagination works ever in free fantasy and large conception. His profound striving to penetrate the mystery of Existence is embodied in purposeful and winged words, furnishing to his nation quotations which form a part of thought and life. Clearness of vision and spiritual insight, together with working imagination, are among his special attributes. Humour he has, but it is attended with one peculiarity—it is humour which extends just so far as it is needed by his art purpose, but never goes beyond that limit. There is, in Goethe, nothing of the frolic fun of humour enjoyed for its own irresistible sake by a born humorist; nothing of Shakspeare's revelry of joy in pure humour. Goethe has it at command for a needful purpose, as, for instance, for the scene between Mephistopheles and Mistress Marthe Schwerdtlein; but he uses it only for his needs, and, indeed, employs it with a certain coy reticence. He loves earnestness better than sportiveness; he thinks all thought rather through gravity than through humour. Life is, to him, in the main, wholly serious. All its sides do not strike upon his mind with the equal force with which they press upon the full-orbed, every-sided mind of Shakspeare. It would be a mistake to expect fun, or more than a stately mirth, from Jupiter; and analysis demands from every man that only which he can give.

Despite some high labour—notably that highest of Carlyle—it cannot yet be said that the full significance and value of Goethe are adequately recognised in England. He has been dealt with in part by such dull commentators that his true image has been all obscured; as the noblest face seems distorted when it is reflected in a spoon. Great art reveals no secrets except to labour of great thought; and it must be long before Goethe can become—if he ever should become—popular in England. His own height stands in his way. You might as well blame a weak man for not having been up the Matterhorn, as blame him for not understanding Goethe; it is not given to all to ascend such ideal altitudes.

Goethe's infinite dramatic poem of *Faust*, the writing of which spread itself slowly over a period of some thirty years, was first printed in 1806. It was the only one of his many works over which he lingered long; he could not hurry the completion of a poem on a quite infinite subject. *Faust* is, indeed, a subject singularly suited to the genius of Goethe. The fulness of meaning in the great Christian mythus had a rare attraction for his magnanimous intellect and wonder-working imagination.

The symbolism involved in the magic fable enabled him to render every line pregnant with meaning; the high, abstract spirit of the legend gave him scope for painting things divine, dæmonic, human. The theme was worthy of the work; the work was commensurate with the theme. Into it he could pour all his thoughts, all his theories, all his wisdom, all his experiences. *Faust* may be said to have been commenced with *Werther;* but the execution of *Faust* outgrew the phase of mind, the *Zeitkolorit,* of that fervid, but feverish frenzy of morbid youth which summed up and exhausted the mental disease of a sickly time in *Werther*. *Faust* survived into his later and his riper years, and includes all that even Goethe felt, and thought, and knew. *Hamlet* was, so far as we know, produced with no more length of labour, with no greater expenditure of time, than were occupied by any of the other works of Shakspeare. Goethe lingered long and lovingly over the great work which is his masterpiece; and worked at *Faust* as he worked upon no other of his poems or his dramas.

The origin and the growth of Goethe's *Faust*, the time at which he first conceived the play, and the different dates at which he executed it, are assuredly subjects of literary interest, if not of great literary importance. It is enough to possess such a work in its entirety; the desire to know the dates and the progress of completion, involves questions which may easily be considered a little too curiously; and this is more especially the case because the evidence, mostly circumstantial, is mainly defective. Still, German *Gründlichkeit* has laboured assiduously in this field of inquiry; though the results, to quote Sheridan's old joke, are voluminous rather than luminous. Wilhelm Scherer, in his 'Aus Goethe's Frühzeit,' is the latest labourer in this highly speculative region of research. His conjectures are many, his discoveries few; but it is yet possible to glean some suggestions of interesting probabilities—nay, even some sure facts, from his inquiries. I pass over, as scarcely worth much attention, the thin and windy theories which would seek to indicate that Herder was the original of Mephisto—or of the *Erdgeist*. Herr Scherer admits that the problem of the growth of *Faust* is one that can never be solved. Asking only, in passing, Why should it be solved?—I shall cite here those few facts in connexion with the subject which seem to be established without much room for doubt by Herr Scherer and by others.

Goethe himself says that *Faust entstand mit dem Werther;* was planned at the same time as was his early romance—that is, his *Faust* was first contemplated when he was a little over twenty years of age. Indeed, the subject is alluded to in a manner which shows that he was then thinking of it, in the *Mitschuldigen*, the work of a youth of eighteen.

From Loeper's *Laroche Correspondenz* it would seem that a sketch of *Faust*, in prose, was made in the winter of 1771-72; and this prose sketch served as the basis of a poetical version begun after 1773. The last scene but two, *Trüber Tag, Feld*—still remains in prose; and Schiller (May 8, 1798) records that Goethe had said that the execution of certain scenes, in prose, was powerfully moving, *gewaltsam angreifend*. Among the side lights thrown upon the subject is an allusion by Wieland (Nov. 12, 1796) to the fact that Goethe had suppressed some interesting scenes—notably one in which Faust became so furious (probably when he discovered the incarceration of Gretchen) that he intimidated Mephistopheles. Gotter says that Goethe was at work on *Faust* in Wetzlar, at the period of his love romance with Lotte. In completing his design, Goethe has let certain of his original intentions drop away; for instance, Gretchen was to have wandered with her child in misery over the earth, until, in her insanity, she destroyed it. Another abandoned project was one of a great public disputation, in which Mephistopheles, as a wandering student, was to have taken a characteristic part. In 1800, Goethe wrote to Schiller that he hoped the great disputation scene would soon be finished. In 1790 was completed that version of *Faust* now known in German literature as ' the Fragment.'

In January or February 1775, Goethe read his

*Faust*, as it then existed, to Jacobi, who noticed but little difference between that version and the fragment of 1790. In 1774, Goethe read *Faust* to Heinrich Leopold Wagner. The heroine was then named Eva. Her name became Margarethe and Margretlein. Gretchen was the latest of the names chosen. In 1776, Goethe speaks of a conception of Helena— a conception reserved for the second part. Theod. Mommsen expresses an opinion that the early prose version still shows through the later poetical form. On March 1, 1788, Goethe writes to Herder that he had found the old thread of *Faust*, and had completed his scheme of the tragedy. In 1777, Goethe visited the Hartz country, and his acquaintance with those mountains is evidenced in the *Walpurgis Nacht*. In 1789, Goethe writes to the Duke that he will produce *Faust* as it stands, as a fragment. He adds that the poem is, in a certain sense, finished for the time. Hence the fragment of 1790. The latest entry in this chronology is 'the first part of *Faust* completed' in 1806. It seems that the witch struck off from Faust the burden of thirty years; so that we may assume him to be fifty-five when a sage, twenty-five when a lover.

Goethe takes an optimistic view of evil; but as the play progressed, the strength of the old tradition moulded the treatment of the modern poet, and he introduces Mephisto's proposal for a compact to be signed with blood. The peaks of the highest mountains seem, at night, to blend with the stars, and

Goethe's pure ideas rise to the divine; but yet the fascination to the imagination of the old wonder-legend exercised a strong influence over his dramatic conception and art treatment. Dropped threads of his early plan, with their ends loose, are sometimes left in his completed work.

In the poem itself, the legend of *Faust* is decided upon, as the subject of a drama, in that prologue which depicts a debate between a theatre director, a theatre poet, and a clown. This deeply, sadly humorous prologue paints the never-ending quarrel between poets and the traders in poetry—a dispute in which a Merry Andrew can act as mediator—and is written with a humour strictly subordinated to its immediate purpose, and with all the sadness of thoughtful satire. Goethe recognises the lets and hindrances which hamper the free activity of the poet, and yet shows that the great poet must and can do his work, despite of all the limitations and difficulties which a theatre, a director, and a mixed public can throw in the poet's way. In spite of a public which desires only to be amused, it is yet possible to deal highly with the high theme of a noble, erring soul to be led, if that may be, *Von Himmel durch die Welt zur Hölle.* Poets do their work through a Spartan training. Earnest effort will, in the end, overcome; but no effort will be wanting on the part of enmity and ignorance to thwart and to oppose the owner of the God-like gift.

Goethe first speaks in his own person, in that matchless, that grandly pathetic *Zueignung*, or Dedication, in which the old man, putting forth his life's highest work to a generation unborn when first he sang, expresses heroic tenderness without a weakling's sentimentalism. After the Theatre Prologue comes one in heaven, in which, following the opening of the Book of Job, Goethe uses the quaint *naïveté* of mediæval conception, in order to lay the frame-work of his *Divina Commedia*. But all prologue ceases, and, with our thoughts full of the mediæval legend, and of the permitted experiment of the Evil One, the curtain draws up on the drama of *Faust*.

Many will probably recollect the emotion with which they saw, for the first time, in some German theatre, the curtain rise and disclose the first scene in Goethe's *Faust*.

In the narrow, high, Gothic chamber, surrounded by books, parchments, skeletons, crucibles, retorts, sits the bowed, worn, prematurely old sage; and the great void space of the theatre becomes filled with the grand declamatory roll of the majestic opening soliloquy. The dark, bearded figure of the life-worn philosopher, who has learned so bitterly that great knowledge is great sorrow, becomes a possession of the mind—a picture fixed in the imagination. The play opens on the eve of Easter Day, and the sad moon shines in through stained glass upon the student's solitary study. Faust's state of mind, or soul, presents to us a spiritual tragedy. His unhappiness is the result of individual dissatisfaction with life. His is the sublime egotism of a scholar, a striver, a thinker, who has exhausted knowledge, but missed all happiness. For him the light of the lamp has replaced the light of heaven. He has turned his back upon the light, and has made his path of life very dark by projecting on to it his own shadow. In his passionate despair he yet yearns madly for truth, and thirsts for fuller knowledge. His recourse to magic is an attempt to reach heaven through hell. He turns to diabolic science in order to attain to divine light. Aspiring and inquiring, half mad with longing, wholly desperate with doubt—sublime, if passionate error impels him into a cavern to seek for light—drives him into darkness with a glass to see his face. The moonbeams make warm gules upon the haggard features and bent figure of the old, life-weary student. As the morning—the morning of Easter Day—greys upon the long vigil of the philosopher, he attempts suicide; but the heavenly tones of the Easter hymn, with all the memories of childhood, of prayer, and of youth, arrest the impious hand. His tears flow, and earth reclaims her son.

In all the early stages of *Faust*, Goethe has used the suggestions—not reproduced the detail—of his own youth's experience. He, too, had pushed knowledge beyond ordinary human limits; he, too, had pined with that sad, high, longing discontent of great and ardent souls, that cannot find in life all that the mind can desire. He knew the unsatisfied desires, the satiety of learning; and he, too, had learned how grey is all theory, and how green alone the golden tree of life. But Goethe remembered and used, though he had long outlived, the feverish discontents of youth. He himself never succumbed to despair. A strong man, he turned his weakness into strength; calmly victorious, he survived into peace and light. He, too, turned to magic; but his magic was divine, and not dæmonic. When, in his *Werther* days, the echo of Jerusalem's pistol sounded through the void heart, the unsatisfied soul, the mock hysterical passion of his brain-sickly time of temporary fever and unrest, Goethe, too, had once contemplated suicide. Basing his only half-sincere plan of operations upon the example of the Emperor Otho, he placed, every night, a sharp dagger by his bedside. Finding, however, after one or two slight trials, that he lacked resolution to drive the keen steel even a little way into his breast, young Goethe relinquished the idea of suicide—nay, parted with it even in laughter. To many human beings the sorrows of life are so many, and so heavy, that, but for the Hamlet dread and doubt, the earth would be strewn with suicides; especially in those times over which a wave of morbid feeling passes. Men shrink from the great and dread Unknown; from the dreams that may come in that sleep of death; and thus remain bound and confined to the ills they know of—ills which, though often almost unbearable, seem to the haggard imagination better than the awful and terrible vagueness of the possibilities that surround death. The dread of death does much to keep men in life.

It is characteristic of Goethe that he draws Faust as always proud of his own image of the Godhead; that he depicts his philosopher scornfully confronting spirits and demons with a haughty assumption of being their peer, if not their superior. Goethe's own residence as a student in Leipzig had made him well acquainted with the Auerbach Keller; his own experience had taught him a contempt for the barren pedantry of University teaching, and for the waste studies of so many ingenuous young souls. His own repugnance to jurisprudence is amply recorded by himself. Indeed, his experience shines through Wagner, through the student, through the mock professorship of mocking Mephistopheles. Goethe records, in his own account of his own University career,—' In logic it struck me as strange that I was, in order to perceive the proper use of them, to pull to pieces, dismember, and, as it were, destroy those very operations of the mind which I had gone through with the greatest ease from my youth.'

Through the whole tragedy of *Faust* shines a deep and distinctive doctrine which Goethe held firmly— I mean his belief in the ultimate supremacy of Good. He did not believe in Ormuzd and Ahrimanes, in two equally powerful potentates, two spirits of the same might, one good, one evil, between which the ultimate issue of the perpetual struggle is uncertain. Goethe believed supremely in the entire supremacy of God ; he held that the shows of evil do but subserve the higher purposes of divine beneficence. The spirit that always wills, and always works for evil, is, as Goethe teaches, always guided and moulded by a Supreme Power, so that its strivings for evil are mainly futile ; and rough-hewn to harm, are, nevertheless, ultimately shaped by God to good. Thus, the seeming victory of Mephistopheles is barren after all—Gretchen and Faust seem, but are not, lost and ruined. They are ultimately snatched from the fiend's grasp ; though ill deeds and impious longings are expiated in time by sore sufferings on earth. Mephistopheles is, unconsciously, but a tool in the hand of the divine ; he walks in a vain shadow, disquiets himself without result—except in so far as he serves divine purposes—and remains, at last, a fooled and baffled fiend. In Goethe's conviction an Omnipotent and All-wise God lives and reigns ; and this conviction is shown through all the scheme and action of his *Faust*. Goethe's Mephistopheles, his ' Squire Satan ' (*der Junker Satan*), is surely one of the supreme products of art ; and in nothing that he has done, has he shown more clearly his spiritual depth of insight. Mephisto gives but a hint, or glimpse, of revelation of things outside human scope and knowledge ; but that hint and glimpse he gives, and gives most wonderfully. The fiend does not wish to tell all he knows ; he says only so much in that sort as is necessary to impress and to mislead Faust; though, at times, by rare pregnant suggestion, he speaks half as if he were thinking his own thought aloud. The fiend is constantly conscious of the supremacy of Deity. The spirit of denial, he knows that he works for good, while always scheming evil. He tells Faust—

> Trust one of us ; this whole of life
> Is made but for a God alone.

At other times—as in the scenes with Marthe and with the student—he cannot restrain his own grim, hellish, cynical humour; he indulges his savage, gross devilish bitterness, his sneering, withering mockery and irony. Always, reader and spectator have before them, through Goethe's magic art, the image of an infra-human, super-human being. In the beginning, light itself created, or evolved, its own shadow—darkness; and of that mystically created darkness Mephistopheles is a part.

Faust sought the stupefaction of doubt ; distraction from vain inquiry—and, hence, he summoned up the fiend. His early passion for knowledge was incapable of being converted into action, was impotent to yield the joys of sense and of life. When magically restored to youth and love, the Titan—the stormer of the skies—is reduced to an ordinary earthly lover, though plunged into a love which, under devils' guidance, could only throb with lust, could only lead to misery and crime. In Faust's devil-guided passion, Gretchen reigns like a fever in his blood. She, when she yields to temptation, illustrates Shakspeare's saying,—

> Lilies that fester smell far worse than weeds.

It is devils' work to lower love to lust. It is noteworthy that Faust, when making his compact with the devil, does not believe in continuance of sensual, or of any other delight. He says,—

> When, to the moment fleeting past
> I cry, ' Oh stay ! thou art so fair ; '
> Then let your chains be round me cast.

Resolved no longer upon the torture of the mind to lie in restless ecstasy, but, in the hope of relief, to plunge into the joy and woe of life, Faust does not even then believe in the possibility of real happiness. The old impulse toward the divine is still left in his breast, but is left vague ; and all his wisdom will soon pale before a glance of Gretchen's eyes. The scenes in the tragedy follow in a somewhat loose order, and great spaces of time are overleaped without reference to them. Thus, we know nothing of Gretchen's child until we learn that she has murdered it. Goethe's large, inexplicable art is rather pregnant with mystic suggestion than precise in careful arrangement of realistic construction ; we must piece out with our imaginations the wild sequence of an unearthly story.

The tragedy is born of that balance of uncommon qualities which forms the divinity of genius.

There is noticeable a certain levity in Goethe's treatment of the character of Mephistopheles; a levity which would assuredly not be found if Goethe had believed in the success of evil. But he seems to regard the Evil One with a certain sarcastic scorn; with a conviction that the restless labours of the devil are futile as impotent. He is full of the belief in the ultimate triumph of enduring Good. Hence it is that, in the drama, der Herr allows Satan to try his best to mislead and ruin Faust; the Lord adding, that the demon will stand abashed at the futility of his attempt to utterly ruin a man to whom, in spite of wildest errors, the way of righteousness is known. Mephistopheles admits to Faust that, despite his long and ceaseless labours, he is sometimes in despair at the smallness of the results he can produce; and Faust recognises, in his hour of most desperate madness, that the Evil One wages fruitless and hopeless war against the source of life and light. Goethe is not didactic; he never distinctly preaches his theory; but until we really understand the profound conviction as to the comparative power and influence of Evil and of Good which Goethe shows throughout the whole poem, we shall miss that great leading idea which lies at the root of all his wonderful treatment of a theme so complex and so high. Mephistopheles can, and does, bring about most damnable mischief, woe, and wrong. Thus, to take a few instances, he transmutes the duel with Valentine into a murder, and causes the hue and cry of the Blood-Ban to be raised against Faust: his devilish arts bring about that which Faust alone could hardly have compassed—the seduction of Gretchen; he gives to Gretchen that sleeping draught which poisons the mother; he drives her to madness with the mocking tones of an Evil Spirit, which sneer down her faith, even when she bends in prayer in the cathedral. He impels her to the murder of her infant; and he leaves her, in the insanity of sorrow, on that night in prison which is to lead to her last morning on the scaffold. Of all this woe, he tells Faust nothing; and few things in this great play are dramatically finer than the cold, devilish indifference with which he replies to Faust's frenzied reproaches that 'She is not the first,' 'Sie ist die Erste nicht.'

Gretchen was the name of Goethe's first love; and the memory of the early, youthful passion survives in the dear, caressing, diminutive of the name of Margaret. In his Gretchen, Goethe has created one of the loveliest, sweetest, saddest women of all poetry. She is divinely and humanly woman. She is not a bundle of attributes; but a living, individual, most human girl—born for love, driven to crime, doomed to sorrow. When first we see her, coming out of the Gothic cathedral, she is pious, innocent, pure, tender; and yet with the simple wiles, the instinctive coquetry, the femine modesty, the little maidenly vanities of her sex, her age, her time. Every man could love, no man—unless moved by the devil—would wrong Gretchen. Faust had sought the fiend; Gretchen would never, of her own free will, have come to him; indeed, she instinctively shuns and loathes Mephistopheles—nor would the demon have had such power over her but for the fatal love of Faust. Mephisto's vain venom, but for her hapless love, would have hurt her no more than the viper could hurt St Paul. When first Faust urges the demon to gain Gretchen for him, Mephistopheles has to confess that he has no power over her. Goethe has used the mediæval respect for rank when he shows how the simple burgher maiden felt flattered by the attentions of a cavalier of noble house. Marthe is a woman

designed express<br>For go-between and procuress;

and she is a tool ready to the demon's hands. Out of Gretchen's own goodness the fiend makes a net to enmesh her. Until her vanity is corrupted by the jewels, his devilish arts have no success; but she yields to the gauds of the tempter. The trials of her virtue—trials both human and infra-human—are too strong for her; she loves, she gives place to the devil, and she falls. One of the best and purest of women succumbs piteously to the powers of hell. Her fate forms the human tragedy of the drama. In the opening of the play we see that spiritual tragedy of Faust's restless soul which leads to the compact with the Evil One; in the later scenes we have the more human tragedy of the love and fate of Gretchen. The sage has become lover—a depraved lover only —earthly, sensual, devilish. In Gretchen's fond arms, Faust might have hoped for the moment in which he could have cried,—

> Oh stay : thou art so fair ;

but the demon who impels while he ensnares, who seems to serve only that he may destroy, is incapable of loyalty to his own victim, of fidelity to his own bargain. He can give ignoble delight, but he cannot, if he would, give happiness, or peace, or rest—even in love. Faust, still the half-god, has only deadened a conscience which he cannot destroy. He is capable of remorse—he cannot shut out pity. Hurried along the infernal path, he obtains his desires only to ensure his misery.

To our human ken, Mephistopheles seems to do much that is against his own interest ; but we must remember Goethe's theory, that he is only the tool of a Higher Power by which he is constantly befooled. Again, we must not forget that his supernatural knowledge is a key to much that he does which seems unwise—that is, unwise as regards his own purposes. Faust is disgusted in the Auerbach Keller, but the demon desired to lead the soaring soul downward to gross and sensual evil through a preliminary stage of flat common-place unmeaningness. Faust resembles a flying fish; his aerial, heavenward flight soon subsides into a return to his more native element. There is, in Goethe, nowhere that attenuated thread of inspiration which is like a waterfall in a dry summer; he is always full, and always full of meaning. It might seem to us that Mephistopheles was thwarting his own ends by transmuting Faust's amour to utter misery; but the fiend had more to hope from Faust's despair and desperation than from his contentment and enjoyment; and then Mephistopheles took a joy in human suffering. Things that happen off the scene are often merely suggested. The art difficulties in the way of picturing ostensible dæmonic interference in human affairs are immense; and if we are puzzled at times on the surface, we always find that Goethe is right in the depths.

The mind lingers with a strange emotion—half of delight, half of sorrow—over Goethe's immortal creation of dear, unhappy Gretchen. *Halb Gott, halb Kind im Herzen*, she is one of the women of fiction who lay hold so strongly of our imaginations, of our sympathies. Her sweet, simple, loving nature; her childlike *naïveté* and trust; her holy innocence, which knows no bashful cunning; her irresistible maiden coquetry, based only upon instinct—all these qualities are fused into a pure and perfect character, which is one of the glories and the charms of great art. Behind the seduction glares the cold, filthy grin of the infra-human Mephistopheles; both Gretchen and Faust are impelled to sweet sin *mit dem Teufel im Leibe.*

The sin of Faust and Gretchen arises from demoniacal possession. Gretchen never wholly loses our respect; and then her error is atoned for by such deep sorrows! When shame and remorse begin in her sweet soul the Nemesis of wrong, she can yet say,—

> Doch—alles was dazu mich trieb,
> Gott! war so gut! ach war so lieb!

She confesses to her lover that she was very angry with herself because she was not more angry with him for having accosted her. Who forgets her playful, childishly superstitious flower-test of love, as she plucks off leaf after leaf of the daisy, murmuring—'He loves me—loves me not'? Compare that moment with the anguish of her bitter prayer in the *Zwinger* to the picture of the *Mater dolorosa*. What a dramatic poem is that in the garden, when cavalier-like Faust and fair Gretchen, Mephistopheles and Marthe, in alternate couples, pass and repass across the working scene! What simple, pious goodness in the girl's tender concern for the soul of the man she loves, when, in Marthe's garden, she questions Faust—

> Nun sag, wie hast du's mit der Religion?

and how characteristic is the reply of the lover-philosopher! Faust's early belief has been turned to mist by devilish obscuration, and yet, in her presence, he who once was *an Hoffnung reich, im Glauben fest*, returns to a faith vital, though obscured by the phraseology of philosophy. Note, too, that Faust declares his love through his vaguely lofty theological profession. Men have often more faith, and a deeper faith, than they themselves know of. In action, in passion, in error, a faith seems dead which is only sleeping. There can be no victory without battle. ' Wer immer strebend sich bemüht, den können wir erlösen.' In the wild anguish with which Faust learns that Gretchen lies in the dungeon which is the porch to the scaffold, he once more addresses direct and burning prayer to the Deity from whom he had strayed so far—whom he had so long forgotten.

In that terrible, most moving dungeon scene, Goethe rises to the very summit of his tragedy. In the insanity of great sorrow, poor Gretchen awaits in the dark prison cell the morrow that shall lead her to the scaffold. When Faust enters to save her, her wandering senses can only recognise him by snatches made up of half memories of their old, their fatal love. She cannot be moved to fly with him. There are, in this scene, touches of pathos that lie too deep for tears. In the madness of her agony, Gretchen can only remember—she cannot act. In her joy at seeing Faust, her warped senses lead her to pray him to stop with her—not to take her away: then she urges that he cannot know that he seeks to free a criminal who has murdered her mother, drowned her child.  Her thought changes, and she next insists that he shall survive in order to provide the graves of herself, of her brother, of her mother, and of their child.  Surely her thought for these graves has rarely been surpassed in pathos—

> The best place you must give my mother,
> And close beside her lay my brother;
> Lay me a little way apart,
> But not too far off!
> On my right breast the little one.

The scene of agony and anguish is ended by the appearance of Mephistopheles.  Gretchen calls upon her Heavenly Father, upon the serried ranks of holy angels, to preserve her from the Evil One.  She trembles at last, not for herself, but for her lover. As her soul flies, the fiend exclaims, exultingly,—

'She is doomed!'

But a voice from heaven says that she

'Is saved!'

And another voice, from within—perhaps the voice of Gretchen on her heavenward flight—exclaims, in tones that die away in distance,—

'Heinrich! Heinrich!'

Faust disappears with Mephistopheles; his fate is left in more doubt, but this is explained partially by the fact that he is reserved for a second part; in which, in some imaginary higher sphere, he will not love and ruin a human-hearted, warm-kissing Gretchen, but will worship in another sense than that of the senses, that Helena of Greece, that

> . . . face that launched a thousand ships,
> And burnt the topmost towers of Ilium.

At the end, the vain fiend, Mephistopheles, is baffled and befooled; and the Enduring Good reigns for ever over all.

The romantic and picturesque side of this great drama is a thing to be noted with delight. Both persons and scenes are in the highest degree picturesque and romantic. The costume is that of the sixteenth century; the architecture is of the same, or of yet earlier times. The two chief figures of Faust and Mephistopheles—a pair as well known in art as are Dante and Virgil—are of most picturesque presence. The old Gothic chamber of the student sage, with its olden furniture, inherited from ancestors, is singularly striking and charming. Take, again, the spring walk of pedant and of sage—of Wagner and of Faust—'outside the gate' of the mediæval city, of some antique Nürnberg, Frankfort, Hildesheim, Leipzig, Lüneberg. They pass through the close streets of olden houses within the narrow limits of the walled town; they pass the great open porch of the Gothic cathedral in which Gretchen prayed and worshipped; they pass through the city gate, with portcullis, probably with drawbridge, and issue into the open country which surrounds the quaint dwelling-place of thickly clustered men. They look back upon the armed town, with its towers, roofs, gables, spires, houses. It is a return, with the bud-bursting opening of the year, to Nature and to life; the snows, and ice, and frosts of winter are melting and disappearing before the gentle breath of hope-giving, life-bearing spring. The gay and active crowd of ordinary men and women, bent on the common-place holiday enjoyments of dancing, drinking, joyous love-making, pass by and talk and walk beside the two philosophers. Note that Wagner is not a particularly stupid man. Goethe's art was too fine to make him that. He is more learned, and as intelligent as is the mass of his compeers; he is the dried, pedantic product of that University professorship which puts on so many coals that the fire cannot burn; which heaps up so much learning — not necessarily knowledge —that the mind is stifled. Goethe had known, in his University career, many a Wagner, and many a student. He knew too, well, what a Voltairian demon would have to say of the course of study, of the choice of a 'faculty.' The whole drama, in its essence, as in its surroundings, is instinct with the romantic and the picturesque, and yet it is classical; for has not Goethe said that everything which is of the highest order of merit is classical? Gretchen, also, in the street, at the well, in the garden, at her spinning-wheel, in the cathedral—nay, even in the dungeon—is a most quaint, lovely, archæological girl figure. The black horses sweep by the ghastly

Rabenstein; the witch's kitchen, with its baser magic and its filthy apes, is a dæmonic picture; and the magic mirror, in which Faust first sees the fair image of Gretchen, replaces the foul wall of the fiend-kitchen by an illusion of beauty and of charm. In short, there is, all through, and all round the drama of *Faust*, that picturesque, objective delight which the genius of Goethe's partly Gothic imagination knew so well how to employ for our enjoyment. We are fascinated by the surroundings, as by the essence of the great Northern tragedy.

In that witch's kitchen a magic draught restores to Faust his youth, and transforms him into the splendidly attired, handsome cavalier of the sixteenth century. It is noteworthy that when the fiend assumes human shape he cannot be beautiful. The Gothic fantasy, so much gloomier in its dark, spectral north than was the Greek imagination, depicted Satan, in the middle ages, as a dusky, terrible phantom with horns, and claws, and tail. Mephistopheles is too modern in spirit for such old-fashioned horrors. He appears as a cavalier, as a Herr Baron, but, in deference to tradition, he retains the red doublet, hose, and cloak, the cock's feather, and the long rapier. When well made up, Mephistopheles is certainly one of the most striking apparitions that the stage can show.*

* Red is the old German colour of the devil, and is worn by Zamiel, as well as by Mephisto.

The profound meanings of this poem do not injure the workings of the drama; so deeply is meaning expressed through action. *Faust* remains, in one respect, a puppet-play; the characters are all *Marionetti*, which are seen moving and acting in the light of a Divine Idea, which shines behind and through all appearance. The high, inscrutable designs of deity are always suggested. Faust was a professor of science, not of art; he acquired knowledge, but did not create beauty. His strivings represented only one phase of human mental activity. He forgot a God who did not forget him. Even in his fall, his flashes of proud, divine manhood are unspeakably noble; they are God-descended. Goethe uses no scalpel to discover a soul by means of the dissection of a body. His art is always spiritual. If stained glass be well-coloured, no spectator regards the intrinsic quality of the glass itself; but in this play of *Faust* the noble colouring covers the finest material; subject and treatment are co-equal. We have the best glass most nobly stained and richly dight. Byron says, finely—

> The Devil speaks truth much oftener than he's deemed;
> He hath an ignorant audience;

and Goethe admired and praised our poet's pregnant saying.

Here we conclude our attempt to measure the incommensurable: here we cease, for the present, to try farther to pluck out the heart of the mystery of

Goethe's 'mystic, unfathomable song' of *Faust*. We shall not have exhausted an infinite subject; we shall not have completed our study of a theme which, like all things divine and high, remains, and will remain, with meanings by no means wholly fathomed, with depths never thoroughly sounded. Like *Hamlet*, *Faust* will ever reserve more than gleanings to reward the labours of future thinkers; but our present attempt may be attended by some gladness, and may yield some profit; since not without delight and gain can men strive to enjoy and to understand one of the world's masterpieces; not without enduring advantage can they seek to love and to admire, through critical comprehension, Goethe's immortal tragedy of *Faust*.

## MADAME ROLAND.

'ET moi aussi, j'aurai quelque existence dans la generation future,' cries Madame Roland, when, in her 'Mémoires,' she appeals, with sublime confidence, to the justice of posterity, and reposes upon the conviction of her fame in the after-time. 'One who will claim remembrance from several centuries—Jeanne Marie Phlipon, the wife of Roland,' says Carlyle, who further terms her, 'genuine, the creature of Sincerity and Nature in an age of Artificiality, Pollution, Cant; there, in her still completeness, in her still invincibility, *she*, if thou knew it, is the noblest of all living Frenchwomen.' Nor will her own countrymen willingly let die the reputation of this heroine and martyr of the Revolution. In 1864, the discovery of various *lettres inédites* gave birth to the 'Étude sur Madame Roland, par C. A. Dauban;' to a new edition of her own 'Mémoires,' edited by Danbau and Faugère. The 'Étude' contained the letters of Madame Roland to Buzot; and in 1867, Dauban produced two volumes of 'lettres en partie inédites de Madame Roland.' In the year

1882, M. Imbert de Saint Amand has produced his picture of the long agony of French royalty during the Revolution (Marie Antoinette et l'Agonie de la Royauté), in which Madame Roland figures as the antagonist of, or the foil to, Marie Antoinette.

M. de Saint Amand is, in sentiment, a royalist. His object is to win sympathy for the royal family by a touching narrative, in which he emphasises their sufferings. His heroine is, naturally, Marie Antoinette. As some historians have conceived the essence of the great civil wars of England as a duel between Charles and Cromwell for sovereign power, so M. de Saint Amand draws Marie Antoinette and Madame Roland as 'deux adversaires qui traitent de puissance à puissance. Le Chateau des Tuiléries et l'Hotel du ministère de l'interieur sont comme deux citadelles ennemies placées à deux pas l'un de l'autre.' He speaks of the 'haine vouée par Madame Roland à Marie Antoinette. Cette haine fut inspirée à la vainteuse bourgeoise par la plus mauvaise, la plus vile de toutes les conseillères, par l'envie.' He says elsewhere, 'Personne ne contribua plus à l'agonie de la royauté que Madame Roland.' But, in truth, Saint Amand is not a critic; nor can we place much reliance upon his pictures or his arguments. He seeks, before all things, effect. His somewhat theatrical method of essaying to write history, impels him to present two distinguished women, one the 'parvenue' of genius, the other the daughter of the Cæsars, in the sharpest dramatic contrast, and to draw the one as the ruthless antagonist who triumphed, and gloried in triumphing, over the other. This is not history; this is not poetry. Saint Amand's is 'that over-hasty work which never seems true work.' His study is not profound; his analysis is not penetrating—nor are his results convincing. He is not a writer of real ability or of genuine conscience. His work may interest but cannot satisfy.

Madame Roland presents herself to us under two aspects—as an historical figure and as a psychological study. Under both aspects she is supremely interesting, and exercises upon our minds an undying charm. A radiant white figure, set in the red frame of the hideous guillotine, her lips are for ever eloquent with her last cry,—'O liberté! comme en t'a jouée!' The child and the victim of the Revolution which once she so dearly loved, from which she hoped so much for humanity, she remains its highest heroine. 'Reader, mark that queen-like burgher woman; beautiful, Amazonian, graceful to the eye; more so to the mind.'

The mass of unedited papers which have been discovered since lofty history, in the person of Carlyle, last essayed to paint her for posterity, will warrant us in an attempt to try a new portrait of the Egeria of the Girondins, of the priestess of the Revolution. She formed a part of a great movement, but yet her soul dwelt apart, and she is well worth being considered as a solitary star, and dealt with in an essay consecrated to her as a most individual woman.

The basis of our knowledge of Madame Roland, from childhood upwards, through all mental growth, to that sad moment in which

> Comes the blind Fury with the abhorred shears,
> And slits the thin-spun life—

is those 'Mémoires de Madame Roland,' written by herself in prison, during her long captivity of five months. She herself says, ' Je me propose d'employer les loisirs de ma captivité à rètracer ce qui m'est personnel depuis ma tendre enfance jusqu'a ce moment.' From the moment of her arrest she foresaw her doom. Her pure love of liberty had rendered her hateful to the tyrants who ruled, and who dreaded a woman so ardent and so noble. She records, proudly, ' Je méprise la mort ; je n'ai jamais craint que la crime, et je n'assurerais pas mes jours au prix d'une lâcheté.' She refused flight, and she despised suicide. In the solitude and the gloom of her prison, it was a refreshment to her weary spirit to re-live, and to depict, the past days of childhood and of youth. As we read her ' Mémoires,' we are under the ghastly impression that her writing might at any moment be interrupted by the summons of the headsman. Perpetually on the blank walls of the prison cell there glooms, in sunlight as in moonlight, the red shadow of the glaive of the guillotine; and these records, addressed to posterity, are touching even beyond their own intrinsic pathos, when we realise the fact that they were written, by a doomed woman, in the Shadow of Death.

She felt the urgency and the hurry of her task. She knew the conditions under which, if achieved at all, it had to be completed; and we can feel how rapidly her fleet pen flew over the patient paper. 'The last infirmity of noble minds,' weighed upon her, and impelled her to secure the record of her life as an appeal to history, before the impending night came in which she could no longer work. Immersed in the thoughts and memories upon which writing such as hers is based, she forgets for a time the Piombi which are closing round her; and old loves, and old antipathies, flash through her mind with all the vividness of the olden time of freedom and of safety. She tells us that she wrote three hundred pages in twenty-two days. What pen was ever more pitilessly driven under the impulse of a danger which was certain, while the time at which it might fall was wholly, was most terribly uncertain? Her papers, as she wrote them, were confided to Champagneux and to Bosc, two faithful friends who obtained opportunities of visiting her in her prison. Champagneux, when himself arrested, thought it necessary, for his own safety, as well as for that of Madame Roland, to destroy a portion of her 'Notices Historiques;' but something was saved. The manuscripts confided to Bosc were well preserved, and they are those which now we read. Both Bosc and Champagneux published, after her death, memoirs in vindication of her fame. The work of Bosc appeared in 1795; that of Champagneux in 1800. These two men were the first that appealed in her behalf to history, and to the judgment of the after-time. Bosc's book was 'imprimé au profit de sa' (Madame Roland's) 'fille unique, priveé de la fortune de ses père et mère.' We may hope that the unfortunate Eudora derived benefit from a publication which reflected honour upon her murdered mother. The confiscation of the property of M. and of Madame Roland does not seem ever to have been reversed. Following the course of her own narrative, and availing ourselves of the labours of later editors, we may now essay to construct some image of the life and death, and of the full space between birth and death, of this extraordinary woman, with her rare gifts, her noble character, and her tragic end.

Marie Jeanne Phlipon was born in Paris, 18th March 1754. Her father was one Gratien Phlipon, a small engraver, who combined with that pursuit occasional excursions into a speculative trade in jewellery; and her mother was one Marguérite Bimont. This couple had seven children, out of which six died in infancy, mostly when put out to nurse, and Marie Jeanne, who was also 'at nurse' till she was two years old, was the only child that survived early childhood. She says of her father, 'Ou ne peut pas dire que ce fût un homme vertueux;' and as our narrative progresses, we shall find cause to agree with her estimate of M. Phlipon. Of her mother, Madame Roland records that she 'avec beaucoup de bonté avait de la froideur.' The young girl was never in full sympathy with her father; but for her mother she felt a strong affection; and all Madame Roland's feelings were always strong and tenacious. Her childhood and early youth were, on the whole, happy. Born in a family of the smaller *bourgeoisie*, in the day of sharp distinctions between classes, she saw intimately the interior of French burgher life; and with an almost unconscious bitterness, she just felt and touched the rim of the insolent, empty, pretentious hangers-on of aristocracy. She witnessed the negligent, scornful injustice and oppression of the French privileged classes of the years during which the coming revolution was silently germinating. She speaks of herself as combining, when a child, une si grande politesse avec quelque dignité; and in her little domestic errands to greengrocers, and the like, she impressed the tradespeople with astonishment at her dignified courtesy. However she might afterwards dislike aristocracy as a French institution, the little girl was by instinct a born aristocrat, with superiority of character softened by grace and refined by noble manners.

As a child, she could be a little obstinate and self-willed, but she was of a generous nature, and was easily touched and won by kindness. The young girl had a most active and inquiring mind, full of distinction and of force, and she was singularly eager for self-culture. She seems to have had early a sense of superiority to her surroundings, and a tendency to retreat alone into her own thoughts and dreams. She read much, and had some dislike for domestic avocations. She says, 'Mon premier besoin était de plaire et de faire du bien.' She was benevolent and charitable ; and she records that the child which read with avidity all the serious books that she could get hold of, was also the best dancer among her young companions. She had originally a fervid religious tendency, which, like all her feelings, was strong and deep. If her own account of her religious ardour read sometimes as if her devotion had been somewhat sickly and affected, it must be borne in mind that such an impression is created by the account written in later life by a Pagan (with just an occasional flicker of conjectural deism) who half scorned a feeling which, while it lasted, was undoubtedly fervent and sincere.

When eleven years and two months old, she astonished her parents by expressing a determined desire to retire for a year into a convent, in order to prepare herself fitly for her first communion. They consented, and she entered (7th May 1765) the convent of Les Dames de la Congrégation, Rue Neuve Saint Étienne, Fabourg de Saint Marcel, an institution situated very near to the prison de Ste Pélagie, in which she wrote her narrative of the event. In the convent she was happy, full of religious fervour, and very successful in all her examinations. Her remarkable ability was fully recognised, and she formed two enduring female friendships with Sophie and Henriette Cannet. She issued from her year of seclusion, and tells us, 'J'avais pourtant le secret dessein de me consacrer à la vie religieuse;' but, being an only child, she could not carry out her purpose, and returned to the world—and to her books.

Reading and thought led to doubt, and doubt darkened to denial. She could not reconcile with her idea of a beneficent Deity the doctrine of the eternal punishment of so many weak and ignorant creatures; and she adds, 'Du moment où tout Catholique à fait ce raisonnement, l'église (Romaine) peut le regarder comme perdu pour elle.' Her first doubt was noble; and it must be remembered that she, like Voltaire, was placed in close juxtaposition with 'L'Infame.'

She became a philosopher, passing, with her wonted ardour, from one set of opinions to the other. Many fluctuations of feeling tended more and more strongly in the direction of scepticism; and it is a characteristic evidence of her change of views that she took to church, in place of her mass book, Dacier's Plutarch.

In proportion as she leaned to denial she turned toward Republicanism. Like her contemporaries,

Madame Roland was deeply attracted by Roman history and by the civic virtues of many of its heroes. Plutarch and Tacitus were her favourite writers; and she indulged in a wide course of miscellaneous reading. Schaftesbury (*sic*) and Thompson (*sic*) were her best loved English authors; and, becoming 'esprit fort et femme savante,' she read with enthusiasm Helvetius and Didérot, Rousseau and Voltaire. The 'Candide' of Voltaire and the 'Nouvelle Helöise' of Rousseau were well known to her. She admired Louvet and his 'Faublas.' Of this licentious writer she remarks, 'Les gens de lettres, et les personnes de goût connaissent ses jolis romans, où les graces de l'imagination s'allient à la légèreté du style; au ton de la philosophie, au sel de la critique.' Truly a wide range of reading for a young French girl of the eighteenth century! Rousseau's 'Confessions' appeared in 1788, and seem to have furnished her with a model for her own 'Mémoires.' She writes of herself with singular frankness and naïveté, and does not shun some subjects upon which a woman might well be reticent.

Thus she paints herself in youth, 'À quatorze ans, comme aujourdhui, j'avais environ cinq pieds ; ma taille avait acquis toute sa croissance ; la jambe bien faite, le pied bien posé ; les hanches très relevées ; la poitrine large et superbement meublée ; les epaules effaceés ; l'attitude ferme et gracieuse, la marche rapide et légère ; voila pour le premier coup d'œil.'

She speaks of her own 'sourire tendre et séducteur.' She adds later, 'Les evenements du mariage me parurent aussi surprénants que désagréables,' adding some further particulars which we will not quote. She records, ' La volupté—je doute que jamais personne fût plus faite pour elle et l'ait moins goutée.' The austerity of Roman manners, as she conceived them, was set before her mind as a model of conduct; and both purity and pride assisted her to control to virtue a sensual temperament—a merit surely great in a woman of her day, who had such a husband—and such a lover!

Fond of self-analysis, and immersed in reflection, high-hearted, ardent, ambitious; devoted to ideals, she felt herself a 'femme d'élite,' and was not without presentiments of a destiny, stormy indeed, but illustrious. Whatever lower inclinations she may have had, she could subdue them; too proud to yield, except ideally, to passion, she would not descend from the heights of purity to the baseness of sensuality; she could not stoop to an illicit 'liaison.' Her name, her reputation, remain stainless and above reproach. Many looked up to her and leaned upon her. Shame she would not know, and she cared for reputation. Her will was firm, and her character was strong, sometimes almost hard; though she is linked to our affections by some of the vanities, the weaknesses even, of woman. With her, the woman was the pedestal upon which to erect the heroine, and she won the place which she deserved in history.  A fair woman flushed with feeling, living in a most grim time, she triumphed over all that was base in herself, or in her times, and her name survives as that of a woman pure, generous, and lofty.

In her girlhood, she ardently desired marriage; but her ideal was high, and she would not marry trivially or unworthily.  Full of sensibility, she was sustained by sentimentalism; but her instincts were noble, and her impulses ambitious. Genius is proud as well as modest, and she had the unrest of superiority, the ardour of conviction, and self-devotion to some ideal life.  A wanton she could never be.  Not one of her portraits pleased her,—'Parceque j'ai plus d'âme que de figure.'  She was right in thinking that her greatest beauty lay in expression; and expression is mastered only by master-painters.  To make a perfect portrait of her, two pictures should have been painted—the one representing her in repose, the other in excitement.  The woman tells us frankly,—' Je plais généralement.'  The flippant Camille Desmoulins wondered that 'avec si peu de beauté,' she had so many admirers.  She is constrained to differ from him.  'Il faut qu'on me distingue et me chérisse; cela ne manque guère quand en me voit souvent, et qu'on a du bon sens et un cœur.'  She can estimate her own value, and says, scornfully, that Camille could only have seen her once or twice, and that she would certainly be cold and stiff towards him.

Madame Roland narrates, with great complacency, that she had, as a young girl, a perfect crowd of suitors. Apart from her own attractions, which were great, she was an only child, and her father was supposed to be well to do as a successful tradesman. Her admirers, according to French custom, did not declare themselves to the young lady direct, but addressed their suits to the father; and Madame Roland describes how she dictated to her parent the letters of refusal which she induced him to write. Her suitors were, naturally, of her own 'bourgeois' order, and not one of the many had for her any strong attraction, though a certain La Blancherie stirred her fancy without succeeding in touching her heart. Among these 'pretendans' we find a butcher and a barrister; the butcher pecunious, if vulgar, the barrister without business and without brains. The mother of the young girl was in failing health, and saw with dismay this wholesale rejection of all offers of marriage. Madame Phlipon argued seriously with the haughty daughter who showed herself so inexorable to lovers. 'Do not refuse a husband,' cried the mother; 'my health is failing. Let me see you secure in the refuge of marriage; think of the happiness it may bring to you!' 'Oui, maman, un bonheur comme le vôtre!' replied the daughter. Now Madame Phlipon was not a happy wife. Of her husband, ' ou ne peut pas dire que ce fût un homme vertueux.' During his wife's illness he became very playful, and sought compensations away from home. Under pretext of stepping out for five minutes to the 'Café,' he remained away from home for times of lengthening duration. When her mother died, the daughter was plunged into the deepest grief ; but the widower was reasonable. He pointed out that the ways of Providence were generally creditable, and that, in the instance before them, peculiar sagacity had been shown, since the defunct had fulfilled the purposes of her life, and was no longer of any use. His daughter dreaded a stepmother ; but M. Phlipon, like George II., could, after the loss of a wife, manage to get on with mistresses, and the good man speedily selected one, and so earned his daughter's gratitude and approval. Her mother dead, Jeanne-Marie plunged even more deeply than before into the reading of many books, and she pursued music, which, indeed, she had always loved, with increasing ardour.

But to Madlle. Phlipon marriage came at last. She had not found her ideal in love ; her tentatives of passion, of affection, of ambition, had all failed her. She would not marry men of her own rank, men 'dans le commerce ;' and at five-and-twenty, in spite of feeling 'des sens très inflammables,' she married, 4th February 1780, M. Roland de la Platière, he being then forty-six years of age. He had known her for five years before he proposed.

M. Phlipon not unnaturally regarded M. Roland as an unsuitable husband for his bright and brilliant daughter, and, at first, treated M. Roland's proposals with great scorn.

But Jeanne-Marie was determined, and had a clear will of her own. When M. Phlipon failed in business, and fell into poverty, he was supported by the son-in-law whom he had regarded with aversion and treated with insult.

The marriage was one of the head and not of the heart. The twenty-one years' difference in age was not in itself a very great matter; but the personality and the character of the 'vénérable époux' were antagonistic to any suggestion of romance, to any idea of love. Madame Roland speaks of 'sa gravité, ses mœurs, ses habitudes, toutes consacrées au travail, me le faisaient considérer, pour ainsi dire, sans sexe, où comme un philosophe qui n'existait que par la raison.' She knew her own objects, but she was under no illusions; and she felt, with keen insight, that, after such a marriage, she might meet with a man who could stir her passion and touch her heart. She did meet with such a man, who even became her lover; but, under the wise governance of her reason, she would discharge duty where she could not give love; and she would use her marriage to subserve her ambition and to afford her a position in which she could render service to humanity. The marriage reminds us somewhat of that entered upon by the nobly erring Dorothea with the loathsome Casaubon. Roland had a pedantry equal to his probity—which latter was great. He was a solemn coxcomb, dictatorial, with all the assumption of a barren philosopher. He was cold, stiff, formal, and required a secretary, a housekeeper—and a blind, deferential worshipper of his talents. He was wealthy and well-placed; Inspector of Manufactories under Government; and had some pretensions to be of respectable old family. He was tall, meagre, bony, with a very yellow complexion, rather bald, with a head 'déjà peu garni de cheveux.' He was pompous, worrying, exacting, and formal. Surely his wife must have seen Othello's visage in his mind; and she may have overrated a mind which was, behind its pretensions, profoundly mediocre. It was a marriage of reason, of duty, and of 'convenance.'

M. Roland was opinionated and dogmatic. His wife records that 'Il tenait si bien à ses opinions, que je n'ai acquis qu'après assez long-temps la confiance de le contrédire.' What spiritual slavery for so bright a spirit! She respected him; she served and aided him; she had a conjugal friendship for him; but of love there could be no question. The advantage to him of such a wife was simply incalculable. She thought for him, worked for him, wrote for him. She enabled him to become minister, and she made his house the most intellectual and most charming in Paris. In his obscure niche in history, he is sustained by the tender hand of a woman, devoted to her duty, immortal in her nobleness, sublime in her heroism, resplendent in her genius, tragic in her destiny. The first few years of marriage were spent in the provinces. Madame Roland's daughter Eudora, her only child, was born at Amiens. They lived at Lyons, and at the Clos de la Platrière. In 1784, Roland solicited, but in vain, 'des lettres de noblesse.' She lived for a time contentedly in the peace and seclusion of the country; she studied, played, and read; she was exemplary in the discharge of all the duties of a mother and a wife; she was kind and charitable to all her poorer neighbours; but at length she began to feel, restlessly, that she was rusting in obscurity. Perhaps, too, the virtuous Roland, lived with in so narrow a circle, may have become unendurable. She followed with interest public events, and began to worship a seeming goddess that was to turn out an adulteress that would hunt for the precious life. For a time she truly loved the country, but when public events aroused her, when ambition began to stir within her, she speaks contemptuously of 'la vie cochonne de la campagne,' and she yearns for Paris. A woman with an empty heart, she longed to plunge into politics. She had confidence in her own genius; she ardently desired the welfare of her country, and with a vast, vague yearning, she adored liberty.

'La revolution survint, et nous enflamma; amis de l'humanité, adorateurs de la liberté, nous crûmes qu'elle venait regénerer l'espéce ..... nous l'accueillîmes avec transport.' 'Le sévère Roland' sympathised with her tendencies, if he could not fully share her aspirations. They burned their ships behind them, and went to Paris—to that Paris which she should only quit upon its revolutionary scaffold. Farewell the quiet life of country calm, of peaceful study, of homely joys! Henceforth, until its end, the life of Madame Roland has merged into the Revolution. 'Les moments de crise produisent un redoublement de vie chez les hommes,' says Chateaubriand. Meanwhile, in the winter of 1787-88, M. Phlipon had died, supported during his last years by his daughter and his son-in-law; and, in 1784, the Rolands had visited England. What Madame Roland says of us is so flattering, that it is worth transcribing :—'Allez, croyez que tout individu qui ne sentira point d'estime pours les Anglais, et un tendre interêt mêlé d'admiration pour leurs femmes, est un lâche, ou un étourdi, ou un sot ignorant qui parle sans savoir.'

They arrived in Paris 20th February 1791.

On 2d April Mirabeau died. The flight of the royal family to Varennes occurred on 20th June. The Convention of Pilnitz met on August 25-27; and Leopold II., Fredrick Wilhelm II., with certain minor potentates, and the emigrant Princes of the Blood, think that the position of Louis XVI. calls upon other Governments for interference. The Constitution is finished, and accepted by the King, 14th September. Legislative

Assembly meets October 1. Massacres in the Ice Tower occurred in October. The country, distracted by anxieties about foreign attack, and by doubts whether France were in a position to meet it. The whole nation agitated, suspicious, turbulent. Meanwhile the Revolution is growing. Such was the Paris into which the Rolands entered.

It was a time that might well develop patriotism into passion; and ardent spirits, indignant at the long rule of imposture, might well hope all things for the State and for humanity, might well yearn for liberty, and might, innocently, further that revolution which, ' sous prétexte de liberté, engendre la tyrannie.' The politics of Madame Roland were, in the main, the politics of noble ideas; but it is difficult to separate, in action, the politics of ideas from the struggles of faction, and from the lust of power; and a woman, immersed in the struggle, may become bitter, vindictive, even cruel. Madame Roland was filled with a hatred of the Court and of Marie Antoinette. Her detractors, as M. de St Amand, allege that her motive was the mere envy of ' la parvenue qui ne sera jamais une grande dame.' This is not just; but it is a curious speculation to think what Madame Roland might have been had she been born an aristocrat, had she taken part in the Trianon fêtes, had she felt the glamour and the grace of the fair young Queen in her day of splendour and of charm. Assuredly such altered circumstances would have produced different feelings—perhaps even a loyal and devoted attachment to the fair woman on a throne. ' As it was, Madame Roland desired, I fear, 'deux têtes illustres.' Lamartine (Cours de Littérature) says, ' Elle anime les Girondins, ses familiers, d'une haine implacable contre la Reine, déjà si humilieé et si menacée ; elle n'a ni respect, ni pitié pour cette victime . . . . elle enflait un mari vulgaire du souffle de sa colère de femme contre une cour odieuse, parce qu'elle ne s'ouvrait pas à sa vanité de parvenue.' Lamartine is fond of rhetorical exaggeration, and the above passage is exaggerated ; but Madame Roland was in power when Marie Antoinette was in the Temple, and the woman of genius certainly felt no pity for the sufferings of the woman born in the purple. No theoretical objection to royalty in the abstract can excuse ungenerous or unwomanly feeling or action toward Marie Antoinette as a woman, as a mother, and a wife. Most queenlike when discrowned, the long agony of Marie Antoinette, the hapless daughter of the Cæsars, showed her, in deep sorrow and sore humiliation, in the very royalty of womanhood. The only excuse for Madame Roland is the bitterness of feeling engendered by a time of fever, hatred, and revenge.

And oh, the whirligig of mocking time! The Queen and Madame Roland occupied the next cells in the Conciergerie, and Marie Antoinette and Jeanne-Marie were executed with an interval of only twenty-three days between their deaths!

When first she arrived in Paris, Madame Roland followed the incidents of the revolution 'avec un intérêt difficile à imaginer. Je courus aux scéances.' She little foresaw how very soon her enthusiasm would change to disgust, to horror, to indignation. Strict, elderly Roland, methodic, rigid, respectable— 'un Quaker endimanché,' was twice minister, and his position offered a career to a wife so immeasurably his superior. Roland owed his position as minister to Brissot, who wanted a laborious and exact coadjutor in office. A fair administrator, Roland would have been, in ordinary times, a decent, honest, head-clerk; but in the Revolution he was swamped and lost. When first (24th March 1792) the virtuous man received the portfolio of the Interior, he presented himself at Court in republican insolence—in shoe-strings instead of buckles. The outraged usher called Dumouriez's attention to the scandal, and the mocking hero of Jemmappes replied, 'Tout est perdu!'

She had opportunity of studying, though through jaundiced eyes, the King and Queen, and her fine feminine pen — always fine, even when her prejudice misled her judgment—records of them in her 'Mémoires':—'Louis XVI., toujours flottant entre la crainte d'irriter ses sujets, la volonté de les contenter, et dans l'incapacité de les gouverner . . . . Toujours proclamant, d'une part, le maintien de ce qu'il faisait saper de l'autre, sa marche oblique et sa conduite fausse excitérent d'abord la defiance, et finirent par allumer l'indignation.'

Her penetrating woman's insight detects the weakness of the well-meaning fatuous King. Had he been a soldier, had Mirabeau lived, had Louis not dismissed Dumouriez—might not the fate of the monarchy have been different? We record with less pleasure her description of the ill-fated Queen. She says the King was 'entrainé par une étourdie, joignant à l'insolence autrichienne la présomption de la jeunesse, l'ivresse des sens, l'insouciance de la légèreté, seduite elle-même par tous les vices d'une cour asiatique, auxquels l'avait trop bien préparée l'example de sa mère.'

The Hôtel of the Minister of the Interior had been rendered splendid by the taste of Calonne, and in this palace Madame Roland reigned. The daughter of Phlipon, the bankrupt engraver, may well have felt some exultation as she moved, a queen, among those handsome rooms; and yet dearer to her than any magnificence was the power for good which, as she thought, her position gave her.

The party of 'la Gironde' then comprised the noblest politicians of the Revolution; men of talent, of character, ardent for liberty, impassioned for humanity; they were orators, were patriots, and were a power. To this party Madame Roland and her husband naturally attached themselves; and she became the soul and inspiration of the party, the life and impulse of their deeds and words. Yet never did she exceed the fine limits of feminine reserve and womanly modesty. She never seemed to rule; her influence was felt, but she assumed no pride of place or power.

She always sought to efface herself in favour of 'le sévére Roland.' His celebrated 'Letter to the King' was her work. She records of her complacent husband, 'Il finissait souvent par se persuader que véritablement il avait été dans une bonne veine l'orsqu'il avait écrit tel passage qui sortait de ma plume.' This little passage, touched with a subtle satire, is curiously characteristic of the pedantic minister and of his able wife. She was always ready to spare his 'amour propre' by retreating behind him when she had done his work; but she left—until she wrote her 'Mémoires'—all the credit to the minister; and he was ready to receive all the praise.

Around them—around her, their Egeria—gathered the young and noble, the pure and ardent of the great Gironde party. She was surrounded by a group of distinguished men—and admirers; as Buzot, Barbaroux, Brissot, Lanthenas, Louvet, Gorsas, de Bancal, Bosc, and many others. Dumouriez said of them: 'They are exiled Romans. The republic, as they understand it, is but the romance of a woman of mind. They are about to intoxicate themselves with fine speeches, while the people will get drunk with blood.' Ah, that getting drunk with blood! Is the

Revolution coming to that? 'In revolutions,' said Danton, 'victory remains with the most wicked.' Will the Girondins be wicked enough to secure victory? They dreamt—under *her* inspiration—of a moderate, firm, incorruptible, ideal Republic; noble, clement, beneficent.

Plutarch was their model—Perfectibility was their illusion—Ruin was their reward. While Madame Roland was minister, she had, beside 'soirées intimes,' twice a week, in her 'hôtel,' dinner parties, at which covers were usually laid for fifteen guests. The hour of dinner was five; and one singularity of these banquets consisted in the fact that, beside Madame Roland herself, no woman was ever present at them. She did not care for 'society,' visited little, and preferred men to her own sex.

Among the constant 'habitués' of Roland's 'hôtel' we find Brissot, Barbaroux, Louvet, Buzot; but all patriotic talent is sure of a welcome from Madame Roland, were it only to test and try men who seem likely to play an important part in that Revolution which tends ever to become more and more mad. Hence Robespierre and Danton are to be discerned among the guests of the fair hostess. Robespierre comes chiefly in consequence of his own request to be invited. He was at first unimportant, and was always repulsive; but Madame Roland generously patronised an obscure but determined deputy, and does not then foresee what warrant that mean-souled

atrabiliar Robespierre will one day sign. Madame
Roland thought him honest :—'Je lui pardonnais en
faveur des principes son mauvais langage et son
ennuyeux débit.' With her, in this case, careless
generosity overrides native insight. Of Danton's face
she says,—'Je n'ai jamais rien vu qui caractérisât si
parfaitement l'emportement des passions brutales, et
l'audace la plus étonnante, demi-voileé par l'air d'une
grande jovialité, l'affectation de la franchise, et d'une
sorte de bonhomie.' Her fine woman's pen recognises the audacity, the brutality, the power of this
debauched, corrupt, bloodthirsty Titan of the Revolution ; but Madame Roland thus paints Danton after
they had become bitter—even deadly—enemies. But
victory remains with the most wicked. Are there
not Marat and Robespierre? The Dantonists shall
succeed the Girondins in the same cells of the Conciergerie. Danton fluctuated for some time between the
Montagne and the Gironde. Perhaps he was repelled
from the Gironde by the subtle scorn shown for him
by Madame Roland. 'They do not trust me,' he said.
He held aloof from the party, and threw his thunder-
voice, his prodigious power, and his ruthless reckless-
ness into the scale of La Montagne.

A fair woman flushed with feeling in the wild
excitement of a raging time, Madame Roland towers
aloft above that roaring sea of a mad democracy, and
seems to guide the whirlwind and direct the storm.
But she, like so many mortals, works blindly, and

contributes unwittingly to the despotism of Marat and of Robespierre, to the massacres of September, to the horrors of the Terror, and to the doom of her party and herself.

Distinctive among her many fine qualities is a bright, high clearness of mind, of heart, of soul; and this is coupled with a calm courage which rises above ordinary heroism. She was effluent of light; she radiated conviction and enthusiasm. Tender she was—but sentimental, never. This high-hearted Pagan woman is always noble. Full herself of ardour for the cause which she held to be holy, she could inspire others with her own lofty purpose. She was able to sorrow, to suffer, to endure unto the death; and she could say, with Brutus,—

> Set honour in one eye and death i' the other,
> And I will look on both indifferently.

She did prefer honour to life; and her high ideals uplifted her above all dread of death. When she thought that the example of her undeserved death might benefit the country that she loved so well, she deliberately accepted, with loftiest courage, the red death of the horrible scaffold of the Revolution. 'The greatest human effort is to wait;' and she could wait through five months of woeful captivity, through the long, long nights in a dreary dungeon, for the bitter end of a noble life of thirty-eight long but intense years.

'Love feareth death,' sings Mrs Browning; and

Madame Roland, like Marie Antoinette, had ties of love that added to the bitterness of death; but she had a proud, defiant fortitude; and yet the willing victim seldom quailed or faltered. Impassioned, ardent, vivacious; with the eloquence of enthusiasm and the influence of example; touching in her sweetness, flaming with her force, she imparted impulse and supplied ideas to the noblest party of the Revolution. Her beauty, flushing with excitement, lighting up with elevated sentiment and sanguine hope for humanity, rendered her the goddess and the martyr of a noble cause and of a glorious dream.

But a sad shadow fell upon her high and ardent hopes. The sceptre began to fall from the hand of her once puissant party, and was seized by Danton, Robespierre, Marat.

'Eloquence, Philosophism, Respectability avail not. Silent, like a queen with the asp on her bosom, sits the wife of Roland. They (the Girondins) wanted a Republic of the Virtues, wherein they themselves should be head; they got only a Republic of the Strengths, wherein others than they were heads.' Victory was to remain with men more wicked than they.

It is sad to read in Madame Roland's retrospect of that time the melancholy with which her noble soul recognises how vain her labours had been—how futile had become her lofty hopes. Her disenchantment was deep as her ardour had been high. It is worth while to extract a few characteristic passages from her 'Mémoires.'

'Vous connaissez mon enthousiasme pour la revolution ; eh bien ! j'en ai honte, elle est devenue hideuse.'

. . . . . . . . .

'Vouloir conduire à la liberté un peuple sans mœurs, qui blaspheme Dieu, et adore Marat, c'est la plus absurde folie.'

. . . . . . . . .

'Le peuple n'est plus fait pour rien sentir que la joie cannibale de voir couler du sang, qu'il ne court pas de risque de répandre.'

'Nôtre gouvernement est une espéce de monstre, dont les formes et l'action sont également révoltantes ; il detruit tout ce qu'il touche, et se dévore lui-même : ce dernier excés fut l'unique consolation de ses nombreuses victimes.'

. . . . . . . . .

'L'histoire peindra-t-elle jamais l'horreur de ces temps affreux, et les hommes abominables qui les remplissent de leurs forfaits? Ils outrepassent les cruantés de Marius, les sanguinaires expéditions de Sylla.'

. . . . . . . . .

'Mais à quoi peut-on comparer la domination de ces hypocrites qui, toujours revêtus du masque de la justice, toujours parlant le langage de la loi, ont crée un tribunal pour servir leur vengéance, et envoient à l'échafaud, avec des formes juridiquement insultantes, tous les hommes dont la vertu les offense' (the Girondins) ' dont les talents leur font ombrage, ou dont les richesses excitent leur convoitise? Quelle Babylone présenta jamais le spectacle de ce Paris, souillé de sang, et de debauches, gouverné par des magistrats qui font profession de débiter le mensonge, de vendre la calomnie, de préconiser l'assassinat? Quel peuple a jamais corrompu sa morale, et sou instinct, au point de contracter le bésoin de voir les supplices, de frémir de rage quand ils sont rétardés, et d'être toujours prêt à exercer sa ferocité sur quiconque entreprend de de l'adoucir ou de la calmer?'

. . . . . . . . . . .

' Ce qu'on appelle, dans la Convention, la Montagne, ne présente que des brigands, vêtus et jurant comme les gens du port, préchant le meurtre, et donnant l'exemple du pillage.'

. . . . . . . . . . .

In these utterances, we have not only opinion but evidence. Madame Roland knew thoroughly that Revolution which she had helped to further, until its excesses and its crimes left her far behind it.

Her view of the Revolution cannot have been unfairly warped by the fact that it had imprisoned her; because an imprisonment so unjust was in itself an act of accusation against the Revolution. She was, of course, a contemporary; she knew all the men in power, and she was well acquainted with every step taken in the furious and bloody march of events. She writes, in prison:—'La femme de Roland, rappelée de temps en temps, par les soins du Père Duchêsne, à la fureur de la populace, en attend les derniers excés dans la même prison d'ou une fille entretenue sort tranquille après avoir payé sa sûreté, et l'impunité de son complice, fabricateur de faux assignats.'

She said, and she in her own person proved the truth of the saying, that 'Les individus qu'on envoie au tribunal revolutionnaire, ne sont pas des accusés qu'on lui donne à juger ; ce sont les victimes qu'il est chargé de faire punir.'

She speaks the 'dernier mot' of history when, describing the rule of the Revolution during the Terror, she exclaims that it was ' Un gouvernement cent fois plus atroce que le despotisme même sur les ruines duquel il s'est élevé.'

To such results do such Revolutions lead. The fire which burned up Imposture was palled in the dunnest smoke of hell. The noblest and best, those who passionately and purely desired liberty, became the victims of the Revolution when that commenced to devour its own children. Victory remained longest with the basest and the wickedest; until outraged humanity, after destroying Robespierre, submitted to military despotism as something better than godless and lawless revolutionary ferocity and outrage.

Alike by temperament and character, by position

and opportunity, Madame Roland, the heroine of the Revolution, was well fitted to understand and to characterise the monster that she, to her sorrow, had helped to create. It was her intention, had she lived, to have written a history of the French Revolution.

Meanwhile the Revolution marched and trod in blood. The 10th August (1792), was the day of the fall of the monarchy and the massacre of the Swiss. The loss of these brave lives was due to the hesitation and the incapacity of the weak King. Napoleon, surely a good judge, said afterwards that a little conduct and courage would have given victory to the Royalists. Pity only to see the noble Queen dragged down through insult to death by so contemptible a husband and a King!

The breach between the Girondins and the Jacobins had widened. The 'Legal' Republicans were opposed by the Unlimited Sansculottes. At the trial of the King (December 11-16) the Gironde made a last bid for power, for the popularity which was passing to the Mountain. They refused to be outbidden, outstripped in the competition for the favour of the populace, and, against their convictions, they voted for the death of Louis. That which the Jacobins desired, the Girondins accomplished, and it was their votes which turned the scale. In an Assembly of 721 voters, death, without appeal, was carried by 7 votes—that is, was carried by La Gironde—the 'Pilates of the Monarchy;' but their immoral action did not uphold their power, or even save their lives. Danton, in his fierce scorn, cried, 'These are your orators! Sublime language and base conduct. What is to be done with such men? Don't talk of them to me. The party is destroyed!' and destroyed it was. The action of the Gironde exposed its weakness as a party; and its enemies were only the more bent upon its destruction.

On September 2, and onwards towards September 6 (1792), occurred the horrible massacres in the prisons. Marat suggested the idea; Danton furnished the butchers; Manuel supplied the victims. In the prisons of L'Abbaye, Les Carmes, Saint Firmin, La Force, Le Grand et le Petit Châtelet, La Conciergerie, Bicêtre, and La Salpetrière, the slaughter was continued during five days and five nights. The number of the paid butchers was 235; the number of victims no man now can reckon, but the lowest estimate would rate them at about 2000. The atrocities of these massacres are too fearful to be again recited. Edgar Quinet ('La Revolution') says,— 'Ce n'était pas une barbarie imprévue, aveugle, c'était une barbarie lentement meditée, curieusement étudieé, par un esprit de sang.' Madame Roland, with her noble indignation, records of these September butcheries:—'Je n'esperai plus que la liberté s'établit parmi des lâches, insensibles aux derniers outrages qu'on puisse faire à la nature.' The Assembly was inactive; La Gironde was silent. There was no interruption to a massacre of five days and five nights; there was no action taken, no protest raised.

During this frightful 'boucherie de chair humaine, chaque maison est inspecteé par les agents de la Commune. Un coup de marteau à la porte fait trembler. La denonciation d'un ennemi, d'une domestique, d'un voisin, suffit pour vous perdre. On ne respire plus!'

Strange! Is not this freed people under a reign of Liberty, Equality, Fraternity? And yet it dares not breathe for terror! Perhaps in the bad days of the old 'régime,' of aristocratic and royal oppression, there was no such terrible time? Noyadings by night, marriages of the Loire, massacres, executions, may, possibly, compose a tyranny more horrible than any that existed of old. Still, we have, at least, got a Revolution.

The blood of September rolls forever between La Gironde and La Montagne. That red flood cannot be bridged over; La Gironde will not pardon those massacres, and La Montagne will not pardon La Gironde for not pardoning. Hence the destruction of the latter party is resolved upon. Danton's loud scorn, Robespierre's stealthy hate, will extirpate the too virtuous Republicans. Marat perished (July 13th) by the hand of the 'angel of assassination,' Charlotte Corday.

Jacobin vengeance rose to the murder pitch. A swift decree is issued against La Gironde. Many deputies, as Guadet, Barbaroux, Buzot, Louvet, Pétion, escaped, and wandered, ruined and in dread of death, hunted and disguised, over France. Vergniaud, Brissot, and the remainder of the 'Twenty-Two,' are incarcerated for their death. Roland flies, and hides near Rouen.

Madame Roland, accused of no crime, of no offence, was suddenly arrested (31st May 1793) and was incarcerated in L'Abbaye; in which prison she occupied the cell which was also tenanted for so brief a time by Charlotte Corday. What a change! From the sumptuous hôtel of the minister to the little, bare, whitewashed cell of L'Abbaye; from troops of friends, to a grim jailor; from communing with and inspiring the beautiful, the brave, the noble, to solitary hours in the coarse, clanging prison! And she knew well what such imprisonment meant. She knew that the gaol was but the ante-chamber to the scaffold. Alone and helpless, she could realise what the end would be. She knew, too, the men in power; men ready to buy popularity at any price of blood; and she felt that Danton and Robespierre would not hesitate to sacrifice their former friend and patroness. She understood fully that mixture of tiger and of monkey which, according to Voltaire, is the basis of French character.

Ah, the first hours of incarceration must have been bitter even to brave Madame Roland! Her child was separated from her. Her husband and Buzot were flying for their lives. Her friends, her party, were to be exterminated, and her hopes and dreams in politics were all dispelled. Her vehement nature, quick to feel deeply, was never ignoble. Hers was not the mere mortification of a baffled partisan; but she felt shamed as a patriot, outraged as an idealist. She had hoped so much for and from France! We can fancy the depression of her first night in L'Abbaye. The dread of death would be to her the least of the sorrows that weighed upon her, and pressed her spirit down, amid the loneliness of that grim and cheerless dungeon.

And her friends, the arrested Girondins, were, as she soon knew, in the Conciergerie—the same prison which contained Marie Antoinette. Sorrow did not destroy the energy of Madame Roland. She could only see the heavens through thickly-barred windows; her room was mean and dirty; the accommodation miserable; but the 'concierge' was not inhuman, and she soon made her cell available for study and for decency:—' Sublimes illusions, sacrifices généroux, espoir, bonheur, patrie—adieu!' She felt the indignation of innocence, the courage of pride, the devotion of heroism; but she was also woman, and she was oppressed by the parting with her child, and by her fears for her country and her friends. They lent her an 'oreiller'—it must have been wet with her tears!

She wrote a protest to the 'Convention Nationale,'

but it remained unanswered. It was addressed to enemies who sought her life. Under the tyranny of Danton and of Robespierre no friend dared to plead for her or for any liberty.

After having been for twenty-four days immured in L'Abbaye, she was suddenly set at liberty. No cause had been assigned for her arrest; none was given for her discharge. Full of the joy of freedom, of the sense of recovered security, she flew to her old home; but when she had ascended four steps of the staircase she was, by a refinement of cruelty, rearrested, and conducted to the prison of Sainte Pélagie. Even her lofty courage almost failed before this shock. Sainte Pélagie was a prison of a lower sort than L'Abbaye. No provision was made for the support of prisoners, and she had to pay for everything—for food as for all other necessaries of life.

Madame Bouchaud, the wife of the gaoler, was touched by the noble resignation and sweet manners of the new captive; and while she could do so, she softened, so far as possible, the prison life of Madame Roland.

'J'ai besoin de me posséder parceque j'ai l'habitude de me régir;' and she soon ruled to submission the despair with which her second imprisonment at first overwhelmed her. She resumed her studies and commenced her 'Mémoires.' With an admirable calm courage, and a lofty disdain, she conquered the terrors of her lot; though she heard the populace shouting under her window, 'A la guillotine!' and listened to the hawkers crying, 'La grande visite du Père Duchêsne à la citoyenne Roland dans la prison pour lui tirer les vers du nez;' and she could hear also the terms, 'Reine Coco,' and 'Veille Guénon,' applied to her by the foul Hébert and his hoarse mob.

A proud woman, terribly in earnest, she underwent sufferings that outrage and insult womanhood. By heavens! 'tis pitiful to think of this splendid creature in Sainte Pélagie!

She entered Sainte Pélagie the 24th June; she remained there until 31st October 1793. At that date she was removed to La Conciergerie—a prison which was but the ante-chamber of the scaffold. Think of the long, long hours, of the crawling weeks, that this bright and active spirit spent in close confinement in Sainte Pélagie! She was the friend of all her fellow-prisoners; she was the soul of the prison. Sublime in her uncomplaining sorrow, her heroism was not insensibility; for she would often, says Riouffe, sit for two or three hours leaning against the window and weeping bitterly. She had so many thoughts, such memories, so many and such deep feelings — and then what baffled hopes and vanished dreams of liberty!

One day, in some wayward mood, half of bitterness, half of sorrow, she wrote a letter to Robespierre with whom, as she well knew, her fate rested. The tone of her letter was proud. She would not ask for life; but yet, reading between the lines, we can detect a suppressed cry for mercy. Like Anne Boleyn, in her celebrated letter to Henry VIII., Madame Roland could not suppress feminine sarcasm, and a desire to irritate and to abase. This letter never met the bilious, bloodshot eyes of Robespierre. Could even he have refused to listen to such a covert appeal from such a woman—a woman who, in the day of her pride and power, had been so friendly to him when he was in such need of help? We cannot know. In a flush of haughty feeling, Madame Roland tore up her letter; but the pieces were preserved and put together; and this unsent letter, which might have changed so much, was never sent to Robespierre. He it was who signed the list for Fouquier Tuirville which contained the name of Madame Roland, and so sent her to certain death.

The cadaverous ambition, and the coward's hatred of Robespierre, could not leave in life a woman that he so dreaded and disliked. Her nobleness, her love of liberty, were qualities fatal to her when Robespierre had to decide upon her death or life. While in Sainte Pélagie, she heard of the execution of Marie Antoinette (Wednesday, October 16), but from Madame Roland, in her prison, this event elicited no word; and she heard also of the execution (October 31) of the Girondins, who sang the 'Marseillaise,' first in chorus, and then with one voice only, as the head of Vergniaud fell last. She learned the flight and sufferings of her proscribed friends; and she knew that her own end could not be far off. She began to be aweary of the sun. The readiness is all; and she was glad to die. When the Girondins perished, she despaired of her country. She thought that the example of her death might serve humanity. Sorrows, sufferings, death she could despise. She looked beyond them, to an immortality—of fame. 'He who fears not death starts at no shadows;' and she, a Pagan, rose to the full height of Christian courage under martyrdom. 'Les tyrans pevrent m'opprimer, mais 'm'avilir? jamais, jamais! . . . . Je puis tout defier; va, je vivrai jusqu'a ma dernière heure sans perdre un seul instant dans le trouble d'indignes agitations.'

And that last hour was at hand. Her tenderness bore its due proportion to the strength of her character; but it never sank to weakness. Her last anguish was the thought of 'Mon enfant, mon ami, mon époux;' but not even such a feeling could for an instant lessen or lower her full possession of the grandeur of her heroic soul. She is almost too great and strong to fully stir our compassion. We admire as much as we pity. She uplifts us to her own elevation; she is so strong, and clear, and calm, that we regard with wonder the spectacle of her splendid courage.

But the last scene is at hand.

She is in the 'Conciergerie,' and her doom is fixed.

She occupied in that fatal prison, for eight days, the next cell to that in which Marie Antoinette had been incarcerated.

' L'accusation porteé contre moi repose entièrement sur ma prétendue complicité avec des hommes appelés conspirateurs.' She knows that the men are not conspirators, but she has no hope of escaping her fate. The murder-bar of the revolutionary tribunal, where Fouquier Thinville dooms under the dictation of Robespierre, is no place that cares for innocence or guilt.

It is with a singular fascination of horror and of charm that we picture to our thought the few last days spent by this noble victim in her last prison.

In the terrible 'Conciergerie,' her cell was the asylum of peace and fortitude. When she descended into the great Gothic hall, in which all the prisoners met, her presence alone restored order and ensured calm. Everyone feared to displease her. Madame du Barry, imprisoned there at the same time, was treated with contempt. To the poor, Madame Roland gave money; to all she gave comfort, counsel, consolation, courage. She was worshipped in her last few days of life.

On the day of her first appearance before the tribunal (which sat above the common hall)—' Elle étoit vêtue avec une sorte de recherche. Elle avait une anglaise de mousseline blanche, garnie de blonde, et rattachée avec une ceinture de velours noir. Sa coiffure étoit soignée ; elle portoit un bonnet-chapeau d'une élégante simplicité, et ses beaux cheveux flottoient sur ses epaules. Sa figure me parut plus animée qu'à l'ordinaire. Ses couleurs étoient ravissantes ; elle avoit le sourire sur les lèvres.' A crowd of women pressed round her to kiss her robe. Everyone was in tears. But as Madame Roland disappeared, apparently unmoved, through the grating, she said only,—'Du courage !'

Comte Beugnot records,—'Je l'avois bien admirée dans les autres moments de sa vie, mais je ne l'appréciai comme il faut que sous les verrous. Quelle dignité elle avoit portée dans sa prison ! elle y étoit comme sur un trône.'

Madame Roland had chosen M. Chaurvau-Legarde as her counsel ; but she was convinced of the inutility of any advocate assistance, and she knew well that the man who should speak for her would incur serious danger for himself. Therefore when he saw her to consult with her about her defence, she absolutely refused his help, and said that, if he appeared at the 'trial' as her advocate, she would disavow him before the judges. 'Demain,' she said 'je n'existerai plus! Je sais le sort qui m'attend.' She drew from her finger a ring, and presented it to her courageous advocate.

She appeared before the Revolutionary Tribunal with serenity, composure, and perfect self-command. The chief judge was Claude-Emmanuel d'Obsent. Antoine Quintin Fouquier Thinville acted as 'accusateur public du tribunal criminel extraordinaire et revolutionnaire.' The result was a foregone conclusion.

The prosecutor asked eagerly where her husband, M. Roland, was. The brave and loyal wife replied,—'Qu'elle le sache ou non, elle ne doit ni le veut le dire.'

Her courage and composure remained unshaken, though at some of Fouquier Thinville's brutal questions the insulted woman wept. The evidence was mere mockery, but she scorned to address the Court. The sentence, dated 'le 18 du mois de Brumaire l'an 11 de la republique Française,' was—death within twenty-four hours.

This was 7th November 1793.

Marie Antoinette had been executed on 16th October—twenty-three days before Madame Roland. As Madame Roland descended into the great court of the prison, in which the prisoners were eagerly waiting for her, she drew her right hand across her throat, to intimate that she had been condemned to death. That action was the accepted sign in the Conciergerie. She appeared radiant, elated, triumphant. Never had prisoner, sentenced unjustly to a bloody death, exhibited such lofty exultation. She wrote in that last night on earth her 'dernières pensées,' which, in addition to the passionate address, meant to be understood of one alone, 'à toi que je n'ose nommer!' contain a most touching apostrophe to that young daughter to whom she wrote,—'Souviens toi de ta mère! Mon exemple te restera, et je sens que c'est un riche héritage.'

On 8th November 1793, at 4.30 P.M., on a dark November day, Madame Roland left the Conciergerie for the scaffold. In the same tumbril with her sat Simon-François la Marche, or Lamarque, who had been denounced and condemned for alleged plots tending to provoke civil war. Lamarche was thirty-five, therefore four years younger than Madame Roland. Both victims sat, with arms tightly bound, in the 'charrette,' which slowly rolled along the usual route by way of 'le Pont au Change, le quai de la Mégisserie,' the 'Rue St Honoré,' to the 'Place de la Revolution.' Lamarche did not excite much popular fury;—that was reserved for Madame Roland. She was 'baited with the rabble's curse,' insulted and outraged by obscene epithets and citations from Hébert, and passed along amid savage howls of 'À la guillotine!

Her death-ride was rendered terrible by the callous cruelty and devilish mockery so characteristic of a French mob. She remained superbly serene. The Spartan heroine of the Gironde never blenched as the tumbril passed through a ferocious, surging crowd which overwhelmed her with injuries. The very 'tricoteuses' of the guillotine could not disturb her lofty calmness. She, dying for no crime, passed to her sacrifice as to a crowning triumph and a regal victory. She was dressed in white, her robe 'parsemée de bouquets de couleur rose;' her long, dark hair flowed below her waist. An eye-witness, M. Tissot, tells us (Histoire de la Revolution) that, when he saw her pass, 'ses yeux lançoient de vifs eclairs, son teint brilloit de fraicheur et d'éclat : un sourire plein de charme erroit sur ses lêvres : cependant elle étoit sérieuse et ne jouoit pas avec la mort.' Her nature was too strong and calm for any levity, or affectation of levity, in that terrible hour. The tumbril passed by the former dwelling of her father at the corner of the 'Quai des Orfèvres et du Pont Neuf.' She gazed —with what feelings?—at the home of her youth, and of the dear dead that she was about to join.

Happily, her woman's tenderness was called forth by the pitiable state of Lamarche. As she was more than woman, so he was less than man. Overwhelmed by the terrors of the death so fast approaching, he succumbed to abject cowardice. She soothed, consoled, animated him. Her soft but penetrating voice gave him all the comfort of which his terror was capable. She had never seen him until they met in the 'charrette.' His fears could not infect her. Her humanity did assist him.

The vehicle stopped. It was backed against the ladder which led up to the platform of the high scaffold; from out of which arose the red upright posts, the cross-beam, and the triangular glaive of the hideous guillotine. Sanson usually executed women first, but Madame Roland, to spare her companion, forewent her privilege. 'Pouvez-vous'—she said to Sanson, who objected to a departure from rule and custom, 'pouvez-vous refuser à une femme sa dernière requête?' She watched and waited while poor Lamarche was beheaded. Then her turn came. With a fine, if unconscious irony, a colossal clay statue of Liberty was erected close to the permanent revolutionary scaffold. When she was strapped to the plank, she looked at this statue of satire, and said, 'O Liberté! comme on t'a jouée!' The plank fell into its place; the red-dripping blade descended rapidly —and Madame Roland had passed into the great mystery of Death. It is said—but the saying rests upon no good evidence—that she asked, when on the scaffold, for pen and paper to write down her last impressions; the story is improbable, as scaffolds are not often furnished with writing materials; but she may, on the road to death, have expressed some wish to record her last thoughts. Goethe says, 'Madame Roland, when on the scaffold, asked for writing materials to note down the singular thoughts that had occurred to her on her last journey. Pity that they were refused to her, because, at the end of life, thoughts come to the composed spirit which before were unthinkable. Such thoughts are like sacred dæmons, which descend shiningly upon the summit of the past.' It is certain that the report was widely circulated. If made, we can only echo Goethe's regretful wish.

A certain M. Bertin, a kind of George Selwyn, was an amateur of executions; and a man with this morbid propensity had unexampled opportunities, during the Revolution, for gratifying his tastes. He was a regular attendant on the scaffold, and he witnessed the execution of Madame Roland. M. Bertin remarks, 'Quand le couteau eut tranché la tête' (of Madame Roland), 'deux jets de sang énormes s'élancerent du tronc mutilé, ce qu'on ne voit guère : le plus souvent la tête tombe décolorée, et le sang, que l'émotion de ce moment terrible avoit fait refluer vers le cœur, jailloissoit foiblement, ou goutte à goutte.' M. Bertin means to argue that, owing to Madame Roland's unusual courage, her blood flowed in an unusual manner ; but, unfortunately, physiology does not support M. Bertin's theory. No supremacy of courage would alter the laws under which the blood circulates and flows. A few days after Madame Roland's death, LA FEUILLE DU SALUT PUBLIC announces to women 'un grand exemple'—the lessons being the execution of three women—

1 Marie Antoinette,
2 Olympe de Gouge,
3 Madame Roland.

The Queen is stigmatised as 'une épouse debauchée,' and the 'Feuille' adds,—'Son nom sera à jamais un horreur à la posterité,' a prediction which has been only imperfectly fulfilled. Of Olympe it is stated that 'La loi ait puni cette conspiratrice d'avoir oublié les vertus qui conviennent à son sexe.' The facts about this unfortunate creature were, that, animated by the pure vanity which creates a desire to be talked about, she had issued placards preaching concord between all parties and factions. The bloody answer was, to shear off her light head.

Of the 'femme Roland,' the 'Feuille' says that she 'fut un monstre sous tous les rapports. Sa contenance dédaigneuse envers le peuple, et les juges choisis par lui; l'opiniâtreté orgueilleuse de ses reponses, sa gaieté ironique, et cette fermeté dont alle faisait parade dans son trajet du Palais de Justice à la Place de la Revolution,' etc., etc. This was addressed 'aux Republicaines.' Madame Roland's courage and irony had evidently irritated as well as impressed the Revolutionary Tribunal. The news of her death reached two men for whom it had peculiar interest—her lover, and her husband.

Roland was in hiding—in danger of certain death if caught—at Rouen. Madame Roland predicted that he would destroy himself when he should hear of her execution; and on 15th November he started from his asylum, and, at a distance of about four leagues from Rouen, the miserable man perished, in a high Roman manner, by running on the blade of a swordstick. He committed suicide most effectually, as he appeared, when found, as if he were 'endormi.' On a piece of paper, found upon the corpse, was written, 'Non la crainte, mais l'indignation—J'ai quitté ma retraite au moment où j'ai appris qu'on alloit égorger ma femme : et je ne veux plus rester sur une terre couverte de crimes.' Such was the unhappy ending of the wretched ex-minister, who, as his great feat in life, had achieved so rare and high a wife.

The news of Madame Roland's death upon the scaffold produced a different and a stronger effect upon Buzot. He was thrown into a state of despair, which touched upon madness, and he remained for some days almost bereft of his senses. He was then in hiding for the dear life ;—hunted from place to place, in want, in misery, in danger. Upon receiving the fatal news, he wrote to M. Jérome Le Tellier,—'Elle n'est plus—elle n'est plus, mon ami! Les scélérats l'ont assassinée! Jugez s'il me reste quelque chose à regretter sur la terre!' Buzot, Petion, Barbaroux kept together in their retreat, but the details of their wretched wanderings are not well known. Half a league from Castillon, they came one day upon a local rustic 'fête,' and thought that they were recognised. Flying into a neighbouring pine-wood, Barbaroux tried to commit suicide with a pistol, but the ball broke his jaw without causing death. He was found, seized, and sent to Bourdeaux, where, mutilated as he was, he was at once flung upon the plank, and guillotined two days later, 20th July 1794. The dead bodies of Petion and of Buzot were found in a field, partially devoured by wild beasts—probably by wolves. They had, at least, escaped the guillotine. A month later, when the revulsion of 9 Thermidor, and the death of Robespierre occurred, these poor Girondins would have been safe ; because, when Robespierre fell, the suspected and proscribed were declared out of danger.

It has seemed good to follow the main current of Madame Roland's life and fortunes, without interrupting the narrative to dwell upon the episode of her life—her profound passion for Buzot—but now it may be in place to devote to this important matter the attention which it so amply merits.

Carlyle ('French Revolution,' chap. iii., Avignon) states that Barbaroux was the lover of Madame Roland ; but this statement, if a natural error, is yet wholly erroneous. Carlyle produced his history in 1837 ; the great discoveries of the correspondence of Buzot and of Madame Roland (discoveries to be more fully alluded to hereafter) were made in 1864.

François - Nicolas - Léonard Buzot was born at Evreux, 1st March 1760 (therefore was six years younger than Madame Roland), came to Paris, as 'Député du Départment de l'Eure,' and in Paris became acquainted with the Rolands. He was chosen deputy in 1792. He was attached, by ardent sympathy, to the party of the Gironde, and this sympathy increased when Madame Roland became the actual leader of this body of politicians. He arrived in Paris at the time of that ferment of ideas, of that passionate partisanship, which were the consequences of the Revolution. He was of a melancholy temperament, tender, sensitive, and of the highest courage. Born in another time, he might have been a poet; placed in the strain of his stormy day, he became, as an orator, the effective mouthpiece of Madame Roland. He was a devotee of justice as of liberty. He loved his country; he worshipped humanity; and the Revolution filled him with sanguine hopes for the future of both. Like most of the Girondins, he was an idealist in politics; like a poet, he found his ideal incorporated in Madame Roland. He was capable of passionate adoration for a woman; and he met the woman that he could, and did adore. With high thoughts seated in a heart of honour, he could love a woman almost desperately, and could yet love honour more. Madame Roland could descend to attract, but could yet never stoop to allure. Both were virtuous in the truest, in the most difficult sense; both could love to the height of highest natures, yet neither could succumb to vice, or become guilty of crime. Their love was noble and was pure. She had a daring, a defiant confidence in her own power to resist a temptation, which yet she felt to be terrible.

Hence the noble, ideal romance of the sad lives of these ill-fated lovers. She was capable of forbearance, of self-control, she had learned 'zu entsagen;' and Buzot was worthy of her. She was the nobler for her love; and he was three times less unworthy. Her vehement nature could not love without passion; but her pure, proud virtue could hold passion in a leash, and restrain it on this side of base indulgence. She loved with the soul rather than with the senses. She foresaw, when she wedded Roland, the possibility of some future passion, but she had a just confidence in her own virtue. Her virtue was individual—it was no part of her stormy and licentious day. Wandering thought was with her never translated into wanton action. She raised her lover to her own altitude, and so they loved ideally, intensely; but without reproach. No stain rests upon the fair fame of either. She could theorise, with the greatest freedom, upon the relations between the sexes—she could feel keenly her own unhappiness—but she would allow to her own conduct no licence. She was not squeamish, but she was essentially virtuous. She was unnaturally linked and tied to the miserable mediocrity of the pompous and venerable Roland; she felt all the love that woman can feel for Buzot; and yet she remained a loyal wife. Characteristically, Madame Roland informed her husband of her love for Buzot. She records,—'Mon mari n'a pu supporter l'idée de la moindre altération dans son empire.' But the thing was not to be altered or avoided, and Roland plunged more actively into politics. She adds,—'Il n'y avait pas parité' (between her husband and herself) 'il y avait de trop l'une ou l'autre de ces superiorités, un caractère dominateur et une différence de vingt années. Roland était doué de toutes les qualités qui commandent l'estime ; il lui manquait celles qui concilient la bienveillance.' Had she been able really to love Roland there would have been no passion for Buzot.

Buzot had a wife, of whom Madame Roland says,— 'Qui ne paroissoit point à son niveau, mais qui étoit honnête.' The poor woman might not be up to the level of her husband's character, but yet she might suffer from his passion for another greater woman. There is nowhere any record to be found of Madame Buzot's feelings. Buzot adopts the same attitude towards his wife that Madame Roland does towards her husband. Both lovers speak of their partners with 'respectful sympathy,' but with no warmer feeling. In the case of Madame Roland this standpoint was natural, or even necessary. Roland was her dreary father. Of him Lemontey says,—'Son mari ressomblait à un Quaker dont elle eût été la fille.' She was devoted to his health, his comfort, his career and reputation—but where was love? Her heart could hold no woman's love for the precise, dictatorial, elderly pedant. Not only his age, but also his character was against the virtuous man. As regards Buzot,—'Il avait la figure noble, la taille élégante.' He dressed well. He was finely courteous, graceful, sympathetic, and he had all the lovely and lofty qualities which could gain her respect and win her affection.

The nature and degree of their mutual passion may best be read in some extracts from those few letters, still extant, which she wrote to him during her long imprisonment, and which were, no doubt, found upon his corpse. These letters paint, with singular clearness, the strong woman and her strong love. Her style in these letters, as indeed in all her writings, is, broadly speaking, simple, sensuous, passionate.

The first is dated ' L'Abbaye, 22 Juin.' She speaks of letters from him which had reached her. ' Combien je les relis ! je les presse sur mon cœur, je les couvres de mes baisers ; je n'espérois plus d'en recevoir ! . . . .' Correspondence with friends was, for the prisoner, always uncertain and even unsafe.

'Quant à moi, je saurai subir les derniers excés de la tyrannie, de manière à ce que mon exemple ne soit pas non plus inutile . . . . Mort, tourmens, douleur, ne sont rien pour moi, je puis tout défier ; va, je vivrai jusqu'à ma dernière heure sans perdre un seul instant dans le treoble d'indignes agitations . . . . . mais ne vois tu pas aussi qu'en me trouvant seule c'est avec toi que je demeure ? Ainsi, par la captivité, je me sacrifie à mon époux, je me conserve à mon ami, il je dois à mes bourreaux de concilier le devoir et l'amour. Ne me plains pas ! '

If she owed it to her executioners to reconcile love and duty, would that duty, under happier circumstances, have resisted for ever the instincts of love?

'Va ! nous ne pouvons cesser d'être réciproquement

dignes des sentimens que nous nous sommes inspirés : on n'est pas malheureux avec cela. Adieu, mon ami ; mon bien-aimé, adieu !'

True woman! how she caresses with her pen the man that she loves.

The second letter is dated 3 Juillet. She says,—'Dis-moi, connois-tu des moments plus doux que ceux passés dans l'innocence et le charme d'une affection que la nature avoue et que règle la delicatesse, qui fait hommage au devoir des privations qu'il lui impose, et se nourrit de la force même de les supporter? Connois-tu de plus grand avantage que celui d'être supérieur à l'adversité, à la mort, et de trouver dans son cœur de quoi goûter, et embellir la vie jusqu'à, son dernier souffle ?—As-tu jamais mieux éprouvé ces effets que de l'attachment qui nous lie, malgré les contradictions de la société et les horreurs de l'oppression?'

. . . . . . . . .

'Va, je sens trop bien ce qui m'est imposé dans le cours naturel des choses pour me plaindre de la violence qui l'a détourné. Si je dois mourir—eh bien ! je connois de la vie ce quélle a de meilleur, et sa durée ne m'obligeroit peut-être qu'à de nouveaux sacrifices. . . . . . Je trouvois delicieux de réunir les moyens de lui être utile à une manière d'être qui me laissoit plus à toi. J'aimerois à lui sacrifier ma vie pour acquérir de donner à toi seul mon dernier soupir.' 'Lui' is, of course, Roland. Noble as is her sacrifice of love to virtue, there is yet something sinister and terrible in this tremendous conflict between passion and duty. Passion strains upon its leash almost to the breaking point. 'Puisse cette lettre te parvenir bientôt, te porter un nouveau témoignage de mes sentimens inaltérables, te communiquer la tranquillité que je goûte, et joindre à tout ce que tu peux éprouver et faire de généreux et d'utile le charme inexprimable des affections que les tyrans ne connurent jamais, des affections qui servent à la fois d'épreuves et de récompenses à la vertu, des affections qui donnent du prix à la vie et rendent supérieur à tous les maux!'

It is observable that, in all these letters, it is the soul that speaks, and not the senses. If Madame Roland were 'faite pour la volupté,' she at least knew how to dominate all ignoble impulses. Again, the letters are written in the sad gloom of a prison, with death hovering near, and ever ready to strike. The only certain object seen through barred windows was the constantly present vision of the red and ghastly guillotine. Love wrote in the shadow of Death. The flying hours were terrible and stern.

The third letter is dated 6th July.

Madame Roland had procured for herself a miniature of her lover, and she writes to Buzot about 'this dear picture.' 'Je me suis fait apporter, il y as quatre jours, *this dear picture*, que par une sorte de superstition je ne voulois pas mettre dans ma prison ; mais pourquoi donc se refuser cette douce image, foible et precieux de dommagement de la présence de l'objet? Elle est sur mon cœur, cachée à tous les yeux, sentie à tous les moments, et souvent baignée de mes larmes. Va, je suis penetrée de ton courage, honorée de ton attachement et glorieuse de tout ce que l'un et l'autre pevrent inspirer à ton âme fière et sensible. Je ne puis croire que le ciel ne réserve que des épreuves à des sentiments si purs et si dignes de sa faveur. . . . . Quiconque sait aimer comme nous porte avec soi le principe des plus grandes et des meilleures actions, le prix des sacrifices les plus pénibles, le dédommagement de tous les maux. Adieu, mon bien-aimé, adieu ! '

This appeal to Heaven is remarkable. She had broken with Catholicism, nay, even with Christianity ; but, though she was a pagan, she could never become a materialist. The lingering traces of her olden faith are visible in this appeal to Heaven, which, if illogical, was, at least, imaginative. But it is only her love for Buzot that can turn her thought, or her fancy, toward a Heaven, long abjured but not quite forgotten. Faith was lost, but a faint memory of it still survived, as does the light of the sun after it has set below the horizon.

The fourth is the last of her letters that have been traced ; and it was certainly received by Buzot. It is dated 7th July.

'Comme je chéris les fers où il m'est libre de

t'aimer sans partage et de m'occuper de toi sans cesse! Ici, toute autre occupation est suspendue : je ne me dois plus qu'à qui m'amie et mérite si bien d'être chéri.'

There is in Madame Roland no coquetry or affectation. Her great heart always dares to speak out the fulness of its meaning.

'Vous embellissez le plus triste séjour, vous faites régner au fond des cachots un bonheur aprés lequel soupirent quelquefois vainement l'habitant des palais.'

All her letters were written in direst haste, and M. Dauban points out the occasional slips of grammar caused by hurry. Facsimiles of these letters are now lying before me. The handwriting is small, but clear. There was no time for corrections. They were written stealthily, under danger of interruption and interference; and they were the chief joy of an imprisoned woman.

'O toi! si cher et si digne de l'être!' She speaks of her position relatively to Roland as one 'où des obligations saintes et terribles contraignoient mes facultés et dechirrvient mon faible cœur.' There is no self-pity in her letters. A 'faible cœur' is only spoken of in connexion with the loathed tie to Roland. Of her cell she says,—'Elle est large de manière à souffrir une chaise à côté du lit. C'est là que, devant une petite table, je lis, je dessine, et j'écris; c'est la que, ton portrait sur mon sein ou sous mes yeux, je remercie le ciel de t'avoir connu, de m'avoir fait goûter le bien inexprimable d'aimer et d'être chérie avec cette générosité, cette delicatesse, que ne connaîtront jamais les âmes vulgaires, et qui sont au dessus de tous leurs plaisirs.'

In her 'dernières pensées,' in those burning lines, written upon the very verge of life, she thus, for the last time, addresses Buzot,—' Et toi que je n'ose nommer ! toi que la plus terrible des passions n'empêcha pas de respecter les barrières de la vertu, t'affligerais-tu de me voir te précéder aux lieux où nous pourrons nous aimer sans crime, où rien ne nous empêchera d'être unis ? '

Love was, with her, a terrible passion, and it was a source of righteous satisfaction to her to think that the barriers of virtue had not been overstepped. Her imagination again plays fondly with the idea that she and Buzot shall meet again after death, in realms in which love shall love its fill, without crime, without sorrow, without remorse. On the day after the above lines were written, death, and what may come after it, were no longer mysteries for her.

The portrait ('this dear picture') had wholly disappeared until, in 1864, M. Vatel picked it up by chance at a 'bric-a-brac' shop. The probability is that, just before her death, Madame Roland had given it to Champagneux to be delivered to Buzot. and that it was found upon him after his death.

Towards the end of November 1863, a young man offered for sale, at a ' librairie quai Voltaire,' several

Girondin manuscripts and letters, for which he obtained fifty francs. Among these were the letters of Madame Roland to Buzot. They also were probably found by peasants on the corpse of Buzot, and were carelessly preserved, without an idea of their value, till some 'young man' knew enough about them to sell them for a few francs. Pictures and letters go through romances of their own.

M. Dauban, in his 'Étude,' gives, as a frontispiece, an engraving of the 'dear picture,' worn so long on the heart of Madame Roland, and on which her loving eyes had so often rested in the reveries of her passionate longing for the dear original. Happily this picture was not buried with her or with Buzot.

The face is rather short and broad, the eyes are large, well-opened, tender; the features are finely modelled, but round the lips plays a kind of sarcastic, sorrowful disdain, the chronic attitude of Buzot's mind towards life, and man, and fate. The portrait expresses an elevated nature, full of capacity for love, full of courage, culture, and of pride. Sorrows of the heart (she says) deepened a constitutional tendency to melancholy in Buzot. The cheek is lean and hollow, like that of a man worn by passion and by grief. The traits speak of sensibility and of gentleness. It is interesting to look upon the effigy of a man so loved by Madame Roland, and so worthy of her love.

The features of Madame Roland are not regular,

but the expression of head and face is singularly striking and attractive; they possess, indeed, a sort of fascination, a mixture of sweetness and of strength, which enable us to realise her influence over contemporaries—over Buzot. The forehead is unusually large and broad. Upon that brow shame were ashamed to sit. The chin is full; the mouth is extraordinarily sweet and mobile; the large eyes are full of genius and of love. Her long, dark hair flows in curls over shoulders and down the back. Not a tall woman, but a creature exquisite in womanly charm and in rare force of character. Frank, fearless, noble, is her most expressive, her eloquent face. The bust is large and well formed. Clear will and heroic courage speak out from the face's sensitive lines. There is nothing ignoble, treacherous, little, in the sublime character of this head—a head which was to be severed by the cruel axe of the ruthless guillotine.

'Natura la fece, e poi ruppe la stampa.' Not easily will the world again need or produce another Madame Roland. She lived in a fatal, a

> ... dark and dreary time,
> The heavens all blood, the wearied earth all crime.

Did Madame Roland forgive her enemies? I think not. She rose superior to them; they could not daunt or even much depress her; but the savage injustice committed against her love, her hope, her life, by the brutal butchers of the Revolution, would rouse indignation in a soul so fiery and so proud.

Marie Antoinette, with wrongs as deep, hurled to death from a much more resplendent position, could, and did, under the influences of Christianity, forgive those who had so unpardonably trespassed against her. She left vengeance to God; but Madame Roland, who could not rise to the Christian valour of humility, had some hope of vengeance from man. She had a great soul, and she possessed it fully. She had a large heart, and Buzot filled it nobly. She had ambition and sense of right—France and Liberty distended these passions to excess—but forgiveness she had not. The combative element was strong in her.

The Girondins 'were not condemnable, but were most unfortunate.' Liberty had no purer or more ardent champions, but in that fierce time of unbridled passions they could not withstand the thunders of Danton, the stealthy guile of Robespierre, or the blood-thirsty ravings of Marat. The 'privileged class' of the Revolution—the mob—demanded more blood than the Gironde would give. They were not coarse or wicked enough to rule in a demented hour, which thirsted for the blood of aristocrats, which dreaded furiously the foe beyond the frontier. Nor had the Gironde a statesman. Vergniaud was an orator; Brissot was a formalist; Madame Roland was an inspiration. With her, politics were a passion. She had the wisdom of genius, but not the strategy of policy. Woman-like, she was a partisan; she felt sympathy or dyspathy; she loved favourites, and she loathed antagonists. Her likes and dislikes were pure in motive, but impolitic in action. To the Girondins, as a party, she did harm. Their strength lay in the confidence of the 'bourgeoisie;' but she did not please the middle class, nor did she care to win the populace. Men resented the only thinly concealed leadership of a woman. But for her, Danton, who preferred the Gironde to Robespierre, Marat, Hebert, would have allied himself to the nobler party; but he found himself repelled by her indignation, degraded by her scorn. He became the dangerous and deadly enemy of the Girondins. In those fierce days, men fought duels with the guillotine for a weapon; Danton turned its blade against the woman-led party which would not forgive or forget the blood of September. 'Les morts seuls ne reviennent pas;' and to oppose a party, meant to exterminate its members. Wholesale massacres became unnecessary owing to the activity of judicial murders. The Gironde was a party fitted only for fairer and for nobler times. The vices of a rampant democracy are only a multiplication by myriads of the selfish vices of an irresponsible aristocracy.

The fate and the failure of the Girondins contain a pregnant lesson for the 'liberals' of all lands who, impelled by theories or actuated by ambition, who, thoughtlessly or wickedly, for party purposes or out of lust for rule, stimulate and develop into frantic action the fierce passions of a demoniac democracy.

Such 'liberals' raise a devil that they cannot lay; they create a monster that they cannot control. After going beyond their convictions in the direction of injustice, cruelty, oppression, such 'liberals' have the mortification of finding themselves passed in the race for popular favour by others wickeder than themselves; and then they see themselves, with a name tainted by history, overthrown and doomed to perish and to fall.

But, before failing and falling, such men may do much to bring about the decadence of a nation, and the disgrace of humanity. They may enfranchise and embolden all lawless passions, mean ambitions, and selfish lusts; they may degrade all authority, all virtue, and all wisdom; they may transfer rule to anarchy, and hand over power to the ruthless hands of an ignorant and conscienceless mob, and of such leaders as *it* may choose. There is a just retribution which sternly awaits all such doctrinaire attempts to rule by trying to govern ungovernable mobs, and to retain influence by pandering to the worst passions of an infuriated people. The errors of the Girondins were terribly expiated. A revolution in France, at the end of the last century, was an event necessary—inevitable; but the pity is, that the revolution, when it came, was so base and bloodthirsty, so demonic and uncreative, that it ended in a military despotism, in an absolute imperialism, and led to the restoration of the old line of kings. Indeed, nothing in the rule or misrule, of the 'ancien régime,' was so inhuman or wicked as the revolution itself. Insolent, selfish, rotten as the old Government was, it was surpassed in wicked cruelty by a Committee of Public Safety, by the revolutionary tribunal, by massacre and murder. The Revolution lasted five years, and committed, during that brief period, more crimes than the monarchy which it shattered. It was no reform. It declined into inhuman ferocity, and lawless outrage. It was ruled by men as mean as they were foul. The tyrants of old had their infamous Bastille, and their abominable 'lettres de câchet ;' the Revolution created many Bastilles, and invented letters of death. The men of the sections, the butchers of the Abbaye, entered the armies of Napoleon ; and sansculottes undoubtedly look better in military uniform. The France of the guillotine became for a time the France of glory, of conquest, of dominion. All high-souled men—men who yet loved liberty—as Burke and Schiller, were revolted by it. It was a time of implacable hatreds, and of most deadly enmities. Goethe says,—'True it is, that I could be no friend of the French Revolution, for I stood too near to atrocities which daily and hourly revolted me, while its beneficial results were not then to be foreseen. I was also fully convinced that no great revolution can be the fault of a people, but must be due to the Government.' These words were spoken in 1824, to Eckermann ; and they may be held to contain almost the 'dernier mot' on the subject.

Madame Roland stands vividly before us as an imperishable instance of sincerity and strength,—'Und was nicht reizt, ist todt,' says the Princess in Tasso; but Madame Roland remains vital in her fulness of womanly charm. Her personality subdues as her character impresses us. Beneath the heroine is the woman; tender, devoted, loving, winning. Those lips can break into a seductive smile, or can become tremulous with moving eloquence. The evidence of her personal influence is overwhelming. Her mind is active with fecundity of idea; is quivering with fulness of vitality. In her life and vigour she is intense. She is always animated, vivacious; and neither in speaking nor in writing can she be reproached with a single dull or trivial sentence. Even large assemblies of men were awed, and were delighted by her. On 7th December 1792, she had a singular triumph in the Convention itself. La Montagne was vanquished by her grace, her talent, her soft eloquence. A certain 'citoyen Achille Viard,' a spy of the Convention, returned from London, and accused Roland of being engaged in a conspiracy for the restoration of the King. Roland denied the preposterous charge, but was wise enough to suggest that his wife should be sent for. She came; 'and with her high clearness, dissipated this Viard into air and despicability.' When she appeared at the bar, she was received with loud applause. Modestly, and yet with firmness, she demented and disproved the lie; and the admiring

President, speaking the voice of the Assembly, invited the citizeness Roland (née Phlipon) to the 'honneurs de la séance.' The Gironde was delighted at the success of its fair ally; and Madame Roland had achieved a public triumph. Had she been a man, 'la Gironde' had not wanted a leader. Condorcet speaks of Robespierre as being 'without an idea in his head, or a feeling in his heart.' Madame Roland had both ideas and feelings.

'Le style c'est l'homme;' et Madame Roland's character is perfectly expressed in her writings. Her vivid, virile style is characteristic of her. She had force, clearness, imagination, irony, wit—but humour never. Reason, perhaps, predominates over imagination; but it must be remembered that the writings by which we now judge her, are all coloured by the fever flush of the day in which she lived and moved and had her being. Much was written with breathless rapidity; but with her, fluency never degenerates into verbosity. It was emphatically not a time for humour. The relations of events to life and death were too serious, and were too terrible—the mind was impressed with a mould of sternness. During the time in which her later letters were written, Charles Henri Sanson, the headsman of the period (see his Memoirs), records that—'I am seized with fever as soon as I enter the Conciergerie. . . . . I do not boast of extraordinary squeamishness—I have seen too much blood not to be callous. If what I feel be not pity, it is a derangement of the nerves. Perhaps I am punished by the Almighty for cowardly obedience to mock justice.' What may this Sanson have felt when he executed Madame Roland?

Her plenitude of talent is always valiant, earnest, intrepid, weighty. She is never sentimental; she is never weak. There is occasional badinage in her letters to Bosc, Bancal des Issarts; there is tenderness in her correspondence with the Demoiselles Cannet; there is passion, deep but never wild, in those last, saddest letters to Buzot; there is frank friendship in her notes to Champagneux ('cher Jany') and to other trusted friends. Ardent for ideal liberty, uplifted above the ignorant present by a sublime patriotism, conscious of power which she, as woman, had to exercise under great restraint, she attained to victory only by means of self-repression. She died at the age of thirty-nine; but nearly six months of those years were spent in captivity, rendered doubly haggard by the chance of death at any moment; while her child was torn from her, her husband was in hiding—and her lover a hunted fugitive. We judge her, from the literary side, chiefly by her Memoirs, and by some of her letters. These were written for the most part under sorrow, danger, difficulties, in the prison of Sainte Pélagie. Marie Antoinette was born 2d November 1755; Madame Roland was born 18th March 1754—they were almost of the same age; and they shared the same doom.

The names of these two victims are inseparably connected with the history of the French Revolution. The 'Zeitkolorit' around them is the dark, red background of a hellish time, against which these two radiant and royal female figures stand out distinctly. One was an aristocrat of birth and rank; the other was an aristocrat of genius and of energy. The one under supernatural, the other under natural consolation, they showed equal courage when the end came.

In the dim darkness of dungeons, in the glare of light on the high scaffold, from out of which the grim apparatus of death affronted the outraged sky, they both stand forth resplendently, and neither blenched beneath the gory guillotine. The daughter of the Cæsars, the daughter of the engraver—both ended their careers in the same tragic way. Each was unworthily and unhappily married; but one only left a mourning lover. They stand on high in history on that lofty platform of the scaffold, round which surges a vast yelling crowd that joyed ferociously in the deaths of two such women. The scene of horror in the 'Place de la Revolution' found the Christian and the Pagan alike calm and undismayed. They are the glory and the shame of the Revolution. They lend it grace, and reflect upon it disgrace. It is a glory to the Revolution that it should have developed a Madame Roland; it is a disgrace to it that it should have murdered her. Such deaths cover with ignominy a movement which suggests salvation carried out by fiends. Martyrs of the Revolution, these women lend to it an imperishable, tragic attraction of great terror and of most splendid courage. That Revolution, in its desire to brand its victims with obloquy, called the one a 'monstre,' the other an 'horreur;' but their sad, high fates stamp the Revolution itself as a monster and a horror. The judgment of posterity has reversed their sentences and rescued their memories.

When first she met the man who was formed to fill up the void in her empty heart, she felt that Buzot 'aurait pu être son amant;' but, while she indulged her ideal passion, she could trust her own virtue, and could resolve that love should never yield to shame. She could not be untrue—even to Roland. 'Jamais l'idée de l'abandonner ne lui vint à l'ésprit.' He was old, was suffering, and he leant on her. Duty constrained her lofty spirit.

A conquest how hard and how glorious! The manners of her time would have sanctioned an ordinary French 'liaison;' but such baseness was not possible to the fervid Madame Roland. And then the contrast between the two men! How terrible must have been the struggle between love and duty in her proud yet passionate heart! And yet she held firmly to the sanctity of the marriage tie—a tie rendered so repulsive by that Roland 'parlant d'un ton monotone et toujours de lui-même, roide et cassant.' While Buzot was an ideal lover, who could fill her heart, stir her imagination, excite her senses. The woman remains glorious!

In the last days of the Gironde in the Convention, Buzot, in the audacity of despair, spoke with her voice, and uttered her thought.

Once she found a false friend; when that Lanthenas, whom she called her brother, terrified by La Montagne, turned traitor to her, and to the cause. Her grief and shame and sorrow were great as was the nobleness of her nature.

Usually, she inspired friends up to the level of her own loftiness. Brave Henriette Cannet, knowing well the risk that she ran, would have sacrificed her own life in order to save that of Madame Roland. She would have exchanged dresses with her friend, and would have remained in Sainte Pélagie, while Madame Roland made her escape from the prison. But Madame Roland was too generous to accept the sacrifice. She thought also of the probable fate of the poor gaoler, who had been kind to her; and she remained voluntarily in her dungeon, and paid the fearful forfeit to which she had looked forward for so long. The example of her death might, she thought, serve liberty.

Then came the Conciergerie, the Revolutionary Tribunal, the mock trial, the dreadful sentence; and then came the long ride to the 'Place de la Revolution,' the last sacrifice to Lamarche, and death by the guillotine. All was over except the fame that never dies, the example of heroism which will never lose its influence, and the human interest in a woman which leads us now to study her life, and to deplore her death. Her longing for justice from posterity is amply gratified. She remains heroine as victim.

'O liberté! s'écria-t-elle, comme on tá jouée. Puis la planche bascula.' . . . .

That France which then erected the colossal clay statue of Liberty close by the guillotine, should now erect there a statue to the woman who so thoroughly understood, and so fully exemplified what French liberty meant—to fair and glorious MADAME ROLAND!

THE END.

www.ingramcontent.com/pod-product-compliance
Lightning Source LLC
Chambersburg PA
CBHW030116240426
43673CB00041B/1297